How Authors Make A Living
An Analysis of Free Lance Writers' Incomes
1953 - 1957

BY

William Jackson Lord, Jr, Ph.D.

The Scarecrow Press, Inc.
New York   1962

338.47
L88h

64321

January, 1969

Library of Congress Card No. 62-19729

Acknowledgment

A debt of gratitude is owed by the author to many:

To Professor Dallas W. Smythe for his guidance, patience, and careful supervision of the thesis in process ...

To the Authors League of America, Inc., New York, for making the study possible, and ...

To his family--Shirley, Michal, David, and Mark--for standing by patiently, giving love, understanding, and encouragement when it was needed most.

Preface

Little or almost nothing is known of how the novelist fares economically from his sale of books, or of how the playwright fares in his market, the theater. For the latter, of course, relatively few plays actually see production from the few hundred optioned each season.

On the other hand, just about everyone thinks he has in his system at least one best selling novel, a Broadway stage hit, or a sure-fire Hollywood movie scenario. Very few of these world-shaking masterpieces, however, ever get into print. Few, in fact, ever even reach the manuscript stage. For one out of every ten novelists earns income from books only one year in five; one in three dramatists earns from playwriting on the same basis.

To be a successful free lance writer today calls, first of all, for ideas. And then stamina. And then--though pro- bably most important of all--freedom from concern about regular income. No matter how capable, a person consider- ing free lance writing as a career should recognize there may be long periods when what he has to offer will find no ready market. To such a person, this book says: free lance writing can be pursued successfully as a subsidiary career ... with one that has a definite salary attached to it.

There are many thousands of men and women who are free lance writers, or are trying to be. Probably no more than a dozen really make a good living at it. Gener- ally, the consensus is that the greater number of writers eke out only a precarious and very modest living.

It is, fortunately, not within the scope of this book to allocate the economic rewards of our civilization--not even to the point of saying whether a writer should receive more than the man who sets his words into type. Nor is it as Cheney discovered in his economic survey of the book industry early in the 1930's, for this investigation to say whether there is any economic or social justice in the fact the writer of popular tripe--stewed in honeysuckle, or of filth, plain--may be showered with golden luxury, while the man who wants only to express seriously the best that is within him through books of real merit, may struggle and starve. But this survey does examine, for the first time statistically, the monetary returns of a large number of honest, earnest, and hard-working writing craftsmen.

While certainly desirable, a comprehensive survey of all aspects encompassed by the writing field is a formidable undertaking even under the full auspices of a foundation or an association. And a study analyzing authorship incomes ought to cover extensive areas of writing other than book writers, playwrights, and magazine writers. This book does not attempt to survey the income of all writers. There are undetermined numbers of writers engaged in various kinds of salaried writing not covered here. Among others are those writing exclusively for the screen--motion picture or television--either on a salaried or original basis, and the bulk of textbook and religious book authors. Apart from these, the writers who are covered make up the entire membership of the Authors League of America. But among these professional free lance writers are numerous television script writers, screen writers, and other kinds in the four hundred and thirty-eight questionnaire returns used for analysis. At the same time, the League (the Clearing House and Advisory Board for professional writers) has one of the most comprehensive, confidential lists of professional writers available. In the majority of cases for the simplicity of organization and mailings, the membership of the League is classified simply as "authors" (book writers and magazine writers) and "playwrights" ... the two best classifications for fiction writers.

To accurately depict the economic situation of the American free lance author, vital statistics concerning his income were prime targets. And, because one is generally somewhat reluctant to divulge such confidential information—even to the Government—the proposal to the League set forth the objectives and procedure of such a study, to be accomplished through the use of a mail questionnaire and follow-up personal interviews. (Since the study originally served as a doctoral dissertation, the particulars of the survey design, execution, methodology, and statistical representativeness of the returns can be secured by those interested from University Microfilms, Inc., 313 North First Street, Ann Arbor, Michigan.)

Seeking to gain some in validity, we gave assurance of anonymity. If you are looking for certain individual's incomes (by name) you will be disappointed; none are here. If you are interested in finding what combinations free lance authors put together to earn a living, how steady that income is from year to year, what the "average" writer is like—as an individual—what the casualness of this labor market is, and a host of other facts unavailable up to now about free lance writers and the profession as a whole ... your search is over.

Adding to the knowledge of the "writing" market--thereby hopefully making a useful contribution to the record of American culture--this book seeks to be of service to would-be authors in giving a thorough-going appraisal of the working conditions and earnings in the profession. It also is relevant to people already in the field, contributing to a greater understanding of their problems--especially income-tax problems.

Thanks are due The Authors League and its staff, particularly Miss Luise M. Sillcox, former Executive Secretary, for making the book possible.

W. J. L.

Urbana, Illinois

Glossary

Professional	-	term used in reference to the independent writer who has the prerogative of deciding <u>what</u> he will or will not write.
Book Writer	-	a writer earning any income from his books between 1953 and 1957, the years covered by the present study.
Playwright	-	a writer earning any income from his plays between 1953-1957.
Other Writers	-	writers not earning personal income from books or plays in the five years between 1953-1957.
Book Writing Specialist	-	a book writer earning his sole personal income from books.
Playwriting Specialist	-	a playwright earning his sole personal income from plays.

<u>Income Concepts:</u>

Personal Income	-	income earned by the writer himself from whatever source.
"Employed"	-	used in reference to the writer actively earning personal income from books, plays, magazines, or whatever source for his livelihood.
Free Lance	-	personal income earned by the writer from books, plays, magazines, or royalties on an independent basis (e.g. non-salaried).

ix

"F. L.-Emp"	-	personal income earned by the writer from original and/or salaried writings for motion pictures and television.
Directed	-	personal income earned by the writer from any salaried or commissioned writing assignment such as staff writing for magazines and newspapers, ghostwriting, advertising copywriting, translations, reviews, etc.
Non-writing	-	personal income earned by the writer from any source not involving writing as the major activity of the job performance.
Yearly Median	-	the mid-point of income earned by all writers reporting in any particular year, 1953-1957, from any particular source.
Mean of Yearly Medians	-	an arithmetic average of the yearly median incomes; same as five years' median.
Five-year Median	-	the mid-point of income of all the earners from any particular source derived by adding an individual's years' incomes together (regardless of whether the writer earned from the source for 1, 2, 3, 4, or 5 years), dividing by five and arraying all averages in frequency.
Spouse's Income	-	income earned by the working spouse of a married writer.
Family Income	-	spouse's income and writer's personal income added together.
Marriage-linked Dependence	-	degree of dependence of the married writer on the working spouse's income.

Table of Contents

Part I

The American Writer: A General Picture

xii

xiii

Spreading of Income
Capital Gains Treatment
Funding of Retirement Provisions

List of Tables

List of Tables

List of Tables

List of Tables

List of Tables

List of Tables

List of Tables

List of Figures

Introduction

"For me ...a writer is a man or woman who writes."
--Malcolm Cowley

It is easy to try to be a writer. All one needs is paper and stamps. There is no license, no defined education, no apprenticeship required. One just sails in and tries. And there are case histories of men and women, verified by the press, who were nobodies yesterday and rich, successful writers today. This anomaly of literary success is confusing, and at the same time one of the reasons for the widespread incompetence in the writing craft ... the millions of banal, ill-written, ill-thought-out words that annually see publication.

This phenomenon induces tens of thousands of others to believe that they, too, can write, that they should write, and so they do write. And as a result every editor has flowing across his desk the most miserable assemblage of verbiage gathered this side of a waste basket, for to judge by the number of manuscripts[1] which editors receive, an appalling portion of the American public fits Malcolm Cowley's definition.

Many of the people aspiring to professional authorship have only a fragmentary knowledge of the writing profession, gathered largely from glamorized accounts of the careers of a few outstanding writers ... of the professional--that wise old bird with the yacht, the Chinese cook, and three divorced wives! The view of the writer by the public is a curious, unstable mixture.

What gives the theme--the position of the writer in A-merica--perennial freshness is that his position is indefin-able. Two factors have joined to produce yet a differing kind of public view of the writer, varying from tolerant con-tempt to active suspicion. They are (1) our passion for the production and exchange of consumable goods, and (2) our passion for mass literacy.

Sanctioning this point, lightly yet with serious over-tones, Clifton Fadiman adds that the writer does not produce consumable goods, though "he may produce non-consumable, useless goods such as the Declaration of Independence."[2] Hence, the writer is looked upon rather uneasily, viewed unconsciously as a kind of second-class citizen--as are his kinsmen, the teacher and the preacher, the artist and the pure scientist ... a somewhat subversive individual, this writer.

Once he enjoyed the small prestige accruing from the possession of talents not generally possessed. Today, though the real writer is still numerically rare, he does not seem to be. Universal literacy has made him appear as perva-sive as light and air.

Universal literacy is an American passion with serious-almost religious--overtones. This passion has been so fer-vently cultivated that now everybody can "read" and "write." What were formerly activities whose essential connection was with thinking have now become universally practiced small-muscle movements of the eyes and fingers, movements into which thought may or may not enter.

We have all become "readers" and "writers" in that we are all proficient in these small-muscle gestures. Hence the writer and the "writer" are confused in the public mind. Most screenplays, advertisements, government speeches,

books--scripts of all kinds--are merely more or less complex word carpentry.

Amid this flurry of wholesale small-muscle activity,
the voice of the old-fashioned writer, who works with real
emotions and real ideas and struggles with most exacting
techniques, may be lost. His value depreciates because he
seems to be doing only what everybody else is doing.

His value is further depreciated by the inevitable consequence of mass literacy--easy printability. Everything
gets into print; and physically all print looks much alike.
Thus a gutter-press editorial and a poem by W.H. Auden
seem to be similar products, though actually they are in no
way connected except that both employ words and are printed
by the same kind of machine.

We have thus a curious mixed-up climate of opinion
within which the writer, a hardy soul, nevertheless manages
to survive, to flourish, and to enjoy himself. On the one
hand he is valued as a kind of seer: his opinions are requested on every subject; they are respectfully printed and
no attention is paid to them. On the other hand, he is
viewed as a harmless, somewhat eccentric[3] nonproducer or
merely as one who does a little better or more visibly what
all of us feel we can do pretty well ourselves.

This incapacity of the writer to make clear what he is
really up to reflects itself in the official attitude toward his
income. A novelist (or playwright) may educate himself for
twenty years, starve for another ten, and then hit the "jackpot" with a bestseller. By law he must pay in taxes the
larger part of the money he makes during his one, two, or
three good years. He is then free to starve again. Under-
lying the public's unconscious feelings is the sense that the
writer is a specialized being whose rewards are other than

monetary, and who therefore is not entitled to exceptional
protection, as for instance are the holders of oil leases.

It is only when it can be shown that a producer of in-
tangible goods can also produce something really useful like
a flying piece of metal with dying dog in it that a public
demand arises that he be given a little extra compensation.

The feeling persists, then, on the one hand that the
writer does not do any real work. On the other is the feeling that the unreal work he does is the spontaneous overflow
of some magical energy. Hence if the writer is a magician
there is no reason why we should not call upon him whenever we wish for a display of his inexhaustible magic. Constant demands, therefore, are made upon writers to "knock
off" (the term is an exact reflection of the view of the writer-
as-magician) a few hundred or a few thousand words to be
used in some undeniably excellent governmental project. The
writer here is regarded as a kind of public utility.

Back of such requests lie two assumptions. The first
is that the writer is a wonder worker, and can therefore
produce his petty miracles without labor.[4] The second is
that, inasmuch as everybody can "read" and "write," we are
not asking him to do anything we ourselves could not do, if
we merely put our minds to it. These two assumptions of
course contradict each other.

"Our friends abroad," writes Archibald MacLeish,[5]
"find it both relevant and interesting that the most audible
and authoritative voices in a Republic which once expressed
itself through Whitman and Emerson should now be the
voices of American men of business, and that the American
people should see nothing odd in this situation. The Europ-
ean mind, which once observed that war is too serious an
affair to be left to the generals, still believes that life is

too important a business to be left to the businessmen. It
still believes that great societies find their voices in their
arts," (e.g. such as the writer). So Samuel Johnson[6] could
not have been more wrong when he remarked that no man
but a blockhead ever wrote except for money. A writer
wants to make as much money as is possible with the kind
of writing he wants to do. But that is not the same thing
as writing for money.

Yet, for at least the past two hundred years the chronic
complaint of authors has been that they have been underpaid.
The paucity and irregularity of statistical data, however, is
one of the basic weaknesses of research in all media of
communications and it is especially so regarding writers.
We do not know, for example, what the supply of authors is
like, nor do we know much more about the demand for writers and the writer's products. There are no year by year
statistics available for comparative purposes.

At the same time, there has been a dearth of information on just how much authors actually do earn. This lack
of information is made further apparent by the fact we do
not know how much authors earn from writing as against
their other sources of income. This is true for both writers of plays and writers of books.

We also have not known how much specialization there
has been among free lance writers as concerns (1) the
author's dependence upon writing for his livelihood, (2) the
practice of writing in more than one field, e.g. an author writing both as a free lance and salaried writer, and also as a
fiction and/or nonfiction writer, or (3) the extent of the casualness in the receipt of income by authors, that is, the degree of
dependence upon the working spouse as sources of income.

Until now, it was also unknown:

(1) what type of book produced the most income for the professional free lance writer

(2) what their total income was from books, or

(3) what the amount of income was from all kinds of writing which these writers do, as part of the writing industry.

We do know that publishers are influenced in their selection of a prospective book for publication by its potential subsidiary earning power; what importance the subsidiary income plays in the writer's total earnings, however, has been another unknown.

It is generally believed by those closest to the field, for example, that there have been important recent shifts in the sources and character of authors' income that probably will have significant consequences in what is written. "Best-sellerdom" and returns from subsidiary rights have materially increased the income possibilities for a small number of popular authors, as have opportunities in television. But relative to the rest of the economy, the income possibilities of all outside that small number may have dimished so that a steadily smaller percentage of writers are able to live on their income from serious writing. Additionally, the economic position of authors is further made insecure by inequities in the taxation of peak incomes, and in the taxation of income from copyrights as contrasted to that from patents, as well as by their ineligibility for tax-favored pension plans.

Such factors limit the number of people who can devote an important part of their time to writing and affect the kind of writing they can afford to do. These economic barriers to authorship hence significantly affect the volume and quality of writing--both scholarly and creative--and probably, therefore, the usefulness to society of the annual output of

books in which that writing is embodied. Yet, in no field
of communications are we less well informed than in the
economics of authorship.

Much can be learned, it is hoped, through this survey
about the relationship of income from authorship of books,
plays, and associated writings, and income from other
sources, for it is through the rewards paid to authors that
the publishing industry stimulates or discourages different
kinds of writing talent. And with the consensus being
generally that the greater number of writers eke out only a
precarious and very modest living, this study somewhat
documents the obvious. It is nevertheless important that we
have these facts and figures available to examine critically,
openly, and analytically to see what implications they hold
for the free lance writer's future and to see what light they
shed on the author's present problems.

The writing market now and for the past hundred or so
years has rewarded best those authors who meet the market
requirement for best sellers. While waiving any value judgment on best-sellerism, it still might be argued that non-
best-sellers may be one of the principal social benefits
derived from the book industry, though an intensive treatment of such a premise is well beyond the scope of this
book. Investigating the cyclical nature of writers' incomes,
however, is not. And it is from the multi-faceted evidence
revealed in the investigation--evidence of a kind that would
seem relevant to an examination of the equity of taxing as
income the "writing" income of writers according to present
practice--which lay bare several important conclusions in
this aspect of the economics of authorship.

Foremost of the results ...

(1) The average professional author earns insufficient

income to live on from his chosen profession.
(His writing career becomes more an avocation
than a profession.)

(2) The professional author, thus, seems to have an
excellent case for tax relief measures. (The
penalty of present taxing practices--particularly
regarding peak incomes--makes it extremely
difficult for him to establish a retirement pro-
gram.)

Several subordinate conclusions tend to support these major
ones: (1) income from writing shows much more irregularity than other professions--year to year in total incomes;
and (2) the professional writing field is limited in the number of new artists and creative works more now than ever
before, which leads to frustration for the writer; what
started out to be fun turns into hack production, for much of
his creative work must be tailor-made to demand.

Serious thought leads to yet a third--though somewhat
unsupported--major conclusion:

(3) The greater portion of income in the writing
field goes to salaried writers; there are fewer
writers in this group, and, therefore, writing
becomes a true profession (not an avocation)
limiting free entry for the free lance author.

Though this investigation is primarily factual, concen-
trating as it does on the incomes of professional free lance
writers from 1953 through 1957 one cannot help raising a few
questions about the writer as an individual. It is in this
latter area, of course, where one finds most of the published
material concerning writers.

Because of such ready references as Farrar's Successful Writers and How They Work, and Cowley's two volumes,
The Literary Situation and Writers at Work, no attempt is
made to answer these questions at length.

For instance, what effect does the economics of authorship have on the author's life and attitude towards his work?
Does the free lancer panic when he hits a spell during which
no one buys his work: What does this panic do to his personal relations? To what extent does it affect his output--
both in quality and quantity? To what extent does the economics of the situation affect him in what he writes and in his
way of writing it? That is, to what extent does the writer
accommodate himself to the market and principles be hanged?

How does the author fare as compared with other
persons associated in his enterprise? For instance, in the
magazine field the amount spent on editorial copy is much,
much less and accounts for a far smaller percentage of the
expense dollar than does what is spent on the printer and
paper-maker.[7] Is this true also in the book field? Does
the publisher make more from a given book than the author?
Does the printer? The bookseller? Similarly, how does
the playwright fare as compared with the backer of the play,
the star, the director, the designer, the costumer?

No attempt was made by the questionnaire to determine
the writers' opinions concerning the points raised by these
questions. Yet, some set forth their personal feelings regarding various matters of deep concern to them. Such comments presented intermittently throughout the book attempt
to put the professional author's income in its rightful pers-
pective.

Notes

1. To cite an example, one survey in 1950 revealed 16
    major high-paying magazines received 182,505 unsoli-
    cited fiction manuscripts, of which 560 were used.
    These same 16 plus 10 others received 79,812 unsoli-
    cited non-fiction manuscripts the same year, using
    slightly less than 1000 of them. Other magazines in
    the same class had no accurate estimates but

indicated they received an astonishingly high number
of unsolicited manuscripts--95 to 99 per cent of which
were rejected. (Kenneth Marne Baker, "Editorial
Requirements for Higher-Paying Magazines," Unpublished Master's Thesis, University of Illinois, Urbana,
1951.)

2.   Material here paraphrased from Clifton Fadiman,
     "Party of One: Ah! The Literary Life," Holiday,
     Vol. 23, No. 3, pp. 11-15.

3.   The term is not without some historical inference.
     William Dean Howell writing of the man of letters
     in 1893, and using the term himself, indicated it
     was already a well-established reference to profess-
     ional writers.

4.   Robert L. Heilbroner ("Mr. Nobody's Byline," The
     Saturday Review, January 14, 1956, p. 9) in his
     study of the magazine writer discovered that this
     opinion is not without support: the magazine free
     lance is the man whom everybody reads and nobody
     knows ... it takes three to six weeks to turn out a
     finished job; few writers turn out as many as twenty
     pieces a year.
        Additionally, Bernard DeVoto ("Writing for Money,"
     The Saturday Review, October 9, 1937, p. 3) learned
     the popular belief even in 1937 was that anyone can
     "toss off a story" (but that editors send back the
     tossed-off stories).

5.   Archibald MacLeish, "The Isolation of the American
     Artist," Atlantic Monthly, Vol. 201, No. 1, January
     1958, p. 57.

6.   Fadiman, op. cit. p. 15.

7.   Theodore Peterson, Magazines in the 20th Century,
     University of Illinois Press, Urbana, 1958.

Part I

The American Writer: A General Picture

Chapter I

Writers' Characteristics

Introduction

While the writer in America has variously been characterized or thought of as an eccentric, a non-producer, a
magician, a ne'r do well, a "sharecropper,"[1] a psychotic,
a dreamer, no one yet has bothered to try and capture him
statistically--to make of him an individual who represents
his profession. One of the difficulties (and perhaps the
reason for the disparaging generalizations of writers), of
course, is in the use of the term "average" for discussing
a profession that includes so many special groups and individuals. Possibly there is no such creature as an _average_
writer just as there is no real _average_ teacher, lawyer, or
engineer.

This chapter, however, structures a picture of the inevitable "average" writer based upon replies to a mail questionnaire and personal interviews used to gather information
concerning (1) the writer as an individual, and (2) the income
he earns.

After first pointing out the methodology used in handling the statistical data here and in later sections, the chapter begins with a look at where authors live. It examines
the citizenship and regional background of writers for those
first formidable ten years of a person's life. Other characteristics reveal the proportion of writers by age, sex,
marital status, and dependent children. And the writer's
education is compared with the population at large.

To learn something of their progenitors, the writers'

fathers' occupations are grouped according to the Bureau of
the Census Occupation Distribution and compared with selected male occupational classifications.

Detailed analysis is made of the casualness of the writer labor market in Chapter II of this section--the sources of
income, the various combinations of sources put together by
the writer to meet his economic obligations, and the degree
of dependence of the writer on non-writing occupations, including his working spouse.

We then proceed, Chapter III, to examine the relative
importance of the different kinds and sources of income for
all writers.

Methodology

Because the median^2 is often more statistically representative than either the mean (arithmetic average) or mode,
it is used extensively here to depict the American writer's
general characteristics and overall income.

Though somewhat tedious and time consuming, arraying by hand from the McBee Keysort Card System is used
for the data in this chapter as elsewhere in the study for
several reasons. The decision to use the "keysort" card for
analysis was determined first of all, because (1) it provides
the advantages of any mechanical punching system whereby
numerical codes can be applied and the data treated statistically, and (2) it has the advantage of "intimacy" with the
data in that each card can be handled, read, and sorted
according to need since each 5 x 8 inch card contains all
facts regarding each respondent either in coded punches or
typed information on the face of the card. (This method combined the advantages of simplicity and ease of handling best
suited to the investigation as mentioned earlier.)

Secondly, this system allows for controls in checking

accuracy of the typed data and coding as well as in determining the exact number of cases applying to any one analysis. And lastly, it was selected because though the Authors
League classifies its membership into Authors and Playwrights, there appeared in the returns no hard and fast
classifications possible--book writers show up as playwrights,
magazine writers, and in other categories; similarly, playwrights show income from book writing or magazine writing,
and/or other sources. Some show no income from book,
magazine, or playwriting but have substantial incomes from
other sources. Therefore, the card system through coded
punches allows a certain freedom in type classifications.

Membership in the League on May 31, 1957, as used in
the mailing of 2250 questionnaires was:

   (a) Active:

Authors of Adult Fiction (Books and
                      Magazines 550
   (Of these, 156 were established authors
   of plays)
Authors of Juvenile books 200
Magazine Writers 497
Dramatists 472
   (Of these, 56 had had books published in
   period covered by study, 1953-1957)

Total Active................................1719

   (b) Inactive:

Dramatists (Marginal) 800
Associate Authors 104

Total Inactive 904

Total Authors and Dramatists 2623

All active members--1719--were sent questionnaires while a
little better than half--531, or 58.7 per cent, to be exact--
of the inactive membership received questionnaires.

From the 2250 questionnaires mailed, 424 writers returned postcards which had been included with the questionnaire. Twenty-three of these cards bore the statement "not
returning questionnaire" ... some carrying explanations of
the why: "ill," "poor health," "retired," and so on. Thus,
401 who returned postcards saying they had mailed the questionnaire actually did mail it. By envelope count of the
questionnaires received, 415 returned them--14 more than
had indicated by card. Of the 415, twelve were unusable
for lack of classifying data or otherwise incomplete information, making a total usable mail return of 403--approximately
an 18-per-cent response. If all responses--the 403 usable
questionnaires, 12 unusable ones, 23 postcards indicating
no questionnaire returned, plus the 35 personal interview--
are considered, the total response is 21 per cent.

Where Writers Live

Roughly, two-thirds of all writers live in New York
and California--approximately the same proportion responding
to the survey.

To learn the geographical location of the writers
responding to the mail questionnaires, the return-addressed
envelopes were kept as they came in, postmarks noted, and
a map plotted to show where the mail sample of authors
reside. (See Figure 1, page 18.) (The thirty-five personal
interviews made as a follow-up--27 in New York City and
surrounding areas, and 8 in Chicago and surrounding areas--
are not plotted but are included in the overall analyses.)

Citizenship and Regional Background

More than 99 per cent of writers are United States Citizens though about seven per cent were either born a-broad or spent the first ten years of their lives in foreign countries.   In their first ten years of life, more than three-fifths of the U. S. born writers have metropolitan back-grounds, while the remaining two-fifths come from small towns (less than 50,000 population) and rural areas;   see Table I, page 19.

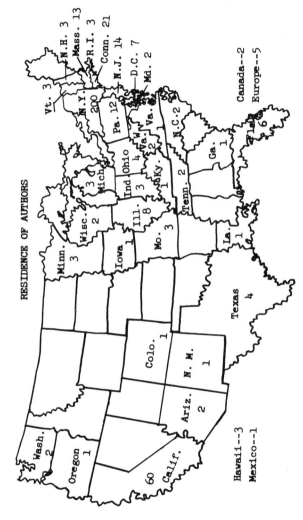

RESIDENCE OF AUTHORS

Wash. 2
Oregon 1
Calif. 60
Ariz. 2
N. M. 1
Colo. 1
Texas 4
Minn. 3
Wisc. 2
Iowa 1
Mo. 3
Ill. 8
Mich. 3
Ind. 3
Ohio 4
Ky. 1
Tenn. 2
La. 1
W. Va. 2
Ga. 1
N.C. 2
Va.
Pa. 12
N.Y. 200
Vt. 3
N.H. 3
Mass. 13
R.I. 3
Conn. 21
N.J. 14
D.C. 7
Md. 2

Hawaii--3
Mexico--1
Canada--2
Europe--5

Fig. 1. Map Showing Location and Concentration of 403 Authors Responding to the Mail Questionnaire.

Table I

Place Of Birth And Present Residence, All Writers

	Metropolitan Areas (Per Cent)	Small Towns And Rural Areas (Per Cent)
Place of Birth:		
U. S. Born (N = 409)	62.1	37.9
Foreign Born (N = 29)	37.9	62.1
	100.0	100.0
Present Residence:		
U. S. Born	73.4	26.6
Foreign Born	69.0	31.0

Foreign-born writers have just the opposite early childhood influences. Three-fifths come from small towns and rural areas, and two-fifths from metropolises. Of the foreign-born American writers, almost seven-tenths now reside in metropolitan areas, as do almost three-fourths of the U. S. born writers.

More than half of the foreign-born writers now call New York City home, with an additional 27.9 per cent living in the New England and Middle Atlantic states. Only 3.5 per cent live on the West Coast and 10.3 per cent in the Midwest.

For the 93 per cent who were born in the United States, regionally the majority--73.8 per cent--come from the Middle Atlantic and Middle West regions as the following breakdown indicates:

Region	Per Cent	Total

New England

Massachusetts	5.8	
Connecticut	2.4	
Rhode Island	1.2	
Maine	.3	
New Hampshire	.3	
Vermont	.3	
		10.3

Middle Atlantic

New York	34.7	
Pennsylvania	7.1	
New Jersey	2.7	
Maryland	.7	
Virginia	.5	
North Carolina	.3	
South Carolina	.3	
West Virginia	.3	
Delaware	-	
		46.5

South

Georgia	1.7	
Kentucky	1.0	
Alabama	.7	
Tennessee	.5	
Florida	.3	
Louisiana	.3	
Mississippi	.3	
		4.6

Southwest

Texas	1.5	
Arizona	.5	
Arkansas	.5	
Oklahoma	.5	
New Mexico	-	
		2.9

Region	Per Cent	Total
Middle West		
Illinois	7.6	
Missouri	4.2	
Ohio	3.9	
Michigan	2.9	
Indiana	2.4	
Kansas	2.0	
Wisconsin	1.7	
Iowa	1.0	
Minnesota	1.0	
Nebraska	.5	
North Dakota	.3	
South Dakota	-	
		27.4
Rocky Mountain		
Colorado	.7	
Montana	.3	
Utah	.3	
Wyoming	.3	
Idaho	-	
Nevada	-	
		1.5
Far West		
California	3.4	
Washington	1.5	
Oregon	.5	
Hawaii	.3	
		5.6
No State Given	1.2	
		1.2
Total		100.0

This early childhood picture also parallels rather closely
the residence makeup depicted in the map on page 18. Native
born New Yorkers are by far the greatest single segment,

and, though 34.7 per cent of all writers were born or spent
the first ten years of their lives in New York, 54.8 per cent
now call this state home. This same growth (population
shift) is true for California where 3.4 per cent are native,
yet 16.6 per cent are now residents. In fact, the New England and Middle Atlantic states are now "home" for 68.7 per
cent of all writers, though only 56.7 per cent were native
born. The Midwest, on the other hand, the native region of
27.4 per cent, is now home to only 5.2 per cent of all writers.

Other Characteristics

Age and Sex
        Sixty-eight per cent of all writers are male. Although
the median age for writers is 49 years, the female average
(median) age is 51 1/2 years, slightly higher than the males
whose median age is the same as for the group as a whole.
        Three-fifths of all writers are between ages 40 and 60,
Table II, page 23. One writer in five is under 40 years of
age, the same ratio as for those 60 and over. For the population at large, only 37.0 per cent are between 40 and 60
years of age. Unfortunately, statistics covering other professions by sex and age are unavailable. Lawyers--the only
profession on which even an age breakdown was obtainable--
in the 40 to 60 age bracket are proportionally larger than the
total population, but considerably less than writers as a
group. While all lawyers age 70 and over approximate closely the population at large, writers in this age group are
about one per cent higher than the population at large and two
per cent higher than lawyers.
        The larger proportion of writers 70 and over simply

means that more writers continue to work at their profession after reaching age 70 than do lawyers--and probably
other professions because of enforced retirement.

Male writers outnumber female writers in all age
groups except ages 50-59 and 70-79. For the population at
large, the proportion of women exceed that for men in the 29
and under, 60 and over age groups.

For the population at large also, the proportion of
male and female under 30 years of age far exceed those of
writers--and all lawyers but to a lesser degree. This fact
only serves to emphasize the length of time required for the
writer, lawyer, or other professional to establish himself in
his chosen field, partly because of the length of required
training, but also as in the case of writers because of the
time required to become "accepted."

Table II.
All Writers By Age And Sex Compared With Population
At Large, And Lawyers

| Age Grouping | All Writers | | | Total Population[1] | | | Lawyers[1] |
	Male	Female	Total	Male	Female	Total	Total
20-29	2.3	1.4	2.1	22.1	22.3	22.2	15.7
30-39	19.5	14.3	17.8	25.2	24.3	24.7	26.2
40-49	32.2	28.6	30.6	21.5	20.7	21.1	25.8
50-59	26.2	35.7	29.4	16.0	15.8	15.9	17.8
60-69	15.1	10.0	13.7	10.4	10.9	10.6	10.0
70+	4.7	10.0	6.4	4.8	6.0	5.5	4.5
Totals	100.0	100.0	100.0	100.0	100.0	100.0	100.0
N =	(298)	(140)	(438)				

1.   Source: Statistical Abstract of the U. S., 1960 Edition

Though statistics are unavailable by professions on a
sex-age breakdown, it is easy enough to determine the proportion of total males and females for various professions.
For the population at large, e.g. the total labor force,
women outnumber men by 1.9 per cent; in only two professions compared in Table III below do women account for as
much as a fourth of the labor force--that of writing, and
other than college teachers. Even for college teachers,
males outnumber females three to one, but for secondary,
elementary, and other teachers, the ratios are reversed.
Female physicians, lawyers, and engineers account for only
a small fraction of these professions.

Table III.

Proportion Of Males And Females By Selected Professions

	Male	Female
Total Labor Force, U.S. (Age 20 and Over)	48.1	51.9
Writers	68.0	32.0
Teachers: College	77.1	22.9
Other	25.5	74.5
Physicians	93.9	6.1
Lawyers	97.3	2.7
Engineers	98.8	1.2

Marital Status

Four-fifths of all male writers are married and living with spouse, while slightly less than three-fifths of all
female writers are married, living with spouse, Table IV,
page 26. Of the married writers, one in four is female;

of the non-married writers, one in two is female. None of
the female writers is married and separated, though two
per cent of the male writers are. Male writers show a
much larger proportion of marrieds than for the population
at large.

Almost two-thirds of the females, 17 years and older,
in the population at large are married, considerably higher
than for female writers. In fact, female writers are less
likely to be married and more likely to be divorced or single
or never married. Widows are about four times as common
as widowers as writers.

We do not know how many children the authors have
because the only request made of them on the questionnaire
was for the number of dependent children. As an average,
however, there are 1.006 children under 18 years of age per
family for those married and living with spouse. If all families are counted (including those married and separated,
divorced, and widowed) the average is .9 per household. The
comparable figure for the population at large is 1.4. (See
Table IVa.)

More than half (52.9 per cent) of the writers' families have no dependent children; for the population at large,
only 44.2 per cent have no children under 18 years of age.
Writers with one or two dependent children approximate all
families as a whole, though only one writer family in 300
have as many as five dependent children, one in 30 have four
children under eighteen. More than twice as many families
at large have four or more children.

The number of dependents, of course, has a direct
bearing on the writer's income tax paid as well as on the
demands in the spending of his net income after taxes.

Table IV.

Marital Status Of Writers By Sex And Children Under 18 Years Of Age, Compared With The Marital Status Of Population At Large

Status	All Writers			(Number of Children, Percent)						Population at Large[1]	
	Male	Female	Total	None	1	2	3	4	5	Male	Female
Married, Living With Spouse	80.5	59.3	73.7	60.2	86.9	98.4	94.0	91.7	100.0	69.8	66.0
Married and Separated	2.0	-	1.4	1.9	1.5	-	-	-	-		
Divorced and Single	4.4	8.6	5.7	6.8	6.1	1.6	3.0	8.3	-	1.8	2.3
Never Married	11.4	25.0	15.8	26.1	-	-	-	-	-	24.5	18.8
Widowed	1.7	7.1	3.4	4.9	1.5	-	3.0	-	-	3.9	12.8
Totals	100	100	100	100	100	100	100	100	100	100	100
N =	(298)	(140)	(438)	(264)	(66)	(61)	(34)	(12)	(1)		

1. Source: Statistical Abstract of the U. S., 1960, p. 40.

26

Table IVa.

Comparison Of Writers With Population At Large By Dependent Children

	Writers (Per Cent)	Population at Large[2] (Per Cent)
No Children Under 18	52.9	44.2
1 Child	17.9	18.5
2 Children	16.5	18.2
3 Children	9.2	10.3
4 or More Children	3.5	8.7
Totals	100.0	100.0

2. Statistical Abstract of the U. S., 1960

Education

Writers as a group are far better formally schooled than the total population.

Better than 50 per cent of the population at large-- both male and female--had in 1957 some high school or less as their entire formal education. (See Table VI, page 30). This proportion was ten times that for all writers.

There are about three times as many in the population as a whole with only a high school diploma as there are writers with only a high school education. More than six times as many writers as all men and women have college degrees. In fact, less than a fifth of the population at large have had any college training at all.

Among writers, three times as many male writers as females have only a grade school education. All these writers are 50 years and older, and they are more likely to be widowed or divorced than married, Table V, page 29.

Those writers with private schooling are younger

writers--most under 30 years of age--and are more likely to
have never married. But of those privately tutored, all are
60 years and over. Twice as many of them are women,
more likely to be divorced and single.

Of all the "married but separated" writers, either these
men have had some high school or some college training.
Half of all widowed writers have college degrees; three-
fifths of those writers single or married do.

Twice as many female writers as males have only a
high school education, though the proportion of males and
females with some college or with a college degree are about
even. Altogether, almost 90 per cent of all writers have had
some college training. Thus, while a formal education is not
a prerequisite to this profession, more than 60 per cent actually have college degrees. Only 1.6 per cent have only a
grade school education, and under five per cent have less
than a high school diploma.

Writers' Fathers' Occupations

About two in every five fathers of professional writers
are or were professional people themselves as compared to
the national male ratio of one in 14.[3] The other major
occupational classification contributing highly to author pro-
geny is that of Managers, Officials, and Proprietors (Table
VII page 31) where three times as many fathers of authors
are in these occupations as there are males proportionally
in the same occupations nationally (Table VIII, page 33).
Together, these two occupational groups account for two-
thirds of the fathers of writers.

Table V.

Writers' Education By Sex, Age, And Marital Status

Education	Sex		Age							Marital Status				
	Male	Female	Under 30	30–39	40–49	50–59	60–69	70–79	80	Marr. Liv.w/ Spouse	Marr. & Sep.	Div. & Sgl.	Never Mar-ried	Wid-owed
Only Grade Schl.	2.4	.7				3.1	5.0	4.0		1.2		8.0		14.3
Some High Schl.	2.7	.7			2.2	.8	6.7	4.0		1.9	16.7	4.0		7.1
Private School	.3	.7	11.1		.7					.3			1.4	
Private Tutor	.3	.7					1.7	4.0		.3		4.0		
High School Graduate	6.4	12.1		6.4	10.4	7.0	11.6	4.0		8.7		16.0	4.3	7.1
Some College	26.5	27.2		32.1	29.6	30.5	15.0	12.0	33.3	26.0	83.3	20.0	28.6	21.5
College Degree	61.4	57.9	88.9	61.5	57.1	58.6	60.0	72.0	66.7	61.6		48.0	65.7	50.0
Total	100.	100.	100.	100.	100.	100.	100.	100.	100.	100.	100.	100.	100.	100.
N =	(298)	(140)	(9)	(78)	(135)	(128)	(60)	(25)	(3)	(323)	(6)	(25)	(70)	(14)

29

Table VI.

Comparison Of Writers' Education With That Of Total Population

Education	All Writers			Total Population		
	Male	Female	Total	Male	Female	Total
Only Grade School	2.4	.7	1.6	30.2	27.4	28.6
Some High School	2.7	.7	2.3	23.9	24.1	23.7
High School Graduate	7.0	13.5	9.1	25.7	31.3	29.0
Some College	26.5	27.2	26.7	9.9	10.3	10.1
College Degree	61.4	57.9	60.3	10.3	6.9	8.6
Totals	100.0	100.0	100.0	100.0	100.0	100.0

Table VII.

Father's Occupation--All Writers

Professional, Technical, and Kindred:

Occupation	%	Occupation	%	Percent of Total
Accountant	1.6	Lawyer-Judge	6.9	
Architect	.5	Minister	3.2	
Artist	.5	Researcher	.5	
Author	.7	Teacher	4.1	
Cartographer	.2	Journalist	2.7	
Chemist	.9	Others	1.1	
Designer	.5			
Doctor	3.9			
Druggist	.9			
Engineer	4.3			
Entertainer	2.5			
Executive	3.0			37.9

Craftsmen, Foremen, and Kindred:

Occupation	%	Occupation	%	Percent of Total
Blacksmith	.2	Mason	.2	
Carpenter	.7	Printer	.5	
Cobbler	.2	Railroading	2.1	
Contractor	1.1	Tailor	1.1	
Decorator	.2			
Electrician	.2			
Foreman	.9			
House Painter	.9			
Jeweler	1.1			
Machinist	.2			9.8

Clerical and Kindred Workers:

Occupation	%	Percent of Total
Clerk	1.1	1.1

Managers, Officials, and Proprietors:

Banker	1.8				
Builder	.9				
Businessman	14.6	Other Retailers	2.1	Manufacturer	6.2
		Government	2.3	Wholesaler	1.8	29.7

Salesworkers:

| Brokers | 3.4 | Salesman | 4.8 | Advertising | 1.4 | 11.2 |

Service Workers, Except Household:

| Barber | .2 | Chef | .2 | Fireman | .2 | |
| Bartender | .2 | | | | | .9 |

Operatives and Kindred Workers:

| Butcher | .2 | Cutter | .5 | Lumberman | .7 | 1.4 |

Farmers and Farm Managers:

| Farmer | 2.3 | Rancher | .7 | Breeder | .2 | 3.2 |

Laborers:

| Laborers | 1.1 | | | | | 1.1 |

Occupations Not Reported--   3.4

Total   100.0

(N=438)

32

Table VIII.

Occupation Distribution: Total Male Employment

			Percent of Total
Professional, Technical, and Kindred:			
Accountant .8	Designer .1	Lawyer-Judge .4	
Architect .1	Doctor .4	Minister .2	
Artist .1	Druggist .2	Researcher .1	
Author .02	Engineer 1.3	Teacher .9	
Cartographer .3	Entertainer .2	Journalist .2	
Chemist .2	Executive .1	Others 1.8	7.3
Craftsmen, Foremen, and Kindred:			
Blacksmith .1	Electrician .8	Mason .4	
Carpenter 2.2	Foreman 1.9	Printer .1	
Cobbler .1	House Painter .9	Railroading .2	
Contractor .02	Jeweler .1	Tailor .2	
Decorator .1	Machinist 1.3	Other 10.2	18.6
Clerical and Kindred Workers:			
Clerk 3.7	Others 2.7		6.4

33

Managers, Officials, and Proprietors: — 10.7

Banker	.2	
Builder	.3	
Businessman	2.9	
Other Retailers	.5	
Government	.3	
Manufacturer	.9	
Wholesaler	.4	
Others	5.2	

Salesworkers: — 6.4

Brokers	.3
Salesmen	5.0
Advertising	.1
Others	.3

Service Workers, Except Household: — 5.9

Barber	.5
Bartender	.4
Chef	.5
Firemen	.3
Others	4.2

Operatives and Kindred Workers: — 20.1

Butcher	.4
Cutter	.3
Lumberman	.4
Others	18.9

Farmers and Farm Managers: — 10.3

Farmer	10.3
Others	.1

Laborers: — 8.1

Laborers	6.8
Others	1.3

Categories Not Included--	6.1
Total	100.0

Source: Statistical Abstract of the U. S., 1960.

34

Within the professional occupations grouping, almost one-fifth of the authors' fathers are lawyers or judges-- particularly disproportionate since the corresponding figure for the national male average is one-seventeenth. Because many of the professional national male group are not fathers, the disproportion looms even larger. (This point is applicable to all Census occupations. Unfortunately, Census occupational distribution figures by marital status are not published.)

Though it is perhaps natural to expect the largest portion of writers to come from professional backgrounds, fathers who are or were authors themselves are not progenitors of authors. The figure is less than one per cent. In contrast, 3.2 per cent of all lawyers had fathers who were lawyers; 2.2 per cent of engineers' fathers were engineers-- the same percentage applicable for doctors, and 2.3 per cent of ministers had fathers who were ministers themselves.[4] Four and two-tenths per cent of other professionals followed in their fathers' footsteps.

Writers' fathers who are or were railroad men (Craftsmen, Foremen and Kindred) outnumber their counterpart nationally 20 to 1 with approximately the same ratio holding for journalists in the professional group. And, writers whose fathers are businessmen (owners, managers, buyers, merchants) account for almost 15 per cent of the total, while nationally, businessmen make up slightly less than three per cent of the male working force.

The Salesworkers grouping is the third and only other occupation distribution category larger for fathers of authors than the Census tally. Thus, the professional, managerial, and salesworking forces account for almost eight-tenths (78.8 per cent) of the occupations of the writers' fathers.

When the Current Writers Became Professionals

Judged by current writers, more women (age 60-69 in 1957, Table IX, page 38) became professional writers earlier--in the decade 1919-1919--when they were in their twenties than did any group of women since. Interestingly enough, this was the decade when the struggle for woman suffrage was at its height.

Such was not the case for male writers, however. A higher percentage (40.6 per cent) of the younger male writers (in their forties in 1957), turning professional in the decade 1930-1939, became professional earlier than for any older male groups. This decade, of course, was that of the great depression.

About the same portion of men aged 50-59 in 1957 turned professional at about the same age--in the decade 1930-1939 when they were in their thirties--as those ten years older (the 60-69 age group who became professional in 1920-1929). For the women in the same age groupings, however, more than twice as many age 50-59 years turned professional (1930-1939) earlier than did their counterpart--those ages 60-69 who became professional in the decade 1920-29. For the 50-year-old female writers, these were also the great depression years; so perhaps more women simply turned to writing as a means of adding to family income. About a fourth (26.4 per cent) of all women writers took up the profession of writing during this period; an equal proportion of men did also.

Men as a whole turn professional earlier than women. The increased percentages in those turning professional during the early postwar (World War II) years--the sudden swing upward for both male writers (31 per cent) and female (35 per cent) over the World War II years--also seem   to point up this fact. A higher percentage of female writers turned professional in the postwar years than did those turning professional during the war. For men, however, only slightly more became professional writers during the war years than immediately afterwards.

Of all writers, only 1.1 per cent turned professional as early as 1910, though almost 50 per cent (47.1 per cent) of our current writers became professional before 1940. Younger writers on the whole are becoming professional earlier than older writers.

Notes

1. The term came into use under the Writers Projects Administration in the mid-thirties in a general comparison of the writer's economic position to that of the farm tenant sharecropper.

2. The median in all instances is determined by arraying in order of size from the smallest to the largest, or from largest to smallest value in any grouping, and selecting the midway point.

3. U. S. Bureau of the Census, Statistical Abstract of the United States: 1960, Eighty-first edition, Washington, D. C., 1960, pp. 218-221.

4. J. Lloyd Warner and James C. Abegglen, Occupational Mobility in American Business and Industry, University of Minnesota Press, Minneapolis, 1955, p. 38.

Table IX.

Age of Writers (1957) And Year They Turned Professional

Age of Writers

Date of Becoming Professional	Male								Female							
	Under 30	30-39	40-49	50-59	60-69	70-79	80+	Total	Under 30	30-39	40-49	50-59	60-69	70-79	80+	Total
1903-1909						16.7	50.0	1.0						7.7	100.	1.4
1910-1919					20.0	41.6	50.0	5.0				2.0	28.6	30.8		6.4
1920-1929			3.1	26.9	40.0	41.7		15.8			2.5	12.0	21.4	46.1		11.4
1930-1939		1.7	40.6	39.7	13.3			25.8		5.0	20.0	48.0	21.4	7.7		26.4
1940-1944		17.3	18.7	12.8	11.1			14.4		15.0	20.0	14.0	7.2			13.6
1945-1949		31.0	17.7	6.4	4.4			14.1		35.0	27.5	12.0				17.9
1950-1957	100.	50.0	19.8	14.1	11.1			23.8	100.	45.0	30.0	12.0	21.4	7.7		22.9
Totals	100.	100.	100.	100.	100.	100.	100.	100.	100.	100.	100.	100.	100.	100.	100.	100.
N =	(7)	(58)	(96)	(78)	(45)	(12)	(2)	(298)	(2)	(20)	(40)	(50)	(14)	(13)	(1)	(140)

38

Chapter II

Casualness Of The Labor Market

Most non-writing occupations appear to be more important to writers than writing, for though 63.9 per cent of all writers reported income from writing of some kind in all five years, 51.4 per cent report receiving more income from non-writing sources (including spouse's income) than writing. And more than 3 out of 5 (61.6 per cent) of those deriving personal income from non-writing sources reported income from the same source for each of the years between 1953 and 1957. This group of writers represents almost a third-- 31.5 per cent--of all writers.

In all but one year--1953-1957--a higher proportion of writers drew personal income from non-writing sources than from any single writing source, Table X, page 41. The questionnaire, designed to allow the writer to report his income from four major areas, included these categories:

(1) Free Lance Writing: (a) from books
(b) from magazines
(c) from plays
(d) from royalties, ASCAP

(2) Free Lance-Employed: (a) television
(b) motion pictures

This category is set up to include originals and/ or salaried writings from either television or motion pictures since there was no way of determining from the questionnaire whether the income reported was for an original work or for an assignment. <u>For convenience, this area of writing income is referred to as "F. L.-Emp." throughout the study.</u>

(3) Directed Writing: (a) staff writing for magazines
                                     and/or newspapers
                        (b) advertising copywriting
                        (c) ghostwriting
                        (d) translations
                        (e) reviews and critiques
                        (f) other special assignments

(4) Non-writing Occupations.

Very few writers it appears from the table are single specialists. That is, many had more than one kind of source of personal income. The pattern of earning personal income from more than one source--either writing or non-writing-- is indicated by the consistency of the percentage of total writers reporting any personal income year to year from a single source. This breakdown does seem to point up more irregularity for the playwright's income from playwriting in that the stability is less year to year; the number reporting drops to less than 51 per cent of the total in 1954 and 1953. Such irregularity is also true for "F. L.-Emp." writing.

Magazine writing, an overlapping field especially for authors of books, shows great stability in the percentage reporting year to year as does the percentage reporting personal income from non-writing occupations.

Cogent comments from the respondents confirm these findings but at the same time indicate the irregularity in income for some whatever the source:

> Mr. A, age 48: I am a playwright and screenwriter, but as you can see, only in one of the five years has this paid off.

> Mr. B, age 77: I have published about 30 plays. Over the thirty years they netted me about $2,200. One book on play production, over 25 years netted $950. Another I have not yet been able to extract a penny from the publisher on though it has sold.

Table X.

Writers Reporting Income, By Source, 1953–1957:
(As Percentage Of Total)

Source	Per Cent of All Writers	Number Reporting	Per Cent Reporting In:				
			1957	1956	1955	1954	1953
Free Lance Writing: Books	65.6	287 = 100%	88.9	84.0	79.8	76.3	70.0
Magazines	46.6	204 = 100	69.6	64.2	66.2	63.2	62.7
Plays	28.3	124 = 100	78.2	70.2	56.5	50.0	43.6
Royalties	3.0	13 = 100	100.0	92.3	76.9	69.2	61.5
Free Lance-Employed	24.4	107 = 100	62.6	66.4	55.1	51.4	42.1
Directed Writing	20.8	91 = 100	74.7	68.1	67.0	60.4	58.2
Non-writing Occupations	51.1	224 = 100	85.3	85.3	85.3	81.7	76.8

(N=438)

41

I published my first book in 1911; it wasn't until
1948 I earned enough to live on from writing,
however.

Mrs. C, age 63: The chief returns from my books
do not show in these years covered by the study.
I do write magazine articles fairly regularly, however, but the pay is not high.

Miss D, age 55: I have published about 100 articles
and the equivalent of 6 books--mostly scientific without remuneration. It (the questionnaire) hardly
applies to me. I received fees for articles especially in the 20's and 30's. One book still pays me
royalties--about $100 a year. I have published a
great deal--almost all non-remunerative.

Mr. E, age 37: This is a hell of a profession!
Look at my 1956 income--$11,374--after deducting
expenses, but for 1957, I had a net loss of $44.17.
It's reported that way on my tax form, too.

Mr. F, age 43: I had a book published in 1947,
have had several reprints--one in 1949, one in
1958, another in 1959; there was no income from
writing during the years 1953-1957.

Altogether, more than one writer in two (51.1 per
cent) reported personal income earned apart from writing of
any kind between 1953-1957. These writers listed 37 occupational classifications--some giving as many as 6 different
occupations in the five years under study. And some writers
held two or more jobs simultaneously. Eliminating the
sources of personal income from Table XI which are obviously not occupations (e.g. investments, stocks, dividends, and
rentals) reveals that there were 1.4 non-writing jobs per
writer in this five-year period. For the population at large,
one out of every 20 employed persons in the United States
were multiple job holders in 1957.[1] The comparable figure
for writers was considerably more than one in 3; these people earned on the average from 1.2 jobs other than their

chosen profession of writing in 1957. Table XI reveals that
for all the non-writing jobs held, almost half (49.4 per cent)
were for the full five years. An additional fourth of the
writers reported steady personal incomes from the same
type jobs--or sources--for three or four of the entire five
years. Other jobs also carry this full-time-employment
inference in that the respondent listing them showed two
years' personal income from the same source before switch-
ing to some other job.

There were, of course, multiple job holders in each
of these year(s) groupings, and those reporting all five years
were no exception. Some had two non-writing sources of
personal income; some had three for the entire five years.
If all multiple sources of personal income are eliminated,
however, and only those writers counted who had a non-
writing source of personal income, 61.6 per cent of the
group had five-year personal incomes from the same non-
writing source.[2]

Other writers' comments typify the writer and his
non-writing pursuits:

Mr. G, age 40: I published a prize-winning novel
in 1941, but if it were not for the fact I had outside income, I couldn't live on my writing income
which averages $350-500 a year.

Mrs. H, age 53: I began as a newspaper reporter, switched to promotion, and did short stories
in my free time from writing promotion for TIME.
In 1941 I quit promotion, began my first novel,
and for 15 years earned all my living as a writer--
4 novels, many novelettes and short stories, a book
column, a newspaper daily column, and fill-in
periods several times a year for the Saturday
Review. I'm now back in promotion.

Miss I, age 53: As you can see, I couldn't
possibly support myself from writing, and so I

Table XI.

Non-Writing Occupations Of Writers And Per Cent Reporting Income From That Occupation Each Year, 1953-1957

Occupation	5 Years	4 Years	3 Years	2 Years	1 Year	Total
Teaching, Coaching, Librarian	17.9	28.6	4.7	21.0	9.1	16.4
Editor, Editing	7.7	8.6	18.6	7.9	9.1	9.5
Lecturing, Speeches	7.7	11.4	-	15.8	6.8	7.9
Acting, Performing, Announcer, Panelist	7.1	2.9	4.7	5.3	13.6	7.0
Executive, Administrator, Owner, Manager	8.3	5.7	7.0	5.3	4.5	7.0
Public Relations	6.4	-	9.3	5.3	9.1	6.3
Consulting	7.7	-	2.3	5.3	4.5	5.7
Investments, Stocks, Dividends	9.6	2.9	-	-	-	5.1
Government Service (Federal, State, Local)	3.8	2.9	9.3	-	2.3	3.8
Secretarial	.6	-	4.7	13.2	4.5	3.2
Rental, Realty	4.5	-	-	2.6	2.3	2.8
Salesman, Promotion, Advertising	3.8	-	4.7	-	2.3	2.8
Medical (Physician, Dentist, Therapist)	3.8	-	2.3	-	2.3	2.5
Producing (TV, Stage)	.6	8.5	-	5.3	-	1.9
Research	.6	-	-	-	9.1	1.6
Military Service	-	2.9	4.7	5.3	-	1.6
Clerk	.6	-	2.3	2.6	2.3	1.3
Artist	1.3	2.9	2.3	-	-	1.3
Director (TV, Stage)	.6	2.9	2.3	-	2.3	1.3
Designing	1.3	2.9	2.3	-	-	1.3
Prizes, Awards	.6	-	2.3	-	4.5	1.3

Occupation	5 Years	4 Years	3 Years	2 Years	1 Year	Total
Illustrating	.6	2.9	2.3	-	-	.9
Farmer, Rancher, Animal Trainer	1.3	-	-	-	2.3	.9
Investigator, Inspector	.6	5.7	-	-	-	.9
Engineer	1.3	-	2.3	-	2.3	.9
Agent	-	-	2.3	-	-	.6
Carpenter, Machinist	.6	2.9	-	2.6	-	.6
Printer, Printing	-	-	2.3	2.6	2.3	.6
Politics	-	2.9	-	-	-	.6
Manufacturing	.6	-	-	-	-	.6
Proofreading	-	-	2.3	-	-	.3
Recording	-	-	2.3	-	-	.3
Photographer	-	-	2.3	-	-	.3
Economist	-	-	2.3	-	-	.3
Unemployment	-	-	-	-	2.3	.3
Unclassified	-	-	-	-	2.3	.3
Totals (Per Cent)	100.0	100.0	100.0	100.0	100.0	100.0
N =	(156)	(35)	(43)	(38)	(44)	(316)

have a job editing books and manuscripts for
publishers and clients which brings me about
$7,000 a year.

Mr. J, age 43: I earned my living exclusively
from writing 1946-1950 ... temporarily diverted
to other occupations.

But actually, occasional non-writing employment is
rare. There were only 13.9 per cent of the jobs listed in a
one-shot capacity, and many of these were done while the
writer held another full-time job. All of the writers reporting jobs on a one-time (e.g. one year only) basis, reported
personal income from writing of some sort, also.

By classifying the 37 occupational classifications listed
in Table XI according to the U. S. Census distribution, we
can see that almost three-fourths of the writers seek non-
writing jobs in the professional, technical and kindred field.
No other single area accounts for as much as ten per cent
of the writers, Table XII.

Table XII.

Non-Writing Occupational Classifications Of Writers

Occupation	Per Cent
Professional, Technical and Kindred	71.2
Managers, Officials, and Proprietors	7.3
Craftsmen, Foremen, and Kindred	2.5
Sales Workers	6.3
Clerical and Kindred Workers	4.7
Farmers and Farm Managers	1.0
Miscellaneous (Awards, Unemployment, Unclassified)	7.0
Total (N=316)	100.0

To explore the extent of casualness in the labor market
among writers, we can examine their "employment" a number

of different ways. For instance, we can first look at a breakdown from the viewpoint of aggregate personal income for all
writers on the basis of five-year earnings. (Note: Personal Income will refer to the writer's writing and non-writing income.
Spouse's income is not included in personal income but is included in family income. See Below.)

A second approach is to analyze specifically the importance of non-writing personal income for that portion of writers
who derive it from non-writing sources.

And, a third view would measure the marriage-linked dependence for family income on writing and non-writing sources
of income--that is, the extent of dependence of the writer on
his spouse's income.

Within each analysis, the major source of total income
(e.g. writing versus non-writing), the median per cent of income, and the dollar income (median) derived are determined.

Based on aggregates, first of all then, for all writers the
largest proportion--not a majority--earn all of their personal
income from writing of some kind, as indicated:

46.6   per cent earned all personal income--1953-1957--
        from writing of any kind.

18.9   per cent earned the majority of their personal in-
        come from writing but also derived some personal
        income from non-writing sources.

32.2   per cent earned the majority of their personal in-
        come from non-writing sources but also earned
        from writing as well.

2.3   per cent reported no personal income earned from
        any source during the five-year period.

Or by way of summary, 65.5[3] per cent of all writers earn the
majority of their personal income from writing of some
kind.   And 51.1 per cent of all writers earn some non-
writing personal income.

But if we add to the writer's personal income that
earned by the working spouse, we find that 51.4 per cent of
all writers report receiving more income from non-writing
sources than from writing.

The median per cent of aggregate personal income
from writing for all writers is 94.2 per cent. This simply
means that half of all writers earn 94.2 per cent or more
of their total personal incomes from writing of any kind--
that this same half of all writers derive 5.8 per cent or less
of their total income from non-writing sources. The opposite side of the coin, of course, is that for the other half
of all writers, these percentages are reversed.

Aggregate personal income (median) for all writers
from all writing totaled $15,277 for the five years between
1953 and 1957, or $3,055 annually. And the aggregate me-
dian personal income from non-writing for all writers was
$298 or $60 annually. Though small, the latter figure as-
sumes added significance when one remembers that 48.9 per
cent of all writers reported no personal income from any
non-writing source at all.

In the second approach--the importance of non-writing personal income to the 51.1 per cent of all writers who
had such income--the median per cent of aggregate personal
income from non-writing sources was 71.3 per cent. Or,
to put it another way, half of all writers deriving personal
income from non-writing sources acquired 71.3 per cent or
more of their total personal income from this source, and
28.7 per cent or less from writing of some kind.

The aggregate personal income (median) from non-
writing for writers deriving non-writing income was $20,390
for the five years, 1953-1957. Or, again, half of all writers

earning from non-writing occupations, drew 71.3 per cent or more of their personal income from this source which totaled $20,390 over the five years, or $4,078 annually.

The personal median earned from writing for the 28.7 per cent (aggregate) was $10,219 for the five years, or $2,044 yearly. Thus, the annual aggregate median personal income earned by writers with non-writing personal incomes from non-writing sources was twice that earned from writing.

A more detailed analysis of the personal incomes earned each year (from the same source) by writers with non-writing incomes emphasizes the crucial importance of this type of personal income to almost a third of all writers. Those writers with regular non-writing jobs, 61.6 per cent of writers with non-writing personal incomes (31.5 per cent of all writers) get more than four-fifths of their personal income from these non-writing jobs. For this group:

a. The median per cent for aggregate personal income from writing is 17.7 per cent;

b. The median per cent for aggregate personal income from non-writing is 82.3 per cent.

The aggregate personal income (median) for writing is $7,305 or $1,461 yearly; the aggregate median for non-writing is $34,780 or $6,956 yearly, for this group of writers who earn steady non-writing personal incomes. The non-writing median personal income is four and three-fourths times as much as the median earned from writing.

Some of the writers were quick to admit that the non-writing job had become primary in their livelihood:

Mr. K, age 60: Even after publishing 7 books, I still make my living in other pursuits.

Mr. L, age 56: I got quite a bit from royalties on three novels for a few years, but I'm a news-

paper man, now, by profession. I was forced
to turn to something; I took a job in writing,
even though it's not the kind I really love doing.

Mr. M, age 37: My main income is from staff
editing of a magazine--I couldn't live on what I
make as a free lance.

Mrs. N, age 51: My writing became incidental
when I was forced to turn to teaching.

Mr. O, age 48: Neither my wife (who writes)
nor I are happy about the present situation we
find ourselves in--both on the staff of a large
circulation magazine. I'd like to just write--
so would she--what I want to [write]; the system
isn't the kind that will let me do that and that
alone ... and live.

Marriage-Linked Dependence

Of the three-fourths (75.1 per cent) of all writers who
are married, more than 98 per cent live with spouses. And
following the current American trend, there are many working
wives. In 1949, the figure for working wives in the population at large was reported to be 46 per cent; by 1959 this
figure had increased to 55 per cent.[4] Married women writers
--comprising a fourth of all married writers--reported 79.5
per cent working husbands.

Altogether, 53.8 per cent of married writers have
working spouses; 46.2 per cent reported non-working spouses.

Age of the writer apparently has little to do with
whether the spouse works or not. There are slightly more
writers under 50 years of age--both male and female--with
working spouses than writers in the same age grouping whose
spouses do not work. (See Table XIII.)

Employed spouses, however, showed steady employment throughout the five years; 70.1 per cent of them earned

Table XIII.

Age Of Writer And Employed Status Of Spouse

Age Grouping	Writer's Spouse Employed (Per Cent)			Writer's Spouse Unemployed (Per Cent)			All Married Writers (per Cent)
	Male	Female	Total	Male	Female	Total	
20 – 29	.9	-	.5	.7	-	.7	.6
30 – 39	21.6	16.7	19.8	14.1	11.8	13.8	17.0
40 – 49	35.1	36.4	35.6	32.6	35.2	32.9	34.3
50 – 59	30.6	31.8	31.1	28.1	41.2	29.6	30.4
60 – 69	9.9	9.1	9.6	17.8	5.9	16.4	12.8
70+	1.8	6.0	3.4	6.7	5.9	6.6	4.9
Total	100.0	100.0	100.0	100.0	100.0	100.0	100.0
N =	(111)	(66)	(177)	(135)	(17)	(152)	(329)

a portion of the total family income every year, Table XIV,
page 52. Only a little more than a tenth of the spouses
worked for just one year between 1953 and 1957. We do not
know the source of the spouse's income, for only total earnings were requested on the questionnaire.

Following the procedure used earlier in detailing aggregate personal income from writing for all writers and aggregate personal income from non-writing for writers with this
source of income, we can again examine (1) the median per
cent for aggregate income, and (2) the income median for
(a) all employed spouses of married writers, (b) the employed husbands of female writers, and (c) the employed wives
of male writers. Comparisons are made with aggregates
for all married writers, all husbands of female writers, and
all wives of male writers.

Table XIV.

Number of Years Writers' Spouses Worked: 1953-1957

Years Employed	Spouses of Male Writers (Per Cent)	Spouses of Female Writers (Per Cent)	Total
5 Years	60.4	86.4	70.1
4 Years	7.2	3.0	5.6
3 Years	14.4	1.5	9.6
2 Years	4.5	-	2.8
1 Year	13.5	9.1	11.9
Total	100.0	100.0	100.0
N =	(111)	(66)	(177)

Annual personal incomes for writers (with employed
spouses) (1) from writing, (2) from all sources, (3) their
spouses income, and (4) total family incomes can then be
compared with writers (without employed spouses) to see
what the writer's dependence is on his spouse's income.

The median per cent of aggregate income from whatever source for all employed spouses was 34.4 per cent for
the five years between 1953-1957. Employed spouses
thus accounted for 34.4 per cent of the total family income
each year. The median for all married writers' spouses
whether working or not working was 1.8 per cent.

Aggregate income (median) for working spouses was
$18,000, or $3,600 yearly, while for all spouses, the comparable figures were $832, or $166 yearly.

For the employed male spouses of female writers, the
median per cent for aggregate income from whatever source
was 66.6 per cent, and the median income for these working husbands totaled $37,600, or $7,520 yearly. Female
writers' aggregate personal income (median) from all sources
was $16,556 or $3,311 yearly, while the median writing
personal income (aggregate) was $12,038, or $2,407 annually. Altogether, the aggregate median family income from
all sources for female writers, including the husband's, was
$63,821, or $12,764 yearly.

For the employed female spouses of male writers, the
median per cent for aggregate income was 17.2 per cent,
and the median income for these working wives totaled
$9,900, or $1,980 yearly. Male writers' aggregate personal income (median) from all sources was $42,414, or $8,483
yearly, while the median writing personal income (aggregate)
was $19,100, or $3,820 yearly. Altogether, the aggregate
median family income from all sources for male writers,
including the wife's, was $58,800, or $11,760 yearly.

By way of summary, for all married women authors,
42.2 per cent earn more money from their writing and/or
other jobs than their husbands, but for all married women
authors with working husbands, only 30.3 per cent make as

much or more money from their writing and/or other jobs
than the husbands do at their jobs.

For all married male authors, 93.9 per cent make
more money with their writing and/or other jobs than their
wives make, but 13.5 per cent of the working wives make
more money from their jobs, than their husbands do from
writing and/or other jobs combined.

While the employed spouse contributes on the average
34.4 per cent of the family income, just how important that
income is to the married writer is readily seen in Table XV,
page 55. The median (five-year average) personal income
from all sources for the married writer whose spouse is employed was $6,210. When the spouse's income is added, how-
ever, the median for family income is almost doubled--
$12,009--even though the median income for all employed
spouses is only $3,600.

By way of comparison, for all married writers the
median five-year average personal income was $7,946; for
married writers without employed spouses, the comparable
figure was $10,637. (See Table XVI, page 56.) And, for
the non-married writer, the median yearly personal income--
$3,243--is slightly more than half that of the married writer
whose spouse works--$6,210--(excluding the spouse's income)
--and slightly more than a third of that of the married writer
whose spouse does not work.

Thus, writers without working spouses are better earners than writers whose spouses must work--or by choice do
work. But, almost 60 per cent (57.2 per cent) of the married writers without working spouses had outside income,
that is, income derived from sources other than writing.
Writers with working spouses also had income from sources
other than writing and their spouses' incomes; 45.7 per cent

Table XV.

Writers With Married Spouses: Writers' And Their
Employed Spouses' Income By Sources
(1953–1957 Averages)

Annual Income (Dollars)	Writers' Writing Income Per Cent	Median	Writers' Total Income Per Cent	Median	Spouses' Income Per Cent	Median	Family Income Per Cent	Median
0 - 1500	30.5	$ 519	14.7	$ 600	31.1	$ 600	2.3	$ 620
1500 - 2500	9.6	1840	6.8	1809	9.6	2000	1.7	1980
2500 - 5000	24.9	3569	21.5	3823	18.6	3600	7.9	4308
5000 - 10000	14.7	6740	24.3	6832	20.3	6755	28.8	6769
10000 - 15000	7.9	12823	13.0	12940	6.2	11900	20.9	12293
15000 - 25000	6.7	19260	10.7	20067	9.6	19200	19.2	18707
25000 - 50000	3.9	33768	5.6	34632	2.8	27442	13.6	32667
50000 - 100000	1.1	66357	1.7	67400	1.7	50000	4.0	62938
100000 & over	.6	115066	1.7	115066	-	-	1.7	152880
Total	100.0		100.0		100.0		100.0	
N =	(177)		(177)		(177)		(177)	
Median		$ 3200		$ 6210		$ 3600		$ 12009

Table XVI.

Comparisons Of Incomes Earned By Writers With And Without Employed
Spouses And Non-Marrieds, All Sources, By Income Classes
(1953-1957 Averages)

Annual Income (Dollars)	Writers' With Employed Spouses Family Income		Writers' Without Employed Spouses Income		Other Writers' (Single, Divorced, Widowed) Income	
	Per Cent	Median	Per Cent	Median	Per Cent	Median
0 - 1500	2.3	$ 620	8.6	$ 38	30.2	$ 620
1500 - 2500	1.7	1980	3.3	1800	14.7	1941
2500 - 5000	7.9	4308	9.9	3659	21.1	3918
5000 - 10000	28.8	6769	27.0	7222	16.5	7660
10000 - 15000	20.9	12293	13.2	12802	9.2	11370
15000 - 25000	19.2	18707	23.7	17640	2.8	21704
25000 - 50000	13.6	32667	9.2	30181	2.8	33988
50000 - 100000	4.0	62938	3.9	66620	1.8	61533
100000 & over	1.7	152880	1.3	153010	.9	167673
Total	100.0		100.0		100.0	
N =	(177)		(152)		(109)	
Median		$12009		$ 10637		$ 3243

reported such income during the five years between 1953 and 1957.

And though writers whose spouses worked and who also derived income apart from writing numbered a tenth less than writers whose spouses did not work but who derived income apart from writing, the latter were also better earners at writing, Table XVII, page 59.

Obviously, then, there are married writers--both men and women--among those with working spouses who devote themselves entirely to writing while the husbands or wives work either (1) as writers, too, or (2) as non-writers. We do not know how many fit which category, as pointed out earlier, but there is considerable marriage-linked dependence for family income.

Two writers' comments about this dependence will illustrate:

> Mr. P, age 47: I became professional in 1936 not by virtue of earning a livelihood but in that year I became associated in the WPA Federal Writers Projects. Being eventually a district supervisor and continuing the employment for four years. Since then--after leaving the project and getting married--I have earned from one to eight hundred dollars each year from writing efforts--a [most] difficult feat in the type of writing I do. Since I never work at anything else when writing income continues (and as long as my wife earns enough for the household) and since I even go into debt regularly to enable myself to do writing, it follows that like an alcoholic takes to the bottle so I take to writing. After all, Van Gogh or Gaugin were no more professional.

> Mr. Q, age 49: I am the author of 6 books among the best known in the field. Do you wonder that I'm giving up juvenile writing? This is all I do, earning about $2,100 a year while my wife (who is not a writer) earns $15,000.

Writers' family incomes on the whole are higher than family incomes for the population at large. For example, 65 per cent[5] of the families at large received incomes under $5,000 in 1959. For writer families, even in 1957, the percentage receiving incomes under $5,000 was only 13 per cent. Those families having incomes in the $5,000 to $10,000 range accounted for 22 per cent of the total number of families in the country; 28 per cent of writer families received between $5,000 and $10,000. Families receiving $10,000 or more made up 12 per cent of all families in 1959, while writer families having $10,000 or more made up 59 per cent of all writer families. The latter is accounted for in good measure, as already indicated, by 65.1 per cent of the women--45.1 per cent who were working wives of male writers, and the 20.0 per cent female writers (with working husbands) --who added to family incomes.

Table XVII.

Writing Income (For Writers With And Without Employed Spouses) By Income Classes (1953-1957 Averages)

Annual Income (dollars)	Writers' (With Employed Spouses) Writing Income		Writers' (Without Employed Spouses) Writing Income	
	Per Cent (Writers)	Median (Income)	Per Cent (Writers)	Median (Income)
0 - 1500	30.5	$ 519	29.6	$ 305
1500 - 2500	9.6	1840	7.2	2052
2500 - 5000	24.9	3569	12.5	3600
5000 - 10000	14.7	6740	17.1	6996
10000 - 15000	7.9	12823	11.2	13566
15000 - 25000	6.7	19260	11.2	17640
25000 - 50000	3.9	33768	6.6	30740
50000 - 100000	1.1	66357	3.9	60788
100000 & over	.6	115066	.7	198020
Total N =	100.0 (177)		100.0 (152)	
Median	$3200		$5478	

Table XVIII.

Proportion Of Writers With Various Combinations Of Income Sources:
(1953-1957)

	Source of Income	(Writers) Per Cent
(1)	Book-Magazine Writing, and Non-writing Occupations	15.5
(2)	Book Writing and Non-writing Occupations	10.0
(3)	Book Writing Only	9.8
(4)	Book and Magazine Writing Only	7.1
(5)	Playwriting and Non-writing Occupations (with some "F.L.-Emp" and/or Directed Writing)	7.1
(6)	Playwriting and "F.L.-Emp" (with some Royalties and/or Directed Writing)	5.7
(7)	Book-Magazine-Playwriting (with some "F.L.-Emp" and/or Directed Writing)	4.3
(8)	Magazine Writing and Non-writing Occupations (with some Directed Writing)	4.3
(9)	Non-writing Occupations Only	4.1
(10)	Book-Magazine Writing (with some "F.L.-Emp" and/or Directed Writing)	4.1
(11)	Book-Magazine, and Non-writing Occupations (with some "F.L.-Emp" and/or Directed Writing)	4.1
(12)	Playwriting Only	3.6
(13)	Book and Directed Writing Only	3.0
(14)	Book-Magazine-Playwriting, and Non-writing Occupations (with some Royalties, "F.L.-Emp" and/or Directed Writing)	2.5
(15)	Book-Playwriting (with some "F.L.-Emp" and/or Directed Writing)	2.5
		2.1

60

Source of Income	(Writers) Per Cent
(16) Book and Non-writing Occupations (with some "F.L.-Emp" and/or Directed Writing	2.1
(17) Magazine-Playwriting (with some "F.L.-Emp" Writing)	1.8
(18) Magazine Writing Only	1.6
(19) "F.L.-Emp" Only (with some Royalties)	1.4
(20) Book-Playwriting and Non-writing Occupations (with some Royalties, "F.L.-Emp" and/or Directed Writing)	1.4
(21) Magazine Writing (with some "F.L.-Emp" and/or Directed Writing)	1.1
(22) Directed Writing Only	1.1
(23) Book and "F.L.-Emp" Only	.5
(24) Magazine-Playwriting, and Non-writing Occupations	.5
(25) Royalties Only	.5
(26) No Income from Any Source	2.3
Total (N - 438)	100.0

61

Not only is the casualness of the writer labor market
revealed by the amount of non-writing "employment" and the
marriage-linked dependence, but it is also evident in the
irregularity of the various combinations--even for writing--
used by writers in earning their incomes. Twenty-six different combinations of personal income sources (1953-1957)
are required to include all writers, Table XVIII.

While this table does not give any indication of how
much of all personal incomes come from the particular combinations, it reveals the combinations most important to the
majority of writers. Specific earnings from the various
combinations are treated in Chapter III following.

Only ten per cent of all writers derive personal income from book writing; three per cent earn personal income
only from playwriting; and less than two per cent derive
personal income solely from magazine writing.

Almost half of the combinations involve non-writing
occupations to some extent. In fact, a bit better than four
per cent of all writers derived their total personal income
solely from non-writing occupations for the five-year period,
1953-1957. On the other hand, however, about one in two
(46.6 per cent) derived all personal income from writing of
some kind.

A majority (55.3 per cent) of all writers derive personal income from six clusters of sources. The largest
cluster is book-magazine-other occupations, which accounts
for less than one-fourth of all writers. The second cluster
is book-other occupations (10.0 per cent). And the third is
book writing only (9.8 per cent). The fourth and fifth clus-
ters--book-magazine writing, and playwriting-other occupa-
tions--account for an equal number of writers (7.1 per cent
each). Completing this group are those writers combining

playwriting-"F.L.-Emp" writing activities (5.7 per cent).

Slightly more than two per cent of the authors reported no personal income from any source for the entire five-year period, though some of these did list titles of non-writing occupations without giving the dollars earned. Of the remainder, some were married and reported their spouses' incomes.

Least common combinations of personal income sources were those involving book-playwriting-other occupations (with other types of writing--1.4 per cent); magazine writing with other types of writing (1.1 per cent); book-"F.L.-Emp" (e.g. either motion picture and/or television writings, salaried or originals); and magazine-playwriting-other occupations.

Summary

Few there are who seem to live solely on personal income earned from free lance writing altogether. This tentative conclusion is based on the number (a little more than a fifth--21.9 per cent) who reported income only from book writing; book-magazine writing; playwriting; magazine writing; and royalties from previous works.

For all writers, 46.6 per cent earn all personal income from writing of some kind, and 51.1 per cent earned some but not all personal income during the years 1953-1957 from non-writing sources.

On the average, 42.5 per cent of all writers found it necessary to add to their personal incomes from non-writing sources each year, though many of the jobs they worked at were closely related to writing. If the 7.8 per cent (average) who report personal income yearly from staff work

for magazines or newspapers (e.g. directed writing) are
added to the 42.5 per cent "other personal income earners,"
better than one in two writers have steady, outside personal
income other than free lance writing. This figure would be
even higher were it possible to separate the <u>salaried</u> writers
of motion pictures and television (e.g. "F.L.-Emp" writing)
from the writers of originals. Including all the latter, however, gives a yearly average of 63.7 per cent--better than
6 in every 10--who seek or have personal income other than
from books, free lance magazine writing, playwriting, and
royalties.

For those writers deriving personal income from non-
writing occupations, 61.6 per cent had steady--each year--
incomes from the <u>same</u> source.

These figures--non-writing and salaried--are high ...
though not surprising when one considers that the profession
of free lance writing on the average "supports" less than one-
fifth of all writers, and that the others must, therefore, do
other kinds of writing and/or have non-writing sources of
personal income.

Non-writing occupations are thus a vital part of the
writer's total income. But occasional non-writing employment is rare, for only about 14 per cent of all the jobs
(other than writing) held by writers in the five years were
on a one-year basis, e.g. stop-gap measures.

For writers who earn personal income from non-writing sources, only 28.7 per cent of their total personal income
comes from writing; the average (yearly) median personal
income from writing of $2,044 is only half of that derived
from non-writing sources.

For the majority of married writers whose spouses
work, a third of the family income is earned, on the average

by the writer's working spouse. Male writers with working spouses earn more--from writing and non-writing--with
a yearly median personal income of $8,483, than working
husbands (of female writers) whose yearly median income is
$7,520. But the family income for female writers with
working husbands is higher--a $12,764 median--than family
income for male writers with working wives, $11,760.

Writers whose spouses do not work are better earn-
ers--both from writing and non-writing sources--than writers whose spouses do work, thus emphasizing the latter's
dependence on this marriage-linked income.

Notes

1. U. S. Department of Commerce, "Current Population
   Reports, Labor Force," (Bulletin), Series P-50,
   No. 79, Washington, D. C., December 1957.

2. Several writers (about 5 per cent) listed other occupations and income sources but gave no figures of
   earnings. Their listings included dividends, rents,
   teaching, medicine, promoting, accounting, directing,
   and producing.

3. This figure is a bit higher than the 63.9 per cent
   who reported income from writing of some kind in
   all five years. Some writers earned income for
   only 1, 2, 3, or 4 years, but still the amount
   derived from writing accounted for the majority of
   their total personal income reported. They are,
   therefore, included in the 65.5 per cent here.

4. "Business Briefs," Illinois Business Review, Vol.
   17, No. 11, December 1960, p. 7.

5. "Business Briefs," Illinois Business Review, Vol.
   18, No. 2, February 1961, p. 9.

Chapter III

Writers' Incomes

Not only are non-writing occupations more regular than writing for writers, but, typically, they pay better. With more than two-fifths of all writers earning non-writing incomes each year, the five-year median of $4,078 is by far the highest earned from any single source.

Table XIX, page 67, a summary table, shows median incomes for the specified source of all individuals reporting income for that source whether they earned such income one year, two, three, four, or all five years and also includes the five-year median incomes.[1] Each individual is counted in each source each year he reported income; thus, the individual five-year medians do not necessarily add to the total indicated for specific sources nor to the total personal income earned by all writers from all sources.

The 1957 median personal income from non-writing sources of $6,000 was almost twice the median for those writers who earned all their personal income from free lance writing, twice as high as the median for all staff writers for magazines and newspapers--or all directed writing combined, and higher than the median personal income for TV writing. Only motion picture writing was more lucrative.

The 1957 median income for those writers deriving personal income only from writing of any kind (in the year indicated) exceeded the 1957 non-writing median personal

66

Table XIX.

Median Incomes For All Individuals Reporting Specified Sources:
(1953-1957)

Source	1957	(Median Income Dollars) 1956	1955	1954	1953	1953-1957 Median
All Free Lance Writing Only	$3689	$4050	$4178	$4000	$3827	$3438
Books[1]	2300	2000	1718	1865	1837	1600
Magazines	850	970	863	724	1000	444
Plays[1]	1548	1400	1692	1337	1477	684
"F.L.-Emp" Combined	8000	5630	5250	5000	6000	1849
Motion Pictures	10000	12250	16000	11200	7650	2700
Television	5250	2000	2500	2650	2195	585
Directed Writing Combined	3250	3200	2020	3750	4200	1893
Staff Writing for Magazines or Newspapers	3000	2750	3000	4500	5675	1200

Table XIX. (continued)

Median Incomes For All Individuals Reporting Specified Sources:
(1953-1957)

Source	(Median Income Dollars)					1953–1957 Median
	1957	1956	1955	1954	1953	
(Writing Only by year indicated (See Table **XXXII**, and discussion)	6300	5990	5706	5150	5606	–)
Non-Writing Income	6000	5408	5452	5710	5225	4078
Personal Income All Sources	8063	6600	6000	5400	5240	6667
Spouses Income	5000	5000	4902	4790	4586	3600
Family Income	10948	10050	9179	9000	9100	9097

1. Individual medians for Books and Plays are detailed in Chapters IV and V.

Table XX.

Proportion Of All Writers Earning From Each Source

	1957	1956	1955	1954	1953
Free Lance Writing:					
Books	30.4	30.0	30.1	30.7	30.2
Magazines	17.0	16.5	17.9	18.2	19.4
Plays	11.5	10.8	9.2	8.7	8.1
Royalties	1.5	1.4	1.2	1.1	1.0
Only From Free Lance:	(16.1)	(16.0)	(17.1)	(17.4)	(18.2)
"F. L.-Emp" Writing:	(8.0)	(8.6)	(7.8)	(7.7)	(6.8)
Motion Pictures	3.2	3.5	3.0	2.5	3.5
Television	5.5	6.3	5.4	5.5	3.9
Directed Writing:	(8.1)	(7.7)	(8.0)	(7.7)	(8.0)
Staff Work for Magazines and Newspapers	4.5	4.2	4.3	4.3	4.7
Other Assignments	3.6	3.5	3.7	3.4	3.3

69

Table XX. (continued)

Proportion Of All Writers Earning From Each Source

	1957	1956	1955	1954	1953
Only From Writing of Any Kind for Particular Year Indicated	(26.5)	(26.9)	(26.6)	(27.7)	(30.1)
Non-Writing Sources:	22.7	23.8	25.1	25.6	25.9
Spouses' Earnings:	(19.6)	(18.7)	(19.9)	(19.9)	(20.2)
Totals	100.0	100.0	100.0	100.0	100.0
N =	(840)	(804)	(760)	(714)	(665)

(Figures in parentheses are subtotals for sources indicated, and are not included in total as a separate count.)

70

income by only $300. This $6,300 figure, however, was
determined by including writers who had motion picture,
television, directed and free lance writing personal incomes
if they had only writing income in 1957. For the entire
five years (median), the non-writing personal median income
is highest of all; even the working spouse's five-year median
is higher than any median for writing.

Perhaps of equal significance are the proportions of
writers earning from each source. In 1957, seven times as
many writers earned from non-writing occupations as earned
from motion picture writing; four times as many as from
television writing; and five times as many as from staff work
for magazines or newspapers, Table XX. When all writing
activities are combined, there are 1.4 times as many non-
writing earners as there are free lance earners; 2.9 times
as many non-writing earners as there are "F.L.-Emp"
earners; and 2.8 times as many non-writing earners as there
are directed writing earners, but 1.2 times as many earning only from writing of any kind in any particular year as
there are earners from non-writing. These proportions are
almost identical each year.

There was, of course, some overlapping of incomes
from the various sources during the years 1953-1957. But
as already pointed out, every writer's income from whatever source was counted in all places where applicable as
the table designations in this chapter indicate.

For example, almost one writer in every two earning
from books also earned from non-writing occupations. One
in every four earning from plays also earned from non-writing sources; one in twenty deriving income from plays, derived income from both books and non-writing. One in four,
also, earning from motion picture writing drew income from

non-writing occupations.

It should be pointed out, however, that "other" occu-
pations--non-writing and other kinds of writing apart from
free lance--do not offer the kind of writing career which the
professional writer seeks.

Total Income

Both the 1957 median personal income of $8,063
(Table XXI, page 73) earned by all professional writers
from all sources and the total family median income of
$9,097 (Table XXII, page74--produced by adding the working
spouse's income to that of the writer's) are larger than estimated by economists in 1957.[2]

The five-year median personal earning of $6,667 for
writers from all sources[3]--slightly higher even than the
$6,261 five-year average[4] derived from Table XXI--approx-
imates the economists' estimates more closely, though none
of these figures alone tell the story.

If only those actually earning income are considered
in Table XXI, the yearly medians are:

1957	1956	1955	1954	1953
$8225	$7332	$6887	$6325	$6031

When the working spouse's income is added to that
of the writer's, the five-year median for all writers is
$9,097, Table XXII.

Table XXI.

All Writers' Total Income From All Sources, By Income Classes:
(1953-1957)

Annual Income (dollars)	1957 Writers Per Cent	1957 Income Median	1956 Writers Per Cent	1956 Income Median	1955 Writers Per Cent	1955 Income Median	1954 Writers Per Cent	1954 Income Median	1953 Writers Per Cent	1953 Income Median
0 - 1500	17.6	$ 347	19.2	$ 242	23.3	$ 154	25.1	$ 0	28.8	$ 0
1500 - 2500	5.7	1965	5.9	1980	5.7	1900	5.9	2000	5.3	2000
2500 - 5000	13.9	3689	14.6	3765	16.2	4000	16.0	3668	13.9	3839
5000 - 10000	21.5	7432	24.2	7008	21.9	7048	21.2	6755	22.6	6889
10000 - 15000	12.0	12023	12.1	11800	10.3	12150	11.2	11359	10.3	11601
15000 - 25000	16.0	19885	12.6	19972	11.4	18606	12.8	19487	12.6	18092
25000 - 50000	7.1	36800	6.9	30675	6.9	31767	4.3	34000	3.9	39400
50000 - 100000	3.9	67200	2.7	60033	2.7	68669	1.8	67850	2.1	62585
100000 & over	1.4	135565	1.8	126237	1.6	133575	1.6	114400	.7	111000
Totals (N=438)	100.0		100.0		100.0		100.0		100.0	
Median		$8063		$6600		$6000		$5400		$5240
Per Cent Having Income	94.5		92.9		89.7		87.0[a]		84.9[a]	

a. Aside from the 2.3 per cent who reported no income in any of the years, part of the decrease in the per cent reporting income in 1954 and 1953--perhaps even in 1955--is due undoubtedly to the writer's inability to supply records that far back.

73

Table XXII.

All Writers' Total Family Income All Sources (Including
Spouses') 5-Year Average (1953-1957)

Annual Income (dollars)		Writers (per cent)	Income Median
0 -	1500	11.4	$ 521
1500 -	2500	5.5	1921
2500 -	5000	11.9	3902
5000 -	10000	25.1	7148
10000 -	15000	15.3	12290
15000 -	25000	16.6	18240
25000 -	50000	9.4	32945
50000 -	100000	3.4	63800
100000 & over		1.4	155440
	Total	100.0	
	N ▪	(438)	
	Median		$ 9097

For a small portion of writers, part or all of their
income came from Social Security Benefits; 35.3 per cent
of writers 65 years and over received such benefits in 1957.
For the population at large, 52.5 per cent of those 65 and
over received Social Security.[5] The proportion of writers
participating appears quite small since all writers age 60
and over make up one-fifth (20.1 per cent) of the writing
profession.

The non-earners among writers were included in the
overall analysis to give a more realistic picture since no
known profession has one-hundred-per-cent employment every
year. Non-earners, however, are not included in the following analyses which portray the writers' activities (e.g. the
various combinations of income sources), the per cent reporting, and the portion of income earned, particular emphasis

being given to 1957 as a typical year.

Free Lance Writing

The situation was a bit brighter in 1957 than indicated previously (Chapter II) for the fifth of all writers earning personal income solely from free lance writing. In
1957, almost a third (30.8 per cent) of all professional writers drew all of their personal income from free lance writing of any kind (e.g. none of it from staff work, special
writing assignments, and so on). Yet, the 1957 median
personal income figure of only $3,689 (Table XXIII) is re-
presentative of these writers; the mean is $10,792--a figure
2 1/2 times the median.

Although no time in the five years did more than 31
per cent of all writers earn all personal income from free
lance writing for any one particular year, there were 42.9
per cent altogether who earned all personal income from
free lance writing for at least one year of the five. Of this
two-fifths of all writers, however, 69.7 per cent are married, more than half (58.8 per cent) of whom had working
spouses during the five years. The working spouse contributed 49.8 per cent of the total family income, or $4,400
yearly, during the five-year period.

More than half (54.5 per cent) of these writers with
working spouses are female and more than 90 per cent of
the spouses were working during the year or years the writer earned all his or her personal income from free lance
writing.

With only slightly fewer writers earning from free
lance writing in 1955 than in 1957, 1955 was by far the best
of the five years for the average free lance writer--a median

Table XXIII.

Income Of Writers Earning All Income From Free Lance Writing Only,
By Income Classes, (1953-1957)

Annual Income (dollars)	1957 Writers Per Cent	1957 Income Median	1956 Writers Per Cent	1956 Income Median	1955 Writers Per Cent	1955 Income Median	1954 Writers Per Cent	1954 Income Median	1953 Writer Per Cent	1953 Income Median
0 - 1500	29.6	$ 482	27.9	$ 648	30.0	$ 600	28.2	$ 463	31.4	$ 404
1500 - 2500	10.4	1973	10.9	1833	9.2	1910	7.3	1900	8.3	2039
2500 - 5000	17.0	3644	17.1	3881	16.9	3852	23.4	3600	16.4	3530
5000 - 10000	19.3	6897	19.4	6754	19.2	7000	19.4	7028	21.5	6750
10000 - 15000	5.9	12549	10.1	11530	10.0	11977	8.9	11100	8.3	11900
15000 - 25000	9.6	19045	8.5	21011	4.6	17810	5.7	20533	8.3	19259
25000 - 50000	4.4	34673	3.9	31250	6.9	33750	3.2	38050	3.3	43767
50000 - 100000	1.5	56937	.8	61267	2.3	58000	1.6	60120	2.5	75272
100000 & over	2.2	145850	1.6	181198	.8	212149	2.4	114400	-	-
Totals N =	100.0 (135)		100.0 (129)		100.0 (130)		100.0 (124)		100.0 (121)	
Median		$3689		$4050		$4178		$4000		$3827
Per cent all Writers	30.8		29.5		29.7		28.3		27.6	

76

of $4,178. All medians were higher than that of 1957 even though a higher percentage of writers earned all their personal income from free lance writing in 1957 than in any other year.

For comparison, Table XXIV, page 78, is a frequency distribution of the averaged yearly personal incomes from free lance writing for the nine-tenths (90.6 per cent) of all professional writers who derived part but not all of their personal income from this source.

Again, however, for all writers earning part but not all of their personal income from free lance writing between 1953-1957, three-fourths (75.4 per cent) are married and 55.7 per cent had working spouses for at least part of this period. The figures for those married who have working spouses are practically the same as for all writers as a whole. But unlike those married writers earning all personal income from free lance writing for one or more of the five years, the majority of these working spouses--63.5 per cent--are wives of male writers.

The "average" writer who had some but not all personal income from free lance writing for only one of the five years between 1953 and 1957 drew a median income of $666 from this source. If the individual figures earned from free lance writing by those who had income from this source for only one year (one-year column, Table XXIV) are totaled for the mean, the figure is $4,149. But since more than four-fifths of this group (82.9 per cent) made less-- much, much less--than $4,000 each, the mean only serves to emphasize the skewness caused by a few high-income earners.

For the 55.5 per cent of all writers who had five-year incomes from free lance writing, the median averaged

Table XXIV.

Yearly Mean Free Lance Writing Incomes For All Writers Reporting Earnings From Free Lance Writing, By Income Classes

Annual Income (dollars)	One Year Writers		Two Years Writers		Three Years Writers		Four Years Writers		Five Years Writers	
	Per Cent	Income Median	Per Cent	Income Median	Per Cent	Income Median	Per Cent	Income Median	Per Cent	Income Median
0 - 1500	71.4	$ 450	63.3	$ 849	60.0	$ 508	50.0	$ 617	28.4	$ 797
1500 - 2500	2.9	2219	10.0	1750	13.3	1896	9.1	1899	11.1	1887
2500 - 5000	11.4	2854	16.7	3160	13.3	3979	22.7	3746	21.8	3679
5000 - 10000	5.7	7907	6.7	7398	6.7	6333	9.1	5687	16.1	6433
10000 - 15000	-	-	3.3	11709	2.2	12550	2.3	10012	9.1	13079
15000 - 25000	-	-	-	-	-	-	6.8	20875	7.0	17640
25000 - 50000	8.6	33250	-	-	-	-	-	-	3.7	31648
50000 - 100000	-	-	-	-	4.4	53916	-	-	1.7	58068
100000 & over	-	-	-	-	-	-	-	-	1.2	125940
Totals N =	100.0 (35)		100.0 (30)		100.0 (45)		100.0 (44)		100.0 (243)	
Median		$666		$975		$1031		$1387		$3670
Per Cent all Writers	8.0		6.8		10.3		10.0		55.5	

78

personal income from this source was $3,670. Yet, the
yearly averaged earnings, which are the basis for Table
XXIV, show two-fifths of all free lance earners (41.0 per
cent) made less than $1,500 annually; their mean income,
however, was $6,792.

And, while a writer cannot in most cases average
his income for tax purposes over a period of years, the
yearly $1,546 median--typical of the free lance writer's
five-year personal income from this source--readily explains why more than half of all writers reported personal
incomes from other (non-writing) occupations, and why about
the same number (45.4 per cent) reported personal incomes
from other kinds of writing.

Magazine writing was a source of free lance personal income for almost half of all writers (46.6 per cent--
or 51.4 per cent of those actually earning free lance income), though no more than a third of them earned from
this source in any one year, Table XXV. Incomes from
books and plays are treated separately in Chapters IV and V.
By way of summary, however, at this point, better than one-
fourth (28.1 per cent) of all writers drew in 1957 more than
half of their personal income from writing of books; 8.2 per
cent from plays; and 4.1 per cent from books and plays
combined.

The five-year median personal income of $444 earned
by all free lance magazine writers is slightly more than
half any individual yearly median shown in Table XXV except for 1953. That year the 29.4 per cent earning such
income drew a median of $1,000.

Almost three-fourths (73.5 per cent) of the writers
earning from free lance magazine work were male, slightly

Table XXV.

Writers' Income From Free Lance Magazine Writing, By Income Classes, (1953-1957)

Annual Income (dollars)	1957 Writers Per Cent	Income Median	1956 Writers Per Cent	Income Median	1955 Writers Per Cent	Income Median	1954 Writers Per Cent	Income Median	1953 Writers Per Cent	Income Median
0 - 1500	58.0	$ 300	60.9	$ 368	62.5	$ 366	63.8	$ 337	60.5	$ 300
1500 - 2500	10.5	2100	8.3	1848	8.1	1900	3.1	1850	11.6	2000
2500 - 5000	17.5	3000	14.3	3200	9.6	4000	16.2	3600	8.5	3672
5000 - 10000	9.1	7850	7.5	6000	11.8	7016	7.7	6247	10.9	7650
10000 - 15000	3.5	12733	6.0	11863	2.9	11488	5.4	12865	7.0	11601
15000 - 25000	-	-	3.0	19876	5.1	20000	2.3	16806	1.5	18192
25000 & over	1.4	32697	-	-	-	-	1.5	28000	-	-
Totals N =	100.0 (143)		100.0 (133)		100.0 (136)		100.0 (130)		100.0 (129)	
Median		$ 850		$ 970		$ 863		$ 724		$1000
Per cent all Writers	32.6		30.4		31.1		29.7		29.4	

80

more than one in four, female. The median age for these
writers was 47 years, or about two years younger than for
all writers as a whole.

A tenth of all writers had no personal income from
free lance writing in any of the five years between 1953 and
1957.

Other Writing Activities

For the more than two writers in five who had personal incomes from other kinds of writing, they earned on
the average yearly $1,871 (five-year median). Other kinds
of writing include, of course, the "F.L.-Emp" writing income, that is, writing for motion pictures and/or television
either on a salary basis or as original works, defined previously. It includes as well directed writing income (e.g.
income such as that from staff work on magazines and newspapers, special writing assignments--ghosting, translations,
reviews, advertising copy)--any kind of writing done whereby
the writer is told or guided in the kind of writing to be done.

"F.L.-Emp" Income

Though almost an eighth of all writers reported earnings from motion pictures (either salary or original) during
the five-year period, only half that number (6.2 per cent)
had personal income from this source in 1957, Table XXVI.
Because the motion picture industry is noted for high sala-
ries and large payments for the material it makes use of,
one would expect the median income for this kind of writing
to be quite high, also. Table XXVI substantiates this as-
sumption. The median personal income for this small and
somewhat exclusive group of writers was $10,000 in 1957.
An even larger median--for about the same number of

Table XXVI.

Writers' Income From Motion Pictures, By Income Classes, (1953-1957)

Annual Income (dollars)	1957 Writers Per Cent	1957 Income Median	1956 Writers Per Cent	1956 Income Median	1955 Writers Per Cent	1955 Income Median	1954 Writers Per Cent	1954 Income Median	1953 Writers Per Cent	1953 Income Median
0 - 1500	7.4	$ 1083	10.7	$ 1000	8.7	$ 875	5.6	$ 300	13.0	$ 914
1500 - 2500	-	-	10.7	1650	-	-	5.6	1500	13.0	1890
2500 - 5000	14.8	3300	7.1	3400	13.0	3800	11.1	3050	4.3	4900
5000 - 10000	25.9	6500	17.9	8000	21.7	8279	22.2	8050	30.4	7200
10000 - 15000	14.8	13150	10.7	13500	4.3	10400	11.1	11200	8.7	12000
15000 - 25000	-	-	3.6	19900	8.7	19250	11.1	16900	4.3	20000
25000 - 50000	22.2	27500	28.6	30750	30.4	35000	22.2	27241	13.0	39000
50000 - 100000	11.1	70000	3.6	66000	13.0	65000	11.1	68700	13.0	66000
100000 & over	3.7	174000	7.1	105006	-	-	-	-	-	-
Totals N =	100.0 (27)		100.0 (28)		100.0 (23)		100.0 (18)		100.0 (23)	
Median		$10000		$12250		$16000		$11200		$7650
Per cent all Writers	6.2		6.4		5.3		4.1		5.3	

82

writers--was earned in 1955 and 1956. Payments to individual writers ranged from a few hundred dollars to a high of $174,000.

Writing for television--a kindred outlet for the motion picture writer's talent--provided personal income for almost a fifth of all writers (18.5 per cent) between 1953 and 1957. But again, only about half this number could report earnings from this source in 1957. For other years--except 1956--the percentage reporting was even smaller, Table XXVII.

Total individual incomes and the yearly medians are not nearly so high for television writing as for motion picture writing. The absolute dollar range is also less, being a few dollars to $54,735.

More than nine-tenths (93.9 per cent) of motion picture writers are male; the median age for both sexes is 45 years. The median age for television writers is even lower--44 years--and slightly more than a tenth (11.1 per cent) are female. All writers for motion pictures were under sixty years of age and only 7.4 per cent of television writers are sixty or over.

More than half (54.2 per cent) of the "F.L.-Emp" writers earned personal income from television writing between 1953-1957; 24.3 per cent earned from motion picture writing; and 21.5 per cent earned from both sources. The latter group with both sources of income accounted for 42.4 per cent of the total personal income earned by all writers from "F.L.-Emp" writing.

Altogether, a fourth of all writers reported personal earnings from "F.L.-Emp" writing during the five-year period, but only 15.3 per cent earned from this source in 1957. They drew a median income of $8,000, Table XXVIII.

Table XXVII.

Writers' Income From Television, By Income Classes,
(1953-1957)

Annual Income (dollars)	1957 Writers Per Cent	1957 Income Median	1956 Writers Per Cent	1956 Income Median	1955 Writers Per Cent	1955 Income Median	1954 Writers Per Cent	1954 Income Median	1953 Writers Per Cent	1953 Income Median
0 - 1500	19.6	$ 1000	33.3	$ 815	34.1	$ 775	38.5	$ 450	42.3	$ 1000
1500 - 2500	19.6	1800	21.5	1575	14.6	1775	5.1	1662	11.5	1990
2500 - 5000	8.7	2715	11.8	3775	14.6	3750	20.5	2875	15.4	2900
5000 - 10000	21.7	7047	11.8	6415	17.1	7200	12.8	6000	19.2	7000
10000 - 15000	6.5	12500	11.8	13732	4.9	11762	-	-	-	-
15000 - 25000	15.2	16400	2.0	15000	2.4	17820	10.3	19240	3.8	15000
25000 - 50000	6.5	40000	3.9	32500	9.8	37500	7.7	30000	7.7	43150
50000 & over	2.2	54735	3.9	53500	2.4	52400	5.1	51500	-	-
Totals N =	100.0 (46)		100.0 (51)		100.0 (41)		100.0 (39)		100.0 (26)	
Median		$5250		$2000		$2500		$2650		$2195
Per cent all Writers	10.5		11.6		9.4		8.9		5.9	

Table XXXVIII.

Writers' Income From All "F.L.-Emp" Activities, By Income Classes, (1953-1957)

Annual Income (dollars)	1953 Writers Per Cent	1953 Income Median	1954 Writers Per Cent	1954 Income Median	1955 Writers Per Cent	1955 Income Median	1956 Writers Per Cent	1956 Income Median	1957 Writers Per Cent	1957 Income Median
0 - 1500	28.9	$ 1000	25.5	$ 500	23.7	$ 775	23.2	$ 887	13.4	$ 1125
1500 - 2500	8.9	1895	5.5	1575	10.2	1775	13.0	1575	11.9	1850
2500 - 5000	11.1	4000	18.2	3250	11.9	3800	10.1	3625	11.9	3300
5000 - 10000	17.8	7200	16.4	6100	16.9	7550	17.4	7163	22.4	7500
10000 - 15000	11.1	12000	3.6	11200	8.5	11700	13.0	13500	9.0	13000
15000 - 25000	4.4	17250	10.9	18640	5.1	17820	2.9	19050	11.9	17350
25000 - 50000	11.1	40000	12.7	27482	17.0	35000	13.0	31500	10.5	30000
50000 - 100000	6.7	66000	7.3	60700	5.1	52400	4.4	66600	7.5	65000
100000 & over	-	-	-	-	1.7	105000	2.9	105006	1.2	174000
Totals N =	100.0 (45)		100.0 (55)		100.0 (59)		100.0 (69)		100.0 (67)	
Median		$6000		$5000		$5250		$5630		$8000
Per cent all Writers	10.3		12.7		13.5		15.8		15.3	

The five-year median for all "F.L.-Emp" writers
was $1,849; if only the yearly medians of earners are con-
sidered, however, the mean is $5,976--more than three
times as large as the yearly median earned by all.

Directed Writing Income

Directed writing, including many more activities than
just staff work for magazines or newspapers, provided earnings for slightly more than a fifth (20.8 per cent) of all
writers.

For the eighth of all writers--three in twenty-five--
who reported personal earnings from staff work in magazines
and/or newspapers, however, almost one in two (4.8 per
cent of all writers) were employed regularly. That is, they
drew income from this source each year. By way of comparison, Table XXIX shows the income stability year to year
for these five-year earners and Table XXX, page 88, includes all who reported any income in whatever year from
staff magazine or newspaper work.

The five-year mean of the yearly median personal incomes for these regular "employees" is $5,700. While the
median age for this group is 51, the same age as for those
writers earning all income from free lance writing, it is
slightly higher than the median for all writers; the educa-
tional level is also a bit higher. Three in five have college
degrees--forty per cent are advanced degrees.

The five-year median personal income for all staff
writers was $1,200, though the mean of the yearly medians
for those earning in any particular year was $3,785--about
two-thirds of that of the five-year earners. 1953 reveals a
considerably larger median personal income (Table XXX)
than for any other year; it is accounted for mainly by the

Table XXIX.

Writers' (Those Reporting Earnings All Five Years Only) Income From Staff Work For Magazines Or Newspapers, By Income Classes, (1953-1957)

Annual Income (dollars)	1957 Writers Per Cent	Income Median	1956 Writers Per Cent	Income Median	1955 Writers Per Cent	Income Median	1954 Writers Per Cent	Income Median	1953 Writers Per Cent	Income Median
0 - 1500	23.8	$ 300	23.8	$ 250	23.8	$ 265	28.6	$ 392	28.6	$ 415
1500 - 2500	4.8	1800	9.5	1925	14.3	1500	4.8	2000	9.5	2100
2500 - 5000	19.1	3250	14.3	3000	9.5	4200	14.3	3750	9.5	3600
5000 - 10000	9.5	7900	9.5	7650	9.5	7650	14.3	7500	14.3	7500
10000 - 15000	14.3	13500	14.3	13000	19.1	12750	23.8	11539	23.8	11579
15000 - 25000	14.3	18500	23.8	21000	14.3	19500	14.3	20000	9.5	18364
25000 & over	14.3	27500	4.8	29500	9.5	27175	-	-	4.8	28350
Totals (N = 21)	100.0		100.0		100.0		100.0		100.0	
Median		$6500		$6000		$6000		$5000		$5000

87

Table XXX.

All Staff Writers' Income From Magazine And Newspapers, By Income Classes, (1953-1957)

Annual Income (dollars)	1957 Writers Per Cent	1957 Income Median	1956 Writers Per Cent	1956 Income Median	1955 Writers Per Cent	1955 Income Median	1954 Writers Per Cent	1954 Income Median	1953 Writers Per Cent	1953 Income Median
0 - 1500	44.7	$ 348	38.2	$ 360	39.4	$ 300	32.3	$ 332	25.8	$ 233
1500 - 2500	2.6	1800	8.8	1600	9.1	1500	6.5	2000	6.5	2100
2500 - 5000	10.5	3250	11.8	3000	9.1	4000	12.9	3975	12.9	3560
5000 - 10000	13.2	6500	11.8	8175	9.1	6000	16.1	7500	22.5	6000
10000 - 15000	10.5	12745	8.8	13000	15.2	12600	16.1	11539	19.4	10789
15000 - 25000	10.5	20250	14.7	21000	12.1	20750	12.9	19750	9.7	18228
25000 - 50000	7.9	27500	5.9	27250	6.1	27175	3.2	31970	3.2	28350
Totals	100.0		100.0		100.0		100.0		100.0	
N =	(38)		(34)		(33)		(31)		(31)	
Median		$3000		$2750		$3000		$4500		$5675
Per cent all Writers	8.7		7.8		7.5		7.1		7.1	

88

regular five-year earners in magazine and newspaper work.

While one would expect some writers for motion pictures to be writers for television material also because of the similarity in demand, one would not expect to see these same writers turn up as staff writers for magazines or newspapers. A few (less than one per cent), however, did just that--specialists enough in their own right to be retained by a magazine or newspaper on a more or less regular basis.

More than two-thirds of all staff writers for magazines and newspapers are men; 29.1 per cent are women; and the median age for this group of writers is 48 years.

When the 8.7 per cent of all writers who had personal income from other kinds of directed writing--ghost writing, advertising copy, translations, etc.--are combined with the staff writers for magazines and newspapers, the five-year median income is almost $700 higher ($1,893) than that for staff writers alone. In contrast, the five-year mean of the yearly medians, Table XXXI, is $3,284--about $500 lower than for staff writers in magazine and newspaper work.

Of all writers earning from directed writing activities, 71.0 per cent are male, 29.0 per cent female. The median age for this group of writers is 48 years--four years older than "F.L.-Emp" writers, but a year younger than all writers as a group.

More writers deriving personal income from directed writing activities earned income in 1957 than in any other year, though for writers deriving income from "F.L.-Emp", 1956 was the year for the greatest number earning. It is the group median, however, for each type of writing that really typifies the individual's income position. And, for

Table XXXI.

Writers' Income From Directed Writing Activities, By Income Classes, (1953-1957)

Annual Income (dollars)	1957 Writers Per Cent	Income Median	1956 Writers Per Cent	Income Median	1955 Writers Per Cent	Median	1954 Writers Per Cent	Income Median	1953 Writers Per Cent	Income Median
0 - 1500	42.7	$ 311	33.9	$ 360	39.3	$ 457	36.4	$ 422	28.3	$ 555
1500 - 2500	4.4	2000	11.3	2000	11.5	1500	5.5	2000	7.6	1763
2500 - 5000	10.3	3500	16.1	3400	14.8	3000	18.2	3875	18.9	3560
5000 - 10000	16.2	7300	16.1	8700	14.8	6000	20.0	7650	24.5	7500
10000 - 15000	11.8	11484	11.3	12500	8.2	12600	9.1	11539	11.3	11000
15000 - 25000	10.3	17000	8.1	21000	8.2	19500	9.1	20000	7.6	18364
25000 & over	4.4	27600	3.2	27300	3.3	27175	1.8	31970	1.9	28425
Totals N =	100.0 (68)		100.0 (62)		100.0 (61)		100.0 (55)		100.0 (53)	
Median		$3250		$3200		$2020		$3750		$4200
Per cent all Writers	15.5		14.1		13.9		12.7		12.2	

motion picture writers that figure in 1957 was $10,000, for television writers, it was $5,250, for staff writers of magazines and newspapers, $3,000, and for all directed writing earners, $3,250.

In summary, the percentage of writers reporting by number of years in each of the other writing areas just discussed, looks like this:

Per Cent Reporting Income For:

Writers For:	One Year	Two Years	Three Years	Four Years	Five Years
Motion Pictures (49=100%)	40.8	18.4	12.2	12.2	16.3
Television (81=100%)	35.8	25.9	7.4	11.1	19.8
Staff Work in Magazines and Newspapers (55=100%)	30.9	12.7	10.9	7.3	39.2
Other Directed Writing (38=100%)	23.7	18.4	7.9		50.0

More than three-fifths of the motion picture and television writers and more than two-fifths of the staff writers for magazines and newspapers and other directed writing earned personal income for only two years or less from these writing activities.

Total Writing Income Only

As many as 50.9 per cent of all writers reported earning all personal income from writing of any kind in any one year's time. Over the five years, 1953-1957 average, however, 46.6 per cent of all writers earned all their personal income only from writing of any kind. For 1956 and 1957, this ratio was about one writer in two: 50.9 per cent of all professional writers drew in 1957 all their personal income from writing; 49.3 per cent drew all their income

Table XXXII.

Writers' Income From Writing Of Any Kind, By Income Classes, (1953-1957)

(Those Reporting All Personal Income Earned From Writing Only For Year Indicated)

Annual Income (dollars)	1957 Writers Per Cent	1957 Income Median	1956 Writers Per Cent	1956 Income Median	1955 Writers Per Cent	1955 Income Median	1954 Writers Per Cent	1954 Income Median	1953 Writers Per Cent	1953 Income Median
0 - 1500	22.0	$ 450	20.4	$ 662	23.3	$ 704	22.2	$ 487	22.0	$ 494
1500 - 2500	7.2	1972	8.8	1867	8.4	1920	6.6	2000	6.5	2000
2500 - 5000	13.9	3644	15.3	3673	15.4	3901	18.7	3500	18.5	3600
5000 - 10000	20.2	7405	18.5	6907	20.3	7032	20.7	6710	21.5	7000
10000 - 15000	9.4	12475	13.0	12130	10.4	12150	12.1	11100	14.0	12000
15000 - 25000	13.9	20150	11.6	21000	6.9	17160	9.1	20464	8.0	19087
25000 - 50000	7.2	36700	6.9	31770	10.4	33750	5.6	34000	5.5	40000
50000 - 100000	4.5	65000	3.2	61267	3.0	57250	3.0	61644	3.5	65000
100000 & over	1.8	173239	2.3	130475	2.0	172862	2.0	135050	.5	111000
Totals	100.0		100.0		100.0		100.0		100.0	
N =	(223)		(216)		(202)		(198)		(200)	
Median		$6300		$5990		$5706		$5150		$5606
Per cent all Writers	50.9		49.3		46.1		45.2		45.7	

92

from this source in 1956, Table XXXII.

More than half of this group of writers are male (57.7 per cent); 42.3 per cent are female. The median age is the same as that for all writers at large--49 years.

Because better than three in five (60.5 per cent) of the writers in Table XXXII are those doing motion picture and television work, staff work for magazines and newspapers, special writing assigments, ghost writing, advertising copy, and so on, the yearly medians--an average of $5,750 for those earning in any year--really overstate the professional writer's free lance income position. Three-fifths had little or no choice in determining what they would or would not write ... they had to earn to live.

Table XXXII shows, for the year indicated, all writers deriving all personal income from writing of any kind. Some of these writers had all income from writing in only one, two, or three years at most. Some of them could have and did have non-writing occupation income for part but not all of the five years. No writer was included as earning all personal income from writing, of course, in the year he reported any non-writing income. For instance, if a writer had only writing income in 1953 and 1954, and non-writing income for 1955-1957, he was included only in the arrays for 1953 and 1954.

In addition, there were other writers earning from writing during this five-year period than the 46.6 per cent average appearing in Table XXXII, but they were excluded simply because they did earn some personal income from non-writing occupations for each year they also reported earnings from writing.

Summarizing, as measures of the dependence on non-writing, we, thus, have (1) 53.8 per cent of the married

writers' spouses working to add to family income as presented in Chapter II, (2) 42.5 per cent of all writers on the
average each year working to earn personal income from
non-writing sources, (3) 61.6 per cent (31.5 per cent of all
writers of 2) deriving personal income from the same non-
writing source each year, and (4) as many as 50.9 per cent
of all writers--but on the average only 46.6 per cent--de-
riving all personal income from writing of any kind.

Writers' Non-Writing Personal Income

On the average, better than eight-tenths of writers
having personal income from other than writing of any kind,
earned from non-writing occupations each year. (See Table
XXXIII, page 95.) Six and seven-tenths per cent (3.4 per
cent of all writers) earned all their personal income from
this source. Non-writing income accounted for 71.3 per
cent of the total personal income earned by these writers,
1953-1957 average; the five-year median income was $4,078.

Of all writers deriving non-writing personal income,
three-fourths (75.4 per cent) are male, one-fourth female.
Their median age is 49--the same as for all writers as a
group.

The mean of the yearly medians--$5,559--is only
slightly less than that for writers reporting all personal income earned in any one year from writing of any kind.
Writers earning from non-writing, however, also, had writing income and the mean of this group's yearly medians for
total personal income all sources was $8,369.

Annual Dollar Income For The Profession

A fourth (25.2 per cent) of the total personal income

Table XXXIII.

Writers' Income From Non-Writing Occupations, By Income Classes, (1953-1957)

Annual Income (dollars)	1957 Writers Per Cent	1957 Income Median	1956 Writers Per Cent	1956 Income Median	1955 Writers Per Cent	1955 Income Median	1954 Writers Per Cent	1954 Income Median	1953 Writers Per Cent	1953 Income Median
0 - 1500	13.6	$ 538	12.1	$ 615	17.8	$ 655	18.6	$ 631	17.4	$ 516
1500 - 2500	6.8	1946	8.4	2000	10.0	2000	6.0	2000	5.8	2000
2500 - 5000	24.6	3600	23.6	3600	19.9	3400	20.8	3881	23.3	3864
5000 - 10000	22.0	8000	27.8	7500	25.6	7000	28.4	7000	28.5	6800
10000 - 15000	14.1	11000	9.4	12080	10.0	12000	8.7	12000	12.2	12000
15000 - 25000	14.1	18938	13.6	18000	13.1	18000	14.8	16300	9.9	16000
25000 - 50000	3.7	37500	3.1	36860	2.6	25000	1.6	25000	1.7	31250
50000 - 100000	.5	65000	-	-	-	-	.6	80000	-	-
100000 & over	.5	100000	1.1	130000	1.1	130000	.6	100000	1.2	100000
Totals N =	100.0 (191)		100.0 (191)		100.0 (191)		100.0 (183)		100.0 (172)	
Median (Median All Sources)		$6000 $10150		$5408 $8673		$5452 $8069		$5710 $7500		$5225 ($7456)
Per cent All Non-writing Earners	85.3		85.3		85.3		81.7		76.8	
Per cent All Writers	43.6		43.6		43.6		41.8		39.3	

95

earned by all writers in 1957 came from books. Only non-writing personal income accounted for a larger portion. Of the estimated $31, 399, 855 annual personal earnings of the profession, Table XXXIV, 8.8 million dollars of it was non-writing income. If the working spouses' incomes are added to the personal income for all writers, the result is an estimated income of $38, 290, 880 to writers and their families in 1957. Thus, the amount received by writers from non-writing sources (including spouses) is 40.9 per cent of total income. Or, to put it another way, less than three-fifths (59.1 per cent) of all income received by writers and their families in 1957 was from writing of some kind.

Total income received by working spouses (1957) is exceeded only by book income and personal non-writing income; it is the third largest amount earned from any one source.

Plays, the third largest portion of personal income, accounted for approximately a sixth of all personal income earned by writers in 1957. While motion pictures accounted for a tenth of all earnings, it was third largest of the total writing incomes. Royalties from previous works and other directed writing activities provided the smallest part of total personal income to professional writers.

Television, with only a tenth of all writers earning from this source in 1957 (see Table XXVII) was much more lucrative than magazines which provided personal income for a third of all writers (Table XXV), or all directed writing from which 15.5 per cent earned (Table XXXI).

Table XXXIV.

Total Incomes Received By All Writers, By Source: 1957[1]

Source	Per Cent of Total	Estimated Income	
Books	25.2	$7,907,095	
Magazines	5.8	1,837,250	
Plays	16.3	5,116,020	
Royalties (from previous works)	.5	167,855	
	47.8		$15,028,220
Motion Pictures	10.7	3,345,800	
Television	6.8	2,135,325	
	17.5		5,481,125
Staff Work for Magazines and Newspapers	4.4	1,374,430	
Other Directed Writing	2.3	730,285	
	6.7		2,104,715
Total Writing Income	(72.0)		(22,614,060)
Non-Writing Income	28.0		8,785,795
Total	100.0		$31,399,855
Spouses Income	(18.0)		6,891,025

1. Figures were computed on basis of writers' and working spouses' 1957 incomes, multiplied by 5, since the response represents about a fifth of profession.

97

Summary

A majority of writers have metropolitan backgrounds and are now resident New Yorkers. In fact, 68.7 per cent of all writers live within the New York area--in the New England and Middle Atlantic states.

The average (median) age of the American writer is 49 years; one writer in five is under 40, one in five is over 60 years of age. Almost seven writers in ten are male.

Three-fourths of all writers--considerably higher than for the population at large--are married. Of the married writers, one in four is female; of the non-married writers one in two is female. More than half of the writer families have no dependent children; 43.6 per cent have 1, 2, or 3 children under 18 years of age.

Far better educated than is the population as a whole, writers with college degrees are about six times as common as writers with only a high school education.

Two writers in five come from professional backgrounds, though less than one per cent of authors' fathers were authors themselves. Lawyers and judges in the professional field are high progenitors of writers as are businessmen in the white collar field.

Men become professional writers earlier than do women and younger writers on the whole are turning professional earlier than older writers did.

Very few writers are single writing specialists; only one writer in ten derives his sole personal income from books; less than one in thirty only from plays, and less than one in fifty solely from free lance magazine work.

Altogether, better than one writer in two earned

from non-writing sources during the years 1953-1957, and
on the average, 42.4 per cent of all writers derive personal
income from non-writing sources yearly. Almost a third
(31.5 per cent) of all writers drew non-writing personal income from the same source each year. Occasional non-
writing employment is rare.

To the writer's credit is the fact that 65.5 per
cent of all writers earn the majority though not all of their
personal income from writing of some kind, the five-year
median (1953-1957) for which was $3,055 writing income
and $60 non-writing for a total of $3,105. The casualness
of the writer labor market, however, is indicated by the
half of all writers who drew 71.3 per cent or more of their
yearly personal income from non-writing (a median of
$4,078) plus that derived yearly from writing ($2,044) for
an annual median income of $6,122--almost twice the in-
come for writers drawing the majority of their personal income from writing.

The casualness is also revealed by the dependence
of the married writer on his working spouse's income.
More than half (53.8 per cent) of all married writers have
working spouses who provide on the average 34.4 per cent
of the total family income--$3,600 yearly between 1953 and
1957.

Writers with working spouses have higher median
family incomes than writers with no working spouses, though
writers without working spouses earn more from both their
writing activities and/or other non-writing sources of income
than do writers with working spouses.

Not only is the casualness of writer employment
shown by the amount of non-writing and the marriage-linked
dependence, but it is also evident from the twenty-six dif-

ferent combinations of income sources put together by writers to meet their economic obligations over the five-year
period covered by the study.

For the writer earning all personal income from
free lance writing only (about a fourth of all writers each
year), his five-year average (median) income was $3,438.
Over the five years, an average of 46.6 per cent of all writers earned all personal income for any one particular year
only from writing of some kind; more than half of these,
however, were those writers earning only from free lance
writing each year.

But while 63.9 per cent of all writers reported personal income from writing of some kind in all five years,
writing provides less substantial support for writers than
other income sources (non-writing, including spouses). The
five-year median personal income for all writers from writing of any kind was $2,828. The non-writing five-year me-
dian income (including spouses) for all writers was $3,103.
Consequently, although there is not necessarily less attach-
ment shown by writers to writing over non-writing, the volume of income from writing is insufficient to meet the average writer's economic obligations and so he seeks additional
income elsewhere.

Through a combination of all sources--excluding the
spouse's--the professional writer drew a five-year median
personal income of $6,667--about the same as the average
for all college teachers, about three-fourths that of the average for lawyers, and less than half that for physicians.

Thus, Malcolm Cowley, writing from his own personal association and knowledge of the writing profession,
seems to have described the average writer rather well,
when he said, "If he (the average writer) did exist and was

established in his calling--

> At the age of forty he would probably be living
> somewhere within a hundred miles of New York,
> unless he was outstandingly successful. In that
> case he would have complete freedom of residence
> and might live anywhere from Arizona to Italy
> and from Tahiti to Cuba (with a concentration
> of glitter in Bucks County, Pennsylvania, and
> Fairfield County, Connecticut), but he wouldn't
> any longer be an average writer. If less famous,
> he would have developed some specialty like
> editing or reading manuscripts or writing some
> particular type of articles or stories on which
> he could depend for part of his income ... His
> total income would vary from year to year, but
> it might average six or eight thousand dollars,
> after deducting his rather high business expenses ...
>
> He would have a wife and one, two, or three
> children, although there are many childless
> marriages ...
>
> From the economic standpoint he belongs to the
> professional segment of the middle classes and,
> as a rule, he has no inherited capital except
> that which was invested in his education. His
> income is smaller on the average than those of
> doctors and attorneys, larger than those of
> clergymen, and roughly equal to those of college
> professors. [6]

Part II, Chapters IV, V, and VI now examine in
detail the book writer's position, the playwright's position,
and that of a small segment of writers who earned neither
from books nor plays in the five years studied.

Notes

1. To determine the five-year median incomes (1953-1957),
   every individual's income for however many years (1
   through 5) were added together and divided by five.
   Since in most cases the largest portion of writers
   earning from any single source for all five years

approaches eighty-five per cent (non-writing) of all writers who earned from that source (and in most cases the percentage of five-year earners is much less) all the five-year median figures are less than the figure derived by adding the yearly medians together and dividing by five.

2. Estimated average earnings for 1956-1957 incomes for selected professions by Professor Seymour E. Harris, Chairman, Department of Economics, Harvard University indicated an average income for authors of $5,325; for college teachers, $5,243; for lawyers, $10,218; and for physicians, $16,017. No explanation, however, was given of how the author's average was calculated or what kinds of income it included. Occupational Outlook Handbook reported an average income for lawyers in 1957 of $10,200; for physicians, $15,000; and for college teachers, $6,198, but gave no listing or estimate for writers.

3. The figure was derived by totaling yearly incomes for all writers, all sources (excluding spouses), arraying for the median, and dividing by five.

4. This figure is simply a mean of the yearly medians.

5. Health, Education, and Welfare Trends, 1960 Edition, U. S. Department of Health, Education, and Welfare, Bulletin, Washington, D. C., p. 74.

6. Malcolm Cowley, The Literary Situation, The Viking Press, New York, 1954, pp. 189-215.

Part II

Types Of Writers

Chapter IV

Book Writers

... The second novel has been the stopping
point for many writers, either because it
marked a backward step--often the author has
used his best material in his first novel--or
else because the improvement wasn't as great
as reviewers had hoped to see. They are
almost always harder on the second book than
on the first. It isn't until the third book
appears that an author can regard himself as
really launched on his career--and even then
he is likely to find that in America today very
few people can earn a living merely by writing
books. (Italics added.)

Cowley

Larston D. Farrar, successful newspaperman, agen-
cy owner, magazine writer, and novelist, when asked the
question, "Who is a successful writer?" replied, "A successful writer," I think, "is a person who has achieved more
than local or regional impact by virtue of his literary efforts
and is earning enough from those efforts alone to meet his
economic obligations without feeling too pinched for money."[1]

While waiving any value judgment on the abstraction
of "success" versus "unsuccess," this chapter sets forth con-
crete facts concerning the two in three writers who earn income from book writing ventures however successful or unsuccessful they may be thought to be.

Specifically, the chapter first briefly sketches a
backdrop portraying almost a universal feeling authors, publishers, and critics alike hold toward books. Next, delving
into the different kinds of books, the chapter establishes the

importance of each type ranked as first by authors according to its earnings in their 1957 personal incomes.

A summary of the five-year median personal incomes earned by original and subsidiary rights to books precedes individual analyses. The latter reveal the importance of each subsidiary source to the book writers' works.

Authors reporting personal income derived only from books are presented separately to show how relatively small this group is among all book writers and all writers as a group.

The rest of the chapter deals with personal income earned by book writers from other kinds of writing, from non-writing sources, and the total personal income earned from all sources.

Up until a short time ago--less than a decade and a half--the author's lot was certainly not thought of pessimistically. Yet, to judge by the comments--so prevalent in the fifties--the view today is almost entirely foreboding:

> ... first novels are being hit harder than ever before. Biographies of little-known figures are eliminated ... all due to the ever-increasing cost of manufacture, selling, promotion and advertising, which works against books where the margin of profit is narrow or nil.[2]

> ... fine novels by excellent authors are being rejected because they are first books, and the cost of promotion and advertising necessary to put a new author over have risen so tremendously that publishers have been forced to reduce their first novels to a minimum.[3]

> ... today the institution [of writing] has a flickering sort of life and poetry seems to be standing still.[4]

> ... not only bad poets but very good ones must subsidize their books, today, unless

they are among the bare dozen or so who have
captured the public's fancy.[5]

Most authors are born to be failures and the
publisher knows it. He makes his living out
of the few successes and if he is indulgent
with less successful writers it is only because there is always the possibility that
today's failure may become tomorrow's bestseller.[6]

... few of the individuals out of the thousands
of authors whose works are published can
make a living simply by writing books.[7]

Even if one is a very, very good poet, he
cannot get his first book published by a
national publisher unless (a) he pays the publisher for it; or (b) he is the publisher's
brother-in-law. The publisher will not take
the risk himself. Until a comparatively few
years ago this situation concerned only poetry.[8]

... though the main audience has turned back
to the play (in all its various forms, both
'live' and filmed), it is, nevertheless, a stoic
consolation for those of us whose first alle-
giance is the novel to know that there will
always be some serious interest in one's
work, that the keys to the kingdom of prose
will continue to be passed on from hand to
hand. And though I suspect that in a century's
time the novel will be as rare and private an
art form as poetry today or that delicate and
laborious process by which dedicated men fire
glass with color, it will always be worth the
doing.[9]

Aside from the hard-working authors of textbooks, standard juveniles, mysteries and westerns, I doubt that two hundred Americans earn
the major portion of their income, year after
year, by writing hard-cover books.[10]

Are these valid statements? Do these authors, publishers, and critics, from their close association with the
book industry, portray the book writer's position accurately?

They unanimously agree that those who write books for publication are somewhat more respected than other types of
authors but that novelists create less wealth of a tangible
sort and hence receive an even smaller reward financially.

C. P. Snow, the distinguished British novelist, scientist, and government official compares[11] the situation of
the writer in England and America in which he points out
that Faulkner was middle-aged, Robert Frost old, before
they drew a modest professional income from their creative
writing. He believes the burden of literary patronage has
fallen onto the universities, for he says, "A great apparatus
of visiting professorships, lectureships, fellowships, has
sprung up which is providing a living, or the best part of a
living, for an astonishing proportion of the best talents in
the country. Without about three exceptions, nearly every
American writer who has been 'heard of' in England, has
had some help--in the simple financial sense--from universities." The results, he points out, is that in America, the
writers don't really know whom they are writing for--apart
from their fellow writer-scholars, but they do earn enough
to get by, and a good deal more than their English equiva-
lents.

Whatever the opinions, the facts are that of the two-
thirds of all writers deriving income from books between
1953 and 1957, only 58.9 per cent had earnings each year
from this source. The remaining 41.1 per cent had income
from books for either one, two, three or four years--9.8,
10.1, 10.1, and 11.1 per cent respectively.

Of all book writers,[12] 15.7 per cent (10.3 per cent
of all writers) are counted also as playwrights. Of these
writers, a tenth are equally successful in either field, that
is, they made approximately the same amount from books

and plays during the five years studied, though not necessarily enough to live on from either one or both together.
Forty-seven per cent made more money from books; forty-
three per cent made more from playwriting. These same
individuals are tabulated both as book writers and as playwrights.

Of all book writers earning personal income from
books in 1957, well over half (58.4 per cent) indicated adult
fiction and general nonfiction as the two kinds of book most
importance to their 1957 incomes. Specialization in juvenile
fiction and juvenile nonfiction were listed by 27.5 per cent
more. These four categories accounted for eighty-six per
cent of the book writers in 1957, Table XXXV.

Table XXXV.

Type Of Book Ranked As Most Important In Book Writers'
1957 Income

Kind of Writing	Per Cent Males	Per Cent Females	Per Cent Total Response
Adult Fiction	36.0	19.8	30.2
General Non-Fiction	28.6	27.4	28.2
Juvenile Fiction	11.0	38.5	20.8
Textbooks	10.4	2.2	7.4
Religious Books	1.8	1.1	1.6
Others:			
Juvenile Non-Fiction	5.5	8.8	6.7
Technical-Scientific	3.7	-	2.3
Biography-Personality	.6	1.1	.8
Verse	.6	1.1	.8
Miscellaneous	1.8	-	1.2
Totals	100.0	100.0	100.0
N =	(164)	(91)	(255)

While for all book writers, males outnumber females almost two to one, proportionally there are over three times as many female as male juvenile fiction writers. But for juvenile nonfiction writers there is almost an even split since there are many husband and wife teams in this field.

As textbook writers, male book writers outnumber females eight to one. And in the religious field male book writers are three times as common as females. Verse is about fifty-fifty.

Arraying the 1957 book incomes by ages and sex adds dimension to the analysis of the book writer's position. More than three-fifths of the book writers (64.7 per cent) were between ages 40 and 60, Table XXXVI. The highest median personal income from books in 1957--$3,798--was earned by the 31.4 per cent between ages 40-49. Book writing income rises with age to a peak in the mid-forties; thereafter it declines, with a striking exception: those in their seventies earn more than those between 50 and 70 and those less than thirty. (The 70-year olds, of course, were the "class of the 1920's"--i.e. they were in their forties then!) It was this same group also (those now in their forties) who had the widest range in absolute dollar amounts earned as well as the highest-paid book writer.

Making up one-third of all book writers--the largest single segment--the fifty-year olds were about 90 per cent "employed", while the 20 year olds were all "employed." The 50 year olds' median personal income from books in 1957 was $3,000 even though the absolute dollar range from the lowest to the highest paid writer was one of the narrowest. Both the 40-and 50-year old groups had more than nine in ten of their number earning.

The extremes of the age scale, the twenty- and

Table XXXVI.

Book Writers' Median Book Incomes By Age And Sex, 1957

Age Scale	Male	Female	Total	Median Age	Median Income	Per Cent Of Group Earning Income	Range
20 - 29	2.4	-	1.6	28	$ 2268	100.0	$692-$26000
30 - 39	11.6	11.0	11.4	36	3565	74.4	100- 71000
40 - 49	32.3	29.7	31.4	45	3798	92.0	40- 76555
50 - 59	32.3	35.1	33.3	54	3000	93.4	10- 36700
60 - 69	16.5	15.4	16.1	62	1065	89.1	7- 64600
70 - 79	4.9	8.8	6.2	72	3073	80.0	75- 50000
Total	100.0	100.0	100.0				
N =	(164)	(91)	(255)				
Median				51	$ 2300		

seventy-year olds, were not the lowest of the lot in median
personal incomes from books. Accounting for slightly more
than six per cent of the book writers reporting in 1957, the
seventy-year olds earned the third highest median income--
$3,073. And, 80 per cent of this group earned from books
in 1957. The sixty-year olds, on the other hand with about
nine in ten reporting income, had the lowest median--
$1,065--from books.

While Table XXXVI shows a sex and age breakdown,
it is restricted to those book writers actually earning personal income from books in 1957, for whom the median age
was 51 years. For that portion of book writers (11.1 per
cent) who did not earn from books in 1957, the median age
was considerably younger--48 years--as Table XXXVII indicates. Two-thirds of these non-earners from books (1957)
were male, three-fifths of whom were under 50 years of
age; for the third female, three-fifths were over 50 years
of age. For all book writers the median age was 50 years.

Table XXXVII.

All Book Writers Not Earning Book Income In 1957 By
Age And Sex

Age Group	Per Cent Male	Per Cent Female	Per Cent Total
20 - 29	-	-	-
30 - 39	38.1	18.2	31.2
40 - 49	23.8	18.2	21.8
50 - 59	14.3	27.3	18.7
60 - 69	23.8	-	15.9
70 - 79	-	36.3	12.5
Total	100.0	100.0	100.0
N =	(21)	(11)	(32)
Median			48

The returns revealed that 77.7 per cent of all

book writers are married and that 56.5 per cent have working spouses. Both figures are slightly higher than for all
writers as a whole.

Book Income

Between 1953 and 1957, 93.7 per cent (better than
nine in ten of all book writers) reported earnings from original editions. It is, in fact, the most important single ele-
ment of income in book activities since the author can not
very well earn subsidiary income without it. At the same
time, it accounts for the largest portion of personal income
earned from books. For example, total personal income
from original editions made up 59.2 per cent of all personal
income derived by all book writers earning from books in
1957. (See below.)

Publication of an original, however, does not auto-
matically guarantee the book writer subsidiary income as
this breakdown readily verifies:

Area of Income	Per Cent of Book Writers Reporting (1953-1957)	Per Cent of Total Book Income, 1957
(1) original editions	93.7	59.2
(2) serializations	18.8	7.5
(3) paperbound reprints	25.1	7.8
(4) bookclubs	19.2	10.6
(5) foreign publications	41.1	5.9
(6) motion picture rights	11.2	5.5
(7) television rights	6.6	2.1
(8) other subsidiary rights	16.7	1.5
Total	(N=287)	100.0

Between 1953 and 1957, only 41.1 per cent of all book writers gained additional income from foreign publication rights--
the most often listed subsidiary source of personal income

from books. And, this source is very unrewarding financially; it accounted for less than six per cent of the total
personal income earned by all book writers deriving income
from books in 1957.

In only one other case--paperbound reprints--did as
much as a fourth show earnings from any one subsidiary income source from book writing ventures during the five-year
period. Publishers, as pointed out earlier, however, view
the new book's acceptance for publication in light of its prospective subsidiary income potential.

The importance of these subsidiary incomes to the
book writers' total personal book income, nevertheless, is
treated in the following section for all five years.

Total personal book income for all book writers by
years, arrayed in frequencies in Table XXXVIII, does not
present a very bright picture. With a 1957 median personal
income of $2,300 for the 88.8 per cent of all book writers
earning from all book sources in 1957, the five-year median
income is $1,600. The mean of the yearly medians is only
a few hundred dollars higher at $1,944. This means, of
course, that throughout the five-year period, half of all book
writers earned $1,600 or less each year from all their
efforts at writing books. Probably the fact that 1953 book
income was reported to be twenty-one-per-cent less than in
1957 is accounted for by the book writer's inability to produce his records. Based on those reporting, however, an
average of 79.8 per cent (or about 4 book writers in every
5) earned personal income from some book source each year.

On the average, a little more than 70 per cent (71.3)
of all book writers earn less than $5,000 a year from their
books. And less than one per cent earns in excess of
$50,000.

Table XXXVIII.

Book Writers' Total Income From Books By Income Classes, 1953-1957

Annual Income (dollars)	1957		1956		1955		1954		1953	
	Writers Per Cent	Income Median	Writers Per Cent	Income Median	Writers Per Cent	Income Median	Writers Per Cent	Income Median	Writers Per Cent	Income Median
0 - 1500	37.3	$ 450	41.5	$ 488	43.7	$ 465	44.3	$ 480	42.3	$ 500
1500 - 2500	16.1	1800	12.9	1810	13.7	1753	13.2	1872	12.9	1791
2500 - 5000	13.3	3769	16.6	3880	16.2	3852	16.4	3616	16.4	3226
5000 - 10000	17.3	6939	15.8	6814	14.4	6920	14.6	6000	14.4	6500
10000 - 15000	5.9	12516	5.0	11944	4.4	12225	3.7	11250	6.0	12482
15000 - 25000	3.5	19000	6.2	19150	3.5	17234	5.5	19900	5.0	16500
25000 - 50000	4.3	34400	1.7	45150	3.1	33589	1.4	34000	3.0	42942
50000 & over	2.4	62538	.4	58200	.9	64400	.9	56500	-	-
Totals N =	100.0 (255)		100.0 (241)		100.0 (229)		100.0 (219)		100.0 (201)	
Median	$2300		$2000		$1718		$1865		$1837	
Per Cent all Book Writers	88.8		84.0		79.8		76.3		70.0	

114

Earlier (Chapter III) the year 1955 for those deriving all income from free lance writing was established as the best year of the five for the average writer. Book writers contributed appreciably to that position in spite of the apparent contradiction in Table XXXVIII where the 1955 median is the poorest. The five-year low of $1,718 for all book writers is due primarily to the fact that more than half of them (57.6 per cent with a median of $1,310) were not included in the free lance group, simply because they earned personal income either from other kinds of writing or from non-writing occupation sources in 1955.

Personal income derived from motion picture rights to books is the only subsidiary source providing a higher five-year median income than originals. And relatively few book writers (11.1 per cent on the average) are fortunate enough to claim it. Table XXXIX is a five-year summary of the yearly median personal incomes derived by book writers earning from the different subsidiary sources each year. A comparison of the five-year median income for all book writers earning (whether they earned in one, two, three, four, or all five years) indicates somewhat the irregularity they experienced in gaining additional income from subsidiary rights.

Only a few hundred dollars are earned each year on the average from foreign publication rights and serializations in magazines or newspapers. Other subsidiary rights account for a little less; paperbound reprints bring in a little more.

Original Editions

For the nine-tenths of all book writers who drew personal income from original editions between 1953-1957,

Table XXXIX.

Yearly Median Incomes Earned By Book Writers From Original
And Subsidiary Rights To Books (1953-1957)

Book Writers' Income From:	5-Year Median Income (1953-1957)	1957	1956	1955	1954	1953
Originals	$1200	$1744	$1800	$1346	$1249	$1511
Serializations	255	587	422	900	750	675
Paperbound Reprints	440	1200	1500	1290	1250	2500
Bookclubs	895	2000	1285	850	1750	1075
Foreign Publications	131	293	300	365	300	340
Motion Picture Rights	1400	5124	6750	7450	10800	7000
Television Rights	200	1630	450	750	375	825
Other Rights	92	142	200	148	143	150
Total from Books	$1600	$2300	$2000	$1718	$1865	$1837

Table XL.

Book Writers' Income From Original Editions By Income Classes,
(1953-1957)

Annual Income (dollars)	1957 Book Writers Per Cent	1957 Income Median	1956 Book Writers Per Cent	1956 Income Median	1955 Book Writers Per Cent	1955 Income Median	1954 Book Writers Per Cent	1954 Income Median	1953 Book Writers Per Cent	1953 Income Median
0 - 1500	44.5	$ 450	47.4	$ 488	52.2	$ 497	52.5	$ 463	47.9	$ 450
1500 - 2500	14.4	1867	13.0	2000	10.7	1790	11.0	1857	16.1	1760
2500 - 5000	16.2	3520	17.2	3850	17.6	3628	18.5	3400	15.6	3195
5000 - 10000	14.4	6500	15.8	6697	12.7	6753	12.0	6055	13.4	6000
10000 - 15000	6.6	11430	3.3	13300	4.9	12000	5.0	11000	3.8	12053
15000 - 25000	1.8	22000	2.3	15205	1.5	18771	.5	15215	2.2	18319
25000 - 50000	1.8	32150	.5	25000	-	-	-	-	1.1	34650
50000 & over	.4	64600	.5	58200	.5	52500	.5	67800	-	-
Total	100.0		100.0		100.0		100.0		100.0	
N =	(229)		(215)		(205)		(200)		(186)	
Median		$1744		$1800		$1346		$1249		$1511
Per Cent all Book Writers	79.8		74.9		71.4		69.7		64.8	

117

more than three-fourths each year made less than $5,000.
(See Table XL.) Thus, with this large a proportion, it is
not surprising that the 1957 median personal income was
$1,744, nor that the five-year median was only $1,200. On
the average, 72.1 per cent of all book writers earned personal income from original editions each year.

Since personal income from original editions accounts
for approximately 60 per cent of the total earned by book
writers from books, obviously then, the remaining 40 per
cent must be spread rather thinly over the field of subsidiary rights.

Serializations

Less than a tenth of the book writers each year earn
additional personal income from serializations in magazines
or newspapers, Table XLI. Almost a fifth (18.8 per cent)
of all book writers could report personal income from this
source at one time or another between 1953 and 1957 but
only about half of this fraction (9.1 per cent) actually earned
from serializations in 1957. The total earned by those deriving income from serializations accounted for 7.5 per cent
of all book income in 1957.

Less than a fifth of the book writers earning from
serializations drew more than $5,000 from this source in
1955, 1956, and 1957. 1953 and 1954 were much better
years when almost a third (31.6 per cent) earned $5,000 or
more. The five-year median for the 18.8 per cent of all
book writers earning from this source, however, was only
$255.

Table XLI.

Book Writers' Income From Serializations By Income Classes,
(1953-1957)

Annual Income (dollars)	1957 Book Writers Per Cent	Income Median	1956 Book Writers Per Cent	Income Median	1955 Book Writers Per Cent	Income Median	1954 Book Writers Per Cent	Income Median	1953 Book Writers Per Cent	Income Median
0 - 1500	65.4	$ 412	80.0	$ 338	73.9	$ 350	57.9	$ 250	52.6	$ 341
1500 - 2500	7.7	1500	5.0	1500	4.4	2250	5.3	2000	-	-
2500 - 5000	7.7	3500	5.0	3150	4.4	4248	5.3	3044	15.8	3600
5000 - 10000	3.9	8100	-	-	13.0	6000	10.5	6131	21.1	6450
10000 - 15000	-	-	-	-	-	-	5.3	10000	5.3	12715
15000 - 25000	7.7	18100	10.0	19000	4.4	20000	15.8	18000	5.3	20000
25000 & over	7.7	28500	-	-	-	-	-	-	-	-
Total N =	100.0 (26)		100.0 (20)		100.0 (23)		100.0 (19)		100.0 (19)	
Median		$ 587		$ 422		$ 900		$750		$ 675
Per Cent all Book Writers	9.1		7.0		8.0		6.6		6.6	

119

Paperbound Reprints

Somewhat better off--both from the viewpoint of the number earning and the median personal incomes--were the fourth of all book writers deriving subsidiary personal income during the five years from paperbound reprints to their original works. Yet, the total personal income earned by these book writers from reprints made up only 7.8 per cent--a fraction more than from serializations--of all the book income earned by <u>all</u> book writers in 1957.

In 1953 with a $2,500 median, Table XLII, was the best year of the five but only 11.5 per cent of all book writers drew personal income from this source that year. On the average, approximately one book writer in eight had yearly reprint earnings, for which the five-year median of $440 was almost twice that for serializations.

Book Clubs

Between 1953 and 1957 Book Club awards went to almost one book writer in five (19.2 per cent). In 1955, the five-year high was reached when a tenth of all book writers drew personal income from this source. Payments that year, however, appear to have been only a token since more than six in ten earned less than $1,500 from this source with a median personal income of $500 and the 1955 median for all was the five-year low of $850, Table XLIII.

1955, nevertheless, was one of the two years in which the top prizes exceeded $25,000. The years 1954 and 1957 produced the highest medians of $1,750 and $2,000 for all book writers earning from this source. Though less than one book writer in ten on the average each year received book club money, the total payments in 1957 to the 11.5 per

Table XLII.

Book Writers' Income From Paperbound Reprints By Income Classes, (1953-1957)

Annual Income (dollars)	1957 Book Writers Per Cent	1957 Income Median	1956 Book Writers Per Cent	1956 Income Median	1955 Book Writers Per Cent	1955 Income Median	1954 Book Writers Per Cent	1954 Income Median	1953 Book Writers Per Cent	1953 Income Median
0 - 1500	56.8	$ 783	47.6	$ 472	56.8	$ 510	54.6	$ 241	42.4	$ 550
1500 - 2500	9.1	1925	23.8	1900	5.4	1862	-	-	3.0	2250
2500 - 5000	20.5	3500	11.9	2700	24.3	3250	30.3	3280	30.3	2700
5000 - 10000	6.8	5100	14.3	5700	10.8	6000	12.1	5825	18.2	5680
10000 - 15000	2.3	10000	2.4	14000	-	-	3.0	14000	3.0	12000
15000 - 25000	4.6	21000	-	-	-	-	-	-	3.0	20000
25000 & over	-	-	-	-	2.7	30000	-	-	-	-
Total N =	100.0 (44)		100.0 (42)		100.0 (37)		100.0 (33)		100.0 (33)	
Median		$1200		$1500		$1290		$1250		$2500
Per Cent all Book Writers	15.3		14.6		12.9		11.5		11.5	

121

Table XLIII.

Book Writers' Income From Book Club Awards By Income Classes, (1953-1957)

Annual Income (dollars)	1957 Book Writers Per Cent	Income Median	1956 Book Writers Per Cent	Income Median	1955 Book Writers Per Cent	Income Median	1954 Book Writers Per Cent	Income Median	1953 Book Writers Per Cent	Income Median
0 - 1500	42.4	$ 648	53.6	$ 647	63.3	$ 500	48.1	$ 675	56.3	$ 342
1500 - 2500	9.1	2000	17.9	1750	10.0	2000	7.4	1843	6.3	2000
2500 - 5000	12.1	4202	10.7	3200	6.7	3375	18.5	3500	18.8	2700
5000 - 10000	21.2	6750	10.7	8000	6.7	6575	18.5	5025	12.5	7000
10000 - 15000	6.1	11750	3.6	11000	3.3	10000	7.4	11975	6.3	10517
15000 - 25000	6.1	18028	3.6	21685	6.7	16000	-	-	-	-
25000 & over	3.0	38500	-	-	3.3	38000	-	-	-	-
Total N =	100.0 (33)		100.0 (28)		100.0 (30)		100.0 (27)		100.0 (16)	
Median		$2000		$1285		$ 850		$1750		$1075
Per Cent all Book Writers	11.5		9.8		10.5		9.4		5.6	

122

cent of all book writers reporting such personal income
made up 10.6 per cent of all income earned from books
that year. The five-year median for all of $895 was twice
that derived from reprints.

Foreign Publications

Subsidiary income from foreign publication rights
went to two book writers in every five between 1953 and
1957. And, on the average, about one in five reported yearly earnings from this source.

Although foreign publications provide an outlet for the
works of more book writers than any other single subsidiary
source, it also is the least remunerative of the major
sources. (See Table XLIV.) In 1955, with a fifth of all
book writers earning from rights to foreign publications, the
five-year high in personal median income from this source--
$365--was realized.

The earnings of almost a third of all book writers
(30.7 per cent) reporting personal income from foreign publication rights in 1957 still accounted for only 5.9 per cent
of the total book income earned by all book writers that
year. The five-year median from foreign publications for
the 41.1 per cent of all book writers earning from this
source was $131--the lowest producer of the major subsid-
iary sources of book income.

Motion Picture Rights

Slightly more than one in ten book writers derived
subsidiary book income from motion pictures during the five
years between 1953 and 1957, but each year less than one
in twenty had income from this source.

By far the most lucrative subsidiary outlet for book

Table XLIV.

Book Writers' Income From Foreign Publications By Income Classes, (1953-1957)

Annual Income (dollars)	1957 Book Writers Per Cent	1957 Income Median	1956 Book Writers Per Cent	1956 Income Median	1955 Book Writers Per Cent	1955 Income Median	1954 Book Writers Per Cent	1954 Income Median	1953 Book Writers Per Cent	1953 Income Median
0 - 1500	80.7	$ 200	89.0	$ 230	79.3	$ 208	81.4	$ 248	84.2	$ 281
1500 - 2500	13.6	2000	5.5	2148	12.1	1888	8.5	1825	8.8	1895
2500 - 5000	3.4	3380	4.1	3278	1.7	2600	8.5	3000	3.5	4138
5000 - 10000	1.1	5257	-	-	5.2	5340	1.7	8405	1.8	5722
10000 - 15000	-	-	-	-	1.7	10000	-	-	-	-
15000 - 25000	-	-	1.4	17788	-	-	-	-	1.8	15716
25000 & over	1.1	30587	-	-	-	-	-	-	-	-
Total N =	100.0 (88)		100.0 (73)		100.0 (58)		100.0 (59)		100.0 (57)	
Median		$ 293		$ 300		$ 365		$ 300		$ 340
Per Cent all Book Writers	30.7		25.4		20.2		20.6		19.9	

124

Table XLV.

Book Writers' Income From Motion Picture Rights By Income Classes,
(1953-1957)

Annual Income (dollars)	1953 Book Writers Per Cent	1953 Income Median	1954 Book Writers Per Cent	1954 Income Median	1955 Book Writers Per Cent	1955 Income Median	1956 Book Writers Per Cent	1956 Income Median	1957 Book Writers Per Cent	1957 Income Median
0 - 1500	33.3	$ 900	27.3	$ 150	16.7	$ 550	30.8	$ 650	27.3	$ 1000
1500 - 2500	-	-	-	-	8.3	2000	7.7	2363	-	-
2500 - 5000	11.1	4500	9.1	4500	16.7	4275	-	-	18.2	2974
5000 - 10000	33.3	9000	9.1	9000	25.0	9000	38.5	9000	27.3	9000
10000 - 15000	11.1	10800	27.3	11250	-	-	7.7	10000	-	-
15000 - 25000	-	-	9.1	16000	33.3	20500	15.4	18000	27.3	18000
25000 & over	-	-	18.2	25000	-	-	-	-	-	-
Total N =	100.0 (9)		100.0 (11)		100.0 (12)		100.0 (13)		100.0 (11)	
Median		$7000		$10800		$7450		$6750		$5124
Per Cent all Book Writers	3.1		3.8		4.2		4.5		3.8	

writers' works, motion pictures provided a 1957 median
personal income--for a very small, select group--that was
more than twice the median for all book writers earning
from all book sources combined in 1957; almost three times
that from original editions and book club awards; and better
than four times that from paperbound reprints. Yet, the
1957 median from motion pictures for the 3.8 per cent of
all book writers earning was the lowest for the five years,
Table XLV.

In only one year (1954) did top payments even approach those made for original rights and book club awards
to books, but even the smallest payment made for motion
picture rights to a book in many cases is well above some
medians earned by entire groups from other sources. That
is why with only 11.2 per cent of all book writers earning
from this source during the entire five years, the motion
picture rights income in 1957 made up 5.5 per cent of the
total book income earned by all book writers. The per cent
of total accounted for by the 3.8 per cent of the book writers earning in 1957 is almost as much as that from foreign
rights, but the group earning motion picture rights income
to books is only a ninth the size of the group earning from
foreign productions.

The five-year median from motion picture rights was
$1,400--highest median for any area from books including
original rights, while the mean of the yearly medians was
$7,425--more than five times the five-year median.

Television Rights

Television rights to books provided an even smaller
demand for the book writers' works than did motion pictures.
Approximately one book writer in every fifteen had a subsid-

iary income from his books for television rights to them in the five-year period. But far fewer actually had earnings each year. By 1956-1957 it appears that television rights brought income to about as large a proportion of writers as did motion pictures. In 1957, the ratio was about one in thirty; in 1953, it was one in a hundred. (See Table XLVI, page 128.)

With the exception of 1957, median personal incomes from television rights were on a par with those from serializations and slightly better than the median personal incomes derived from foreign publication rights.

The per cent of total book income contributed by the 3.5 per cent of all book writers earning from television rights in 1957 was slightly better than 2 per cent (2.1).

On the average, the few book writers who do receive additional personal income from television rights to their books receive approximately $200 yearly (five-year median) --a little less than that received from serializations, a little more than that received from foreign publication rights.

Other Subsidiary Rights

Other subsidiary rights gave approximately the same number of book writers income as those earning from serialization rights to their books. The median personal earnings each year for serializations, however, was several times more. Almost one hundred per cent of the book writers earning from miscellaneous subsidiary sources, Table XLVII, page 129, earn less than $1,500 yearly; the average yearly earning is about $92. As a portion of the total book income earned by all book writers in 1957, miscellaneous subsidiary sources accounted for only 1.5 per cent of it.

Table XLVI.

Book Writers' Income From Television Rights By Income Classes,
(1953-1957)

Annual Income (dollars)	1957 Book Writers Per Cent	1957 Income Median	1956 Book Writers Per Cent	1956 Income Median	1955 Book Writers Per Cent	1955 Income Median	1954 Book Writers Per Cent	1954 Income Median	1953 Book Writers Per Cent	1953 Income Median
0 - 1500	50.0	$ 900	72.7	$ 450	71.4	$ 450	100.0	$ 375	100.0	$ 825
1500 - 2500	20.0	2205	9.1	2250	14.3	1700	-	-	-	-
2500 - 5000	10.0	2500	9.1	4527	-	-	-	-	-	-
5000 - 10000	-	-	-	-	-	-	-	-	-	-
10000 - 15000	20.0	11250	9.1	10500	14.3	10500	-	-	-	-
15000 & over	-	-	-	-	-	-	-	-	-	-
Total	100.0		100.0		100.0		100.0		100.0	
N =	(10)		(11)		(7)		(6)		(2)	
Median		$1630		$ 450		$ 750		$ 375		$ 825
Per Cent all Book Writers	3.5		3.8		2.4		2.1		.7	

128

Table XLVII.

Book Writers' Income From Other Subsidiary Rights By Income Classes, (1953-1957)

Annual Income (dollars)	1957 Book Writers Per Cent	Income Median	1956 Book Writers Per Cent	Income Median	1955 Book Writers Per Cent	Income Median	1954 Book Writers Per Cent	Income Median	1953 Book Writers Per Cent	Income Median
0 - 1500	93.8	$ 136	100.0	$ 200	100.0	$ 148	100.0	$ 143	100.0	$ 150
1500 - 2500	-	-	-	-	-	-	-	-	-	-
2500 - 5000	3.1	2500	-	-	-	-	-	-	-	-
5000 - 10000	-	-	-	-	-	-	-	-	-	-
10000 - 15000	-	-	-	-	-	-	-	-	-	-
15000 & over	3.1	15000	-	-	-	-	-	-	-	-
Total N =	100.0 (32)		100.0 (17)		100.0 (21)		100.0 (15)		100.0 (21)	
Median		$ 142		$ 200		$ 148		$ 143		$ 150
Per cent all Book Writers	11.1		5.9		7.3		5.2		7.3	

The Book-Writing Specialists

There is a very small group of authors who earn all their personal income only from books. These, for the laymen, may be thought of as the writers' writers--the stereotypical novelists. But very few book writers make their living simply as authors of books. Separate treatment is given here to show how relatively small the group is that earns only from this one specialized kind of writing. All book writers as a group make up more than 65 per cent of all writers, but book writers earning personal income solely from books accounted for just a fraction more than a seventh of all book writers between 1953 and 1957. Among all writers they account for less than a tenth (9.8 per cent).

Approximately one in four deriving his sole personal income from books is male, each of whom reported earning yearly for a five-year median income of $4,670. Only one in twelve is under 45 years of age; the median is 59 years for this group of male book writers.

Three-fourths of these male book writers are married and more than half had working spouses during the five-year period.

Of the female book writers reporting personal income earned only from books, two-thirds of them earned such income every year. Though considerably less than for males, the five-year median personal income for female book-only writers was $3,077. Females, like males who earned only from books, are older than book writers as a whole. The median is 52 years for this group of female book writers. Almost two-thirds of the females (64.5 per cent) are married and 65 per cent reported working spouses.

For all book writers earning solely from books

there was rather steady "employment" for the five years--
an average of 86.0 per cent each year. A fourth or more
of the group, however, earned less than $1,500 yearly.
(See Table XLVIII.)

More than eight-tenths of the group reporting less
than $1,500 yearly personal income solely from books were
women. Nine in ten are married and housewives ... perhaps in the profession simply as "something to do." This
latter is not meant to belittle their position, for on occasion
about 15 per cent realized substantial returns--more than
$5,000--for their efforts.

Of book writers earning personal income solely from
books, almost two-thirds (65.1 per cent) are married (lower
than for all writers) but 64.3 per cent of them have working
spouses--considerably higher than for all writers as a whole.

Book writers deriving personal earnings solely from
books were more dependent on the working spouse's income
than were other book writers or all writers as a whole. The
working spouse contributed 59.7 per cent, or $4,543, to the
family income yearly. The extent of dependence is readily
apparent when the five-year medians--personal and family--
are compared for this 15 per cent of all book writers. For
personal income the median is $3,646; for family income it
is $5,474. Both figures, however, are lower than those for
all book writers and all writers.

Other Writing Income

Free Lance

More than one book writer in every two (56.8 per
cent) earned income from free lance magazine writing between 1953 and 1957 in addition to that from his books.
And slightly more than one in six (15.7 per cent) earned

Table XLVIII.

Personal Income Of Book Writers Earning Solely From Books, By Income Classes, (1953-1957)

Annual Income (dollars)	1953 Book Writers Per Cent	1953 Income Median	1954 Book Writers Per Cent	1954 Income Median	1955 Book Writers Per Cent	1955 Income Median	1956 Book Writers Per Cent	1956 Income Median	1957 Book Writers Per Cent	1957 Income Median
0 - 1500	32.4	$ 590	25.0	$ 451	27.0	$ 520	26.3	$ 838	26.8	$ 465
1500 - 2500	8.8	2250	11.1	2205	10.8	1988	7.9	1793	14.6	1770
2500 - 5000	20.6	3837	22.2	3599	24.3	4000	26.3	4143	14.6	3673
5000 - 10000	35.3	6442	27.8	6083	21.6	7000	21.1	6577	24.4	6115
10000 - 15000	-	-	11.1	11100	13.5	12150	10.5	11016	9.8	12744
15000 - 25000	-	-	-	-	-	-	5.3	19150	2.4	15622
25000 - 50000	2.9	38800	2.8	44900	2.7	37500	2.6	45300	4.9	36700
50000 & over	-	-	-	-	-	-	-	-	2.4	50000
Total N =	100.0 (34)		100.0 (36)		100.0 (37)		100.0 (38)		100.0 (41)	
Median		$3504		$4023		$4000		$4326		$4000
Per Cent all Book Writers	11.8		12.5		12.9		13.2		14.3	

from playwriting activities.

Magazines.--Free lance magazine writing is not particularly lucrative for book writers though on the average,
36.2 per cent of them earned yearly from this source, Table XLIX, page 134. Only in two of the five years--1954
and 1957--did the top-paid book writer earn as much as
$25,000 for his magazine writing. In contrast, 60 per cent
or more each year earned less than $1,500, and thus the
mean of the yearly medians from this source hovered around
$800. The five-year median was much less--$284.

The trend seems to be toward lower payments for
the book writers' efforts in the magazine field, for with
more book writers reporting income from this source in
1957 than in any other year, far fewer of them (less than
14 per cent) earned $5,000 or more. In 1953 and 1955
twenty-one per cent received $5,000 or more and with only
a few less book writers deriving personal income from magazine work than did so in 1957.

Plays.--"The play's the thing," or so it would appear in Table L, page 135. Here, the trend is toward an
increasing proportion of book writers earning $5,000 or
more from plays--22.3 per cent in 1957 compared with the
5.9 per cent earning similar income in 1953--just the opposite of what happened in magazine writing. More book writers, of course, reported income from playwriting activities
in 1957 as was true for magazine writing, but the number of
book writers earning from plays more than doubled from
1953 to 1957 while magazine earners increased by only 15
per cent. The percentage earning in excess of $10,000 from
plays--none in 1953--increased steadily; 1957 was also the
top playwriting year in median personal income for the group.
(1953 had been for magazine writing.)

Table XLIX.

Book Writers' Income From Free Lance Magazine Writing By Income Classes, (1953-1957)

Annual Income (dollars)	1957 Book Writers Per Cent	1957 Income Median	1956 Book Writers Per Cent	1956 Income Median	1955 Book Writers Per Cent	1955 Income Median	1954 Book Writers Per Cent	1954 Income Median	1953 Book Writers Per Cent	1953 Income Median
0 - 1500	60.0	$ 300	58.6	$ 336	61.2	$ 477	67.7	$ 337	62.0	$ 300
1500 - 2500	9.6	1948	9.1	1848	6.8	1800	2.9	1875	11.0	2000
2500 - 5000	16.5	3000	13.1	3000	10.7	4000	11.8	3600	6.0	3353
5000 - 10000	7.8	7850	9.1	6000	12.6	7065	8.8	6600	12.0	7890
10000 - 15000	4.4	12733	7.1	12300	3.9	11488	4.9	12865	8.0	11796
15000 - 25000	-	-	3.0	18752	4.9	20725	2.0	16153	1.0	16885
25000 & over	1.7	32697	-	-	-	-	2.0	28000	-	-
Total N =	100.0 (115)		100.0 (99)		100.0 (103)		100.0 (102)		100.0 (100)	
Median		$ 750		$ 970		$ 930		$ 624		$ 989
Per Cent all Book Writers	40.1		34.5		35.9		35.5		34.8	

Table L.

Book Writers' Income From Playwriting By Income Classes,
(1953-1957)

Annual Income (dollars)	1957 Book Writers Per Cent	1957 Income Median	1956 Book Writers Per Cent	1956 Income Median	1955 Book Writers Per Cent	1955 Income Median	1954 Book Writers Per Cent	1954 Income Median	1953 Book Writers Per Cent	1953 Income Median
0 - 1500	47.2	$ 440	57.6	$ 320	60.7	$ 585	71.4	$ 500	58.8	$ 520
1500 - 2500	13.9	1576	-	-	10.7	2075	4.8	2000	11.8	1500
2500 - 5000	16.7	4120	6.1	4730	7.1	3950	14.3	3600	23.5	2853
5000 - 10000	8.3	7500	21.2	6140	-	-	-	-	5.9	6790
10000 - 15000	-	-	-	-	7.1	12690	4.8	15745	-	-
15000 - 25000	2.8	18000	6.1	17205	-	-	-	-	-	-
25000 - 50000	2.8	48461	3.0	48500	3.6	49645	-	-	-	-
50000 - 100000	5.6	74750	3.0	94000	7.1	58000	-	-	-	-
100000 & over	2.8	123052	3.0	126830	3.6	111000	4.8	135000	-	-
Total N =	100.0 (36)		100.0 (33)		100.0 (28)		100.0 (21)		100.0 (17)	
Median	$1543		$1200		$1237		$ 665		$1200	
Per cent all Book Writers	12.5		11.4		9.8		7.3		5.9	

135

The 1957 median personal income ($1,543) from plays is characteristic of the average (median) personal income derived by book writers from paperbound reprints and book club awards. About the same number, roughly, earned from the three sources. But the fact remains that only about a third as many book writers were earning from playwriting as from magazine writing in 1957.

For the 15.7 per cent of all book writers who derived personal income from playwriting between 1953 and 1957, the five-year median earned was $740; the mean of the yearly medians was only a few hundred dollars higher--$1,169.

"F. L. -Emp"

A much better financial position was achieved by the book writers who derived personal income from motion picture and television writing apart from their books. (See Table LI.) Motion picture writing and television writing for this group--18.1 per cent of all book writers, or about three per cent more than the number of book writers writing plays --were not subsidiary outlets but special writing assignments either on a salary basis or as an original work.

The 1957 median of $5,118--very nearly the same as for 1955, and 1956--was more than twice the median income for all book writers from books, though the per cent of all book writers deriving income each year from "F. L. - Emp" writing was indeed quite small--about 10 per cent in 1956, less than 10 per cent in 1955 and 1957.

As substantial as these median incomes from "F. L. - Emp" writing appear, they account for but a third or less of the total personal income earned by this 18.1 per cent of all book writers. In other words, book writers earning per-

Table LI.

Book Writers' Income From "F.L.-Emp" Writing By Income Classes, (1953-1957)

Annual Income (dollars)	1957 Book Writers Per Cent	1957 Income Median	1956 Book Writers Per Cent	1956 Income Median	1955 Book Writers Per Cent	1955 Income Median	1954 Book Writers Per Cent	1954 Income Median	1953 Book Writers Per Cent	1953 Income Median
0 - 1500	11.1	$ 1000	33.3	$ 657	25.0	$ 625	34.8	$ 338	41.7	$ 909
1500 - 2500	14.8	1712	6.7	1918	8.3	1787	13.0	1575	12.5	1800
2500 - 5000	14.8	3434	10.0	4050	16.7	3600	13.0	3500	8.3	3400
5000 - 10000	22.2	6149	13.3	8163	16.7	7739	17.4	7050	20.8	7199
10000 - 15000	7.4	13850	13.3	13550	8.3	12600	-	-	4.2	11400
15000 - 25000	11.1	15500	3.3	19900	4.2	22500	-	-	4.2	20000
25000 - 50000	11.1	25000	13.3	29500	12.5	36000	17.4	27241	4.2	31500
50000 - 100000	7.4	73037	3.3	80000	4.2	72289	4.4	68400	4.2	66600
100000 & over	-	-	3.3	106013	4.2	105000	-	-	-	-
Total N =	100.0 (27)		100.0 (30)		100.0 (24)		100.0 (23)		100.0 (24)	
Median		$5118		$5100		$5033		$3000		$1900
Per cent all Book Writers	9.4		10.4		8.4		8.0		8.4	

137

Table LII.

Total Income Earned (All Sources) By Book Writers Deriving "F.L.-Emp" Writing Income, By Income Classes, (1953-1957)

Annual Income (dollars)	1957 Book Writers Per Cent	Income Median	1956 Book Writers Per Cent	Income Median	1955 Book Writers Per Cent	Income Median	1954 Book Writers Per Cent	Income Median	1953 Book Writers Per Cent	Income Median
0 - 1500	-	$ -	3.3	$ 1329	4.2	$ 800	-	$ -	4.2	$ 1200
1500 - 2500	-	-	6.7	2254	-	-	8.7	2085	4.2	2415
2500 - 5000	3.7	4980	6.7	4136	16.7	4250	21.7	3033	20.8	3000
5000 - 10000	25.9	7180	16.7	7234	12.5	7342	21.7	8500	29.2	8250
10000 - 15000	14.8	12587	10.0	11737	8.3	13182	17.4	11342	12.5	11400
15000 - 25000	25.9	18440	23.3	20278	12.5	19000	8.7	18828	12.5	21800
25000 - 50000	14.8	39010	20.0	32485	20.8	36000	12.0	43450	12.5	31950
50000 - 100000	14.8	77790	6.7	80552	12.5	65050	8.7	77362	4.2	67244
100000 & over	-	-	6.7	118326	12.5	133575	-	-	-	-
Total N =	100.0 (27)		100.0 (30)		100.0 (24)		100.0 (23)		100.0 (24)	
Median		$16000		$16586		$21652		$8939		$8891
Per cent "F.L.-Emp" Income is of Total Income	32.0		30.8		23.2		33.6		21.4	

138

sonal income from "F. L.-Emp" writing also earned quite
well from other sources as Table LII indicates, page 138.
In 1957, for instance, the $16,000 median total personal
income (all sources) included the $5,118 median (Table LI)
from "F. L.-Emp" writing, but the latter amount is only
32.0 per cent of the total. The $5,033 median personal in-
come earned from "F. L.-Emp" writing in 1955 (Table LI)
by slightly more than a twelfth of all book writers was less
than a fourth of this group's total median income from all
sources--a high of $21,652. Impressive as the figures are,
still in 1955, about one in every five of this group had less
than $5,000 total income; the five-year median income from
"F. L.-Emp" writing was $1,565, however, almost the same
as that earned by all book writers from books.

Directed

Slightly more than a fifth (21.3 per cent) of all
book writers earned from assigned writing projects including
staff work for magazines and newspapers between 1953 and
1957, but on the average, only 14 per cent of them earned
yearly from this source. Generally much better than playwriting in terms of yearly medians for the book writers'
efforts, directed or staff writing projects were far less
lucrative than "F. L.-Emp" writing. (See Table LIII.)

1953 was by far the best year of the five for directed writing personal income but the least number of book
writers also reported earning from this source that year.
The $4,000 median personal income was more than three
times that earned in 1957.

Book writers doing directed writing show much
more regularity in income than those doing plays, though top
payments for the latter are far greater. In no instance do

Table LIII.

Book Writers' Income From Directed Writing By Income Classes,
(1953-1957)

Annual Income (dollars)	1957 Book Writers Per Cent	1957 Income Median	1956 Book Writers Per Cent	1956 Income Median	1955 Book Writers Per Cent	1955 Income Median	1954 Book Writers Per Cent	1954 Income Median	1953 Book Writers Per Cent	1953 Income Median
0 - 1500	51.1	$ 312	29.3	$ 275	37.2	$ 457	39.5	$ 500	31.4	$ 500
1500 - 2500	6.4	2000	14.6	1988	11.6	1500	5.3	2000	8.6	1800
2500 - 5000	12.8	4000	22.0	3400	16.3	2950	18.4	3750	20.0	4000
5000 - 10000	10.6	6000	14.6	8475	14.0	5600	13.2	9000	20.0	8500
10000 - 15000	12.8	11995	9.8	12500	11.6	12500	13.2	12000	14.3	10000
15000 - 25000	4.3	21351	7.3	21000	9.3	20750	7.9	19500	5.7	18364
25000 & over	2.1	32000	2.4	25000	-	-	2.6	31970	-	-
Total N =	100.0 (47)		100.0 (41)		100.0 (43)		100.0 (38)		100.0 (35)	
Median		$1310		$3000		$2500		$2954		$4000
Per cent all Book Writers	16.4		14.3		15.0		13.2		12.2	

140

payments for staff or directed work exceed $50,000; in 1953 and 1955 they did not exceed $25,000.

As was true for book writers doing free lance magazine writing, playwriting, and "F.L.-Emp" writing, a large portion deriving income from directed writing earn very little from their efforts. In 1957, more than 50 per cent earned less than $1,500. The five-year median earned by all book writers reporting personal income from directed writing was only $630.

Non-Writing Income

Like all writers, more than half of all book writers derived income from other sources than writing (1953-1957).

Altogether, more than three-fifths of the book writers deriving non-writing personal income were regularly engaged in their jobs the full five years, though we do not know the amount of time required by these jobs. One writer, however, was quite specific on his return when he wrote, "Eighty per cent of my time is devoted to writing (average $3,100) and twenty per cent to business consulting (average $31,000 a year)." The occupation title itself does suggest in many instances a "full time" connotation.

Less than a tenth listing non-writing occupations reported them for only one year of the five, about the same portion reporting two- and four-year personal incomes from non-writing sources.

In cases where a book writer listed multiple jobs, the one providing the major portion of his non-writing income was tabulated in Table LIV, page 142.

Teaching was the most often listed non-writing

Table LIV.

Type Of Job Held By Book Writers To Supplement Writing Income And Degree Of Regularity (1953-1957)

Occupations	Per Cent Reporting	Per Cent Reporting				
		5 Years	4 Years	3 Years	2 Years	1 Year
Teaching	21.4	24.5	42.9	-	14.3	14.3
Editing, Editors	11.0	7.4	7.1	27.8	14.3	14.3
Executive, Director, Manager	8.4	9.6	7.1	5.6	7.1	7.1
Consulting	7.8	10.6	7.1	-	7.1	-
Public Relations & Promotion	7.1	8.5	-	11.1	7.1	-
Lecturing	6.5	6.4	7.1	-	-	7.1
Real Estate & Investments	5.8	8.5	-	-	21.4	-
Artist, Illustrator	5.2	3.2	14.3	-	7.1	-
Government (Fed, State, Local)	3.9	3.2	-	11.1	-	7.1
Secretarial, Clerical	3.2	2.1	-	11.1	7.1	-
Medical	3.2	5.3	-	5.6	7.1	7.1
The Arts--Radio, TV, Stage	3.2	2.1	-	5.6	7.1	7.1
Selling, Advertising	2.6	3.2	-	-	-	7.1
Military Service	1.9	-	7.1	5.6	7.1	-
Inspector, Investigator	1.3	2.1	-	-	-	-
Manufacturing	1.3	1.1	7.1	-	-	-
Research	1.3	-	-	-	-	14.3
Ranching	.7	1.1	-	-	-	-
Literary Agent	.7	-	-	5.6	-	-

142

Table LIV. (continued)

Type Of Job Held By Book Writers To Supplement Writing Income And
Degree of Regularity (1953-1957)

Occupations	Per Cent Reporting	Per Cent Reporting				
		5 Years	4 Years	3 Years	2 Years	1 Year
Printer	.7	-	-	5.6	-	-
Economist	.7	-	-	5.6	-	-
Proofreading	.7	1.1	-	-	-	-
Miscellaneous	1.3	-	-	-	-	14.3
Totals	100.0[1]	100.0	100.0	100.0	100.0	100.0
N =	(154)	(94)	(14)	(18)	(14)	(14)

1. In addition, about a fifth were multiple job holders; almost a third of these held multiple jobs the entire five years, about a tenth for four of the five years, an eighth for three years, about a fifth for two years; and almost a third for one year. Teaching and lecturing were the most often listed occupations.

143

occupation by more than a fifth of the book writers earning from non-writing sources. It accounted for almost a fourth of book writers reporting personal income from non-writing sources for the entire five years, and almost half of those reporting four-year incomes from this source.

Though consulting was listed by only 7.8 per cent of the book writers as the fourth most common non-writing occupation, it was second to teaching by those reporting five-year incomes. Editing or editorships was the second most popular non-writing occupation selected by book writers to supplement their writing incomes--an occupation closely allied to books. And editing was reported most frequently by more than a fourth of those earning non-writing personal incomes three out of the five years.

The number of book writers deriving personal income from non-writing sources was slightly higher (53.7 per cent) than for all writers (51.1 per cent) as was the per cent of book writers earning each year from this source (44.6 per cent); see Table LV, page 145. But, unlike all writers deriving non-writing personal income who drew 71.3 per cent (five-year median) of their total personal income from non-writing sources, book writers derived 60.3 per cent of their total personal income over the five years from this source. The five-year median for book writers, however, was a few hundred dollars higher--$4,479.

Emphasizing the importance of non-writing personal income, again, the total yearly median personal income from all sources for book writers deriving non-writing income (Table LVI, page 146) exceeded that of all book writers as a whole (Table LVII, page 147) by almost $2,000 each year.

All book writers (representing 65.5 per cent of all

Table LV.

Book Writers' Total Non-Writing Income By Income Classes,
(1953-1957)

Annual Income (dollars)	1957 Book Writers Per Cent	Income Median	1956 Book Writers Per Cent	Income Median	1955 Book Writers Per Cent	Income Median	1954 Book Writers Per Cent	Income Median	1953 Book Writers Per Cent	Income Median
0 - 1500	17.8	$ 506	15.7	$ 600	19.1	$ 721	22.7	$ 555	20.3	$ 539
1500 - 2500	7.0	1946	8.2	1975	9.9	1838	3.1	1766	5.1	1820
2500 - 5000	20.9	3600	20.9	3550	16.8	3272	18.8	3695	17.0	3820
5000 - 10000	20.2	8000	26.9	7550	26.0	7025	28.1	7428	28.8	7090
10000 - 15000	14.0	10573	8.2	11910	9.9	12600	7.8	12000	15.3	12100
15000 - 25000	16.3	18500	16.4	17500	15.3	16062	17.2	16502	11.0	16500
25000 - 50000	3.1	38750	3.0	31000	2.3	25000	1.6	26500	1.7	34125
50000 - 100000	.8	65000	-	-	-	-	.8	80000	-	-
100000 & over	-	-	.7	160000	.8	160000	-	-	.9	100000
Total N =	100.0 (129)		100.0 (134)		100.0 (131)		100.0 (128)		100.0 (118)	
Median		$6700		$5000		$5720		$5855		$6000
Per cent all Book Writers	44.9		46.7		45.6		44.6		41.1	

Table LVI.

Total Income All Sources For Book Writers Deriving Non-Writing Income,
By Income Classes, (1953-1957)

Annual Income (dollars)	1957 Book Writers Per Cent	1957 Income Median	1956 Book Writers Per Cent	1956 Income Median	1955 Book Writers Per Cent	1955 Income Median	1954 Book Writers Per Cent	1954 Income Median	1953 Book Writers Per Cent	1953 Income Median
0 - 1500	3.1	$ 1096	3.0	$ 965	3.8	$ 1000	5.5	$ 785	5.9	$ 730
1500 - 2500	4.7	1899	3.7	1960	4.6	1617	5.5	1921	5.1	2008
2500 - 5000	11.6	4057	11.9	4168	18.3	4190	14.1	3633	8.5	4155
5000 - 10000	24.8	7688	35.1	7000	27.5	7215	27.3	6871	35.6	6912
10000 - 15000	19.4	11867	12.7	11426	11.5	12236	14.8	11600	8.5	11415
15000 - 25000	20.9	20212	19.4	20060	23.7	19640	25.0	19223	29.7	17600
25000 - 50000	10.1	36800	10.5	29051	6.1	30040	5.5	32750	5.1	35661
50000 - 100000	5.4	67200	3.0	63750	3.8	77000	1.6	69400	.9	58400
100000 & over	-	-	.7	162500	.8	185000	.8	106000	.9	145000
Total N =	100.0 (129)		100.0 (134)		100.0 (131)		100.0 (128)		100.0 (118)	
Median		$10800		$9087		$9290		$9050		$9322

146

Table LVII.

Book Writers' Total Income All Sources By Income Classes,
(1953-1957)

Annual Income (dollars)	1957 Book Writers Per Cent	Income Median	1956 Book Writers Per Cent	Income Median	1955 Book Writers Per Cent	Income Median	1954 Book Writers Per Cent	Income Median	1953 Book Writers Per Cent	Income Median
0 - 1500	14.2	$ 513	12.7	$ 675	14.4	$ 600	14.8	$ 500	16.0	$ 585
1500 - 2500	7.1	1972	6.9	1894	7.0	1805	7.6	1961	6.0	2079
2500 - 5000	11.0	3646	13.0	4027	16.6	4050	17.5	3633	14.4	3586
5000 - 10000	23.1	7405	27.2	7000	24.0	7000	23.6	6871	27.2	7000
10000 - 15000	14.9	12474	13.0	11859	12.6	12268	14.1	11440	12.0	11460
15000 - 25000	17.0	19700	15.2	20005	14.4	19318	15.6	19675	18.4	18214
25000 - 50000	7.8	36700	8.3	31250	7.0	31684	4.6	34340	4.8	38541
50000 - 100000	4.3	69925	2.2	73237	2.9	74644	1.5	70712	.8	62822
100000 & over	.7	135565	1.5	123175	1.1	133575	.8	133765	.4	145000
Total N =	100.0 (282)		100.0 (276)		100.0 (271)		100.0 (263)		100.0 (250)	
Median		$8766		$7975		$7000		$6620		$7000
Per cent all Book Writers	98.3		96.2		94.4		91.6		87.1	

147

professional writers) on the other hand, have a higher median personal income each year (all sources) than do all writers as a group, although in 1957 the $8,766 median was
only $700 higher. All other years are better by at least a
$1,000 or more. And, the five-year median was $6,952.

Whether the book writer earns from books, magazines, plays, other kinds of writing or from non-writing
occupations, on the whole, book writers have a high incidence of "employment" each year. In 1957, for instance,
98.3 per cent of all book writers earned income; only in
1953 did the figure drop below 90 per cent. Again, however,
a third or more each year earn less than $5,000, regard-
less of the source of income.

For comparative purposes, Table LVIII presents
the yearly median personal incomes compared with the five-
year median earned by book writers from the different areas
of writing, non-writing, and total personal income from all
sources. The table also includes the working spouses' income for married book writers.

Married book writers (77.7 per cent of all book
writers) are a bit more common than married writers as a
whole, and slightly more of them (56.5 per cent) have working spouses.

On the average, the book writer's working spouse
with a five-year median income of $3,478 (lower than for
working spouses of all writers) contributed 34.9 per cent of
the total family income--about the same portion as for writers as a whole. Of the working spouses of book writers,
87.3 per cent reported five-year earnings.

Forty-eight and eight-tenths per cent of all working
spouses of book writers are wives of male book writers and
account for $2,279 yearly (five-year median) or 20.9 per

Table LVIII.

Book Writers' Yearly Median Personal Incomes From All Sources And Spouses' Income (1953-1957)

Book Writers' Income From:	5-Year Median Income (1953-1957)	1957	1956	1955	1954	1953
Books	$1600	$2300	$2000	$1718	$1865	$1837
Magazines	284	750	970	930	624	989
Plays	740	1543	1200	1237	665	1200
"F.L.-Emp" Writing	1565	5118	5100	5033	3000	1900
Directed Writing	630	1310	3000	2500	2954	4000
Non-Writing Sources	4479	6700	5000	5720	5855	6000
Total Personal Income	6952	8766	7975	7000	6620	7000
Spouses' Income	3478	5200	4500	4000	4680	4777
Family Income	9935	11715	10750	10345	10244	9707

cent of the family income. This figure is higher than for working wives of all writers (45.1 per cent); the amount contributed yearly to total family income is also slightly higher. For all working wives that figure was $1,980 (Chapter III, Part I).

In contrast, 77.0 per cent of married female book writers had working spouses, less than for all married female writers as a whole; the number with working husbands was 79.5 per cent. Yet, the portion of family income contributed by working husbands of female book writers was very nearly the same as for working spouses of all female writers--$7,740 or 63.7 per cent.

From Table LVIII it is obvious that the largest portion of personal income (for more than half of all book writers) is earned from non-writing sources. And on the average, book income accounts for less than a fourth of the personal income earned by all book writers each year. Book income amounts, moreover, to only 16 per cent of the writer's family income.

Summary

Two in every three writers are book writers--that is, they earned some personal income from books at one time or another between 1953-1957.

Adult fiction and general non-fiction are the two trade book types most important to more than half of the book writers; juvenile fiction is the most important as an income producer for another fifth.

While the general feeling among book writers, publishers, and critics alike is not one of promise, almost three-fifths of all book writers earn from books each year. Yet, with an average (median) yearly income of only $1,600 earned by the book writer from this source, it would seem there is good cause for such feeling.

Between 1953-1957, 1 book writer in 4 drew personal income from paperbound reprints; 1 in 5 earned from bookclubs; 1 in 9 earned from motion picture rights to books; and 1 in 15 drew income from TV rights. Motion picture rights to books are by far the most lucrative subsidiary source for book writers but less than four per cent of all book writers each year realize such income.

About 15 per cent of all book writers earn all their personal income solely from books, but three-fourths of these are women almost two-thirds of whom are married and housewives. The one in four of this group who is male fares fairly well from his books--$4,670 yearly--as compared to all book writers.

Free lance magazine writing provided a source of income to 57 per cent of the book writers (1953-1957) though it was a meager addition to their incomes in most instances--a five-year median of $248. Playwriting was an additional source of income to approximately 16 per cent of all book writers and 9.4 per cent earned yearly from this source. The five-year median income earned, however, was less than half of that for books.

Other kinds of writing--"F.L.-Emp" and directed combined--gave more than a third (34.4 per cent) of all book writers personal income during the five-year period. Although the yearly median (five-year) earned by 18.1 per cent of all book writers from "F.L.-Emp" writing was almost as high ($1,565) as that by all book writers from books, staff work and other directed writing assignments for a fifth (21.3 per cent) of all book writers was less than half as much.

Altogether, 46.3 per cent of all book writers derived all their personal income from writing of some kind-- a five-year median income of $4,804. Three-fourths are married, almost two-thirds of whom had working spouses who contributed 47.2 per cent of the total family income, or $4,947 yearly.

This means that for about a fourth of all book writers (24.0 per cent) who earned their sole income only from writing of some kind, the yearly income (five-year median) typical of this average book writer's earnings was $5,474. The fourth includes those married but who had no working spouse.

Like book writers earning only personal income from writing and greatly dependent on the working spouse's income, the remainder of all book writers (53.7 per cent) were dependent in large measure on non-writing sources of personal income. Sixty per cent of it--$4,479--was derived yearly from these non-writing sources.

There was also some dependence on the working spouse's income by book writers earning from non-writing sources, but not to the extent applicable to those earning only from writing.

Of those book writers earning personal income from non-writing sources, for instance, 80.5 per cent are married; half have working spouses who contribute on the average $2,890, or 27.0 per cent of the family income yearly.

Altogether, about one book writer in four earns between $5,000 and $10,000 from all personal sources of income each year; close to a third between $10,000 and $25,000; and less than a tenth earns in excess of $25,000.

On the average, book writers earn $6,952 yearly (five-year median) personal income from all sources, and

93.4 per cent report income earned each year.

How playwrights fared--better or worse than book writers--is the subject of the following chapter.

Notes

1. Larston D. Farrar, Successful Writers and How They Worĸ, Hawthorn Books, Inc., Publishers, New York, 1959, p. 52.

2. Basil Woon, The Current Publishing Scene, Exposition Press, New York, 1952, p. 21.

3. Ibid., p. 59.

4. Malcolm Cowley, The Literary Situation, The Viking Press, New York, 1954, p. 3.

5. Woon, op. cit., p. 58.

6. Chandler B. Grannis, ed., What Happens in Booĸ Publishing, Columbia University Press, New York, 1957, p. 43.

7. Ibid., p. 6.

8. Woon, op. cit., p. 58.

9. Gore Vidal, "The Perils and Rewards of Going Into Trade," The Reporter, July 11, 1957, p. 34.

10. Cowley, op. cit., p. 170

11. C.P. Snow, "Which Side of the Atlantic?", Harper's Magazine, October 1959, pp. 165-166.

12. Because it is difficult to categorically determine who is a novelist, who is a dramatist, who is a magazine writer on the basis of the returned questionnaires, all who reported income from booĸs--however small the amount--are included in the analyses in this chapter as booĸ writers. Even the League's own breakdown (Chapter I) shows "multiple" writers ... equally "successful" in two or more fields.

Chapter V

Playwrights

> The theater and its writers are seriously, perhaps
> fatally, hampered by economic pressure. Because
> it costs too much to put on a play, one works in
> a state of hysteria. Everything is geared to suc-
> cess. Yet art is mostly failure. And it is only
> from a succession of daring, flawed works that
> the occasional masterwork comes ...
> Vidal

"A literary form which depends on the combined
excellence of others for its execution can hardly be worth
the attention of a serious writer" might well be the prevail-
ing philosophy of the modern playwright. In the theater, to
fail is death, and in an atmosphere so feverish it is difficult
for the playwright to work with much objectivity.

Through the years, the playwright's position has
changed to conform with the molding circumstances attendant
the three distinct outlets for his talents--the theater, motion
pictures, and television. Each of the latter in turn has been
the "industry" giant--fighting each other to maintain an ex-
istence. And the playwright has moved somewhat tremulous-
ly from the turn of the 20th Century when he was little more
than a hack turning out new vehicles each theater season to
order, through the twenties when the theater made room for
the serious, experimentalist--epitomized in Eugene O'Neill--
to combat motion pictures.

Motion pictures in turn had its heyday with its
standard formula writers and has now been forced by the
new giant--television--to turn to new and better stories.

Television, having won first place in the entertainment field, now has the burdens of the victor. It has become the staple. It is standard brand.

Do these changes--the shifts in the playwright's position--automatically mean more work and thus more dollars in his pocket? How has he fared economically?

Following generally the format set forth for book writers, this chapter first establishes the importance of the personal income earned by playwrights[1] from plays. Next, beginning with a summary table comparing yearly personal earnings from subsidiary rights to plays with five-year median incomes, the importance of each subsidiary source is analyzed in detail.

To show how relatively small is the number of playwrights who derive their sole personal income from plays, again separate treatment is given this group.

Other areas of personal income--the different kinds of other writing and the non-writing occupations--are examined before taking a look at the playwright's total personal income from all sources. How the playwright fares in comparison to book writers as well as the playwright's dependence on his working spouse's income is scrutinized throughout.

Altogether, 28.3 per cent of all writers derived personal income from plays between 1953 an 1957. Though playwrights number less than half that of book writers, playwrights had even less regularity in yearly earnings from plays than did book writers from books. For example, only 31.5 per cent of the playwrights derived personal income from plays each year against 58.9 per cent of book writers earning from books. Almost three times as many playwrights--28.2 per cent--had income from plays only one of

the five years as did book writers from books. The same
portion of playwrights--16.1 per cent--had personal income
from playwriting for two and three years of the five. Less
than a tenth--8.1 per cent--earned from plays for four years.

When the 1957 play incomes are arrayed by age and
sex, Table LIX, page 157, reveals that playwrights' median
incomes and the per cent of each age group earning were
much lower than was the case for book writers. The median age for the 78.2 per cent of all playwrights earning in
1957 was much younger also--46. While the majority of
playwrights, like book writers that year, were between ages
40 and 60, a third were under forty years of age, almost
three times the proportion of book writers in this age group.
Only one playwright in 10 earning in 1957 was over 60 years
of age.

Curiously enough the same pattern of earning exists
for playwrights as for book writers. Though the 70-year
olds have the highest median personal income from plays
and the 40-year olds are second, still they are the same two
age groups (the forties and seventies respectively) who are
highest in 1957 median personal income from books.

The 31 per cent of playwrights between 40 and 49
years of age earning from plays in 1957, had a median income of $2,658--second highest of any group; the widest
range of actual dollars paid was also reported by these 40
year olds. With a median less than half that of the 40-49
age group, the 50 year olds--a fourth of the playwrights--
had one of the narrowest ranges from lowest paid to highest
paid playwright as was true for book writers. The 30 year
olds, and about three-fourths in that age group earning, had
a $1,548 median personal income from plays, the same as
for all playwrights earning from plays in 1957. Accounting

Table LIX.

Playwrights' Median Play Income And Dollar Range By Age And Sex, 1957

Age Group	Per Cent Male	Per Cent Female	Total	Median Age	Median Income	Percent of Age Group Earning	Range
20 - 29	4.9	6.3	5.2	28	$ 666	71.4	$ 300 - 123052
30 - 39	30.9	12.5	27.8	37	1548	73.0	100 - 59500
40 - 49	30.9	31.2	30.9	46	2658	83.3	25 - 200628
50 - 59	22.2	43.7	25.8	54	1120	86.2	20 - 39044
60 - 69	7.4	6.3	7.2	64	1200	70.0	25 - 48461
70 - 79	3.7	-	3.1	74	3000	60.0	1200 - 4619
Total	100.0	100.0	100.0				
N =	(81)	(16)	(97)				
Median				46	$1548		

157

for the highest median and the narrowest range of dollar income, the 70 year olds also had the lowest proportion of
their age group earning.

Playwrights on the whole in each age group drew a
lower median personal income from plays and less of each
age group earned in 1957 than did book writers from books
that year in the same age group.

As with some book writers not earning from books,
a certain portion of playwrights (21.8 per cent) did not earn
personal income from plays in 1957. These appear in Table LX. The majority of male playwrights in this group,
like book writers, are younger writers under 50 years of
age. Female playwrights, accounting for less than a third
of the group, are older than males; the majority of them
are between 40 and 60 years of age. For playwrights not
earning play income in 1957, the median age was 44--the
youngest for any group of writers.

Table LX.

Playwrights Not Earning From Plays In 1957, By Age
And Sex

Age Group	Per Cent Male	Per Cent Female	Per Cent Total
20 - 29	5.3	12.5	7.4
30 - 39	52.6	-	37.0
40 - 49	15.8	37.5	22.2
50 - 59	10.5	25.0	14.8
60 - 69	10.5	12.5	11.1
70 - 79	5.3	12.5	7.4
Total	100.0	100.0	100.0
N =	(19)	(8)	(27)
Median			44

Combining all playwrights--those that did not earn from plays in 1957 with those that did--produces a median age of 46, four years younger than for all book writers.

All male playwrights out-number females four to one--twice the ratio of book writers. More than three-fifths of the male playwrights are between ages 30 and 50; for females, more than three-fifths are between ages 40 and 60.

The returns show that 66.9 per cent of all playwrights are married and that 51.8 per cent have working spouses. Both figures are well below those for book writers and all writers as a whole.

Play Income

For the five years (1953-1957), 7 in 10 earned income from original plays during one or more years in the period. The number earning this income each year, however, at no time reached as high as 50 per cent of the total playwrights. As with book writers, originals account for the largest portion of personal income from plays, and in 1957, income from this source accounted for 59.0 per cent of all personal income derived by all playwrights from plays. This percentage is the same as that for book writers from original books. Other subsidiary rights to plays (see below) gave almost half of the playwrights additional income between 1953 and 1957. It was the most often listed subsidiary source of play income. Motion picture rights provided almost a fourth (24.2 per cent) with additional income from their original plays:

Area of Play Income	Per Cent of Playwrights Reporting (1953-1957)	Per Cent of Total Play Income, 1957
(1) original scripts	71.8	59.0
(2) foreign productions	18.5	5.0
(3) motion picture rights	24.2	20.6

Area of Play Income	Per Cent of Playwrights Reporting (1953-1957)	Per Cent of Total Play Income, 1957
(4) television rights	18.5	3.7
(5) other subsidiary rights	46.0	11.7
Total	(N=124)	100.0

The importance of these subsidiary incomes as well as the income from original rights for the playwrights' total personal play income is detailed below for all five years.

Total personal play income arrayed by years, Table LXI, presents an even less bright picture for playwrights than did total book income for book writers in Chapter IV. On the average, three playwrights in five (59.7 per cent) earned from playwriting activities each year and the mean of the yearly medians was $1,491. But the five-year median income for all playwrights from plays was only $684.

The year 1957 was the best of the five from the viewpoint of the number of playwrights earning personal play income; slightly more than three-fourths (78.2 per cent) drew income from this source that year. 1955 was the best year, however, for median income when 56.5 per cent of the playwrights earning derived a median personal income from plays of $1,692.

Income from playwriting was not a major portion of the playwrights' total income in any of the five years studied. As indicated in Table LXI, playwriting income accounted for 22.1 per cent or less of the total personal income earned by playwrights reporting each year.

Like book writers, personal income derived from motion picture rights to plays is the only subsidiary source providing a higher five-year median income than originals, as seen in Table LXII. This five-year summary table of

Table LXI.

Playwrights' Total Income From Plays By Income Classes,
(1953-1957)

Annual Income (dollars)	1957 Playwrights Per Cent	Income Median	1956 Playwrights Per Cent	Income Median	1955 Playwrights Per Cent	Income Median	1954 Playwrights Per Cent	Income Median	1953 Playwrights Per Cent	Income Median
0 - 1500	47.4	$ 450	51.7	$ 540	50.0	$ 585	59.7	$ 526	50.0	$ 487
1500 - 2500	9.3	1800	5.7	1893	8.6	2027	6.5	2003	11.1	1700
2500 - 5000	17.5	3347	9.2	3648	12.9	3015	11.3	3553	13.0	2900
5000 - 10000	10.3	7500	16.1	6193	7.1	6100	3.2	6600	7.4	6245
10000 - 15000	-	-	4.6	10750	4.3	14025	-	-	1.9	13000
15000 - 25000	2.1	17750	3.5	19310	1.4	20300	1.6	15745	3.7	19250
25000 - 50000	7.2	34900	1.2	48500	5.7	41534	6.5	34227	3.7	46104
50000 - 100000	4.1	61687	4.6	59383	5.7	58000	4.8	53500	9.3	75272
100000 & over	2.1	161840	3.5	188000	4.3	212149	6.5	124700	-	-
Total N =	100.0 (97)		100.0 (87)		100.0 (70)		100.0 (62)		100.0 (54)	
Median		$1548		$1400		$1692		$1337		$1477
Per cent all Playwrights	78.2		70.2		56.5		50.0		43.6	
Per cent Median is of Total Income	14.7		14.0		20.4		15.6		22.1	
Median (Total Income)		$10530		$10000		$8300		$8575		$6670

Table LXII.

Yearly Median Incomes Earned By Playwrights From Original
And Subsidiary Rights To Plays, (1953-1957)

Playwrights' Income From:	5-Year Median Income (1953-1957)	1957	1956	1955	1954	1953
Originals	$ 680	$2040	$1820	$2758	$1076	$1600
Foreign Productions	420	1756	2010	1701	1392	1214
Motion Picture Rights	2400	15000	7500	8201	1660	8000
Television Rights	100	927	500	840	500	1000
Other Subsidiary Rights	270	985	942	993	1100	975
Total from Plays	$ 684	$1548	$1400	$1692	$1337	$1477

the yearly median personal incomes derived by playwrights
earning from the different subsidiary sources each year
shows motion picture rights income to be almost four times
as much as that earned from original plays by all playwrights
during the period. Comparisons of the five-year median incomes for all playwrights earning (whether they earned in
one, two, three, four, or all five years) points up the irregularity they experienced in realizing additional income
from subsidiary rights. Only a few hundred dollars were
earned each year from foreign production rights, television,
and other subsidiary rights to plays.

Original Plays

For the 7 playwrights in 10 earning from original
plays during one or more years in the period, 1957 was the
best year when 43.5 per cent of all playwrights had income
from this source. The largest median, however, was earned in 1955--$2,758, Table LXIII. Only a third of the play-
wrights earned that year; a fourth had such income in 1953.

Income derived from original plays, nevertheless,
accounted for 59.0 per cent of the total play income earned
by all playwrights reporting in 1957. But of greater significance is the percentage of playwrights who earn less than
$2,500 annually from original plays. More than half each
year--except in 1955--drew less than $2,500 for their ef-
forts. On the more positive side was the fact that close to
a fifth earned $25,000 or more each year.

As was true for book writers (with 93.7 per cent
earning), a greater portion of playwrights (71.8 per cent)
drew income from originals than from any other single playwriting source. Subsidiary rights, thus, provided only a
small portion with additional income.

Table LXIII.

Playwrights' Income From Original Plays By Income Classes,
(1953-1957)

Annual Income (dollars)	1957 Playwrights Per Cent	Income Median	1956 Playwrights Per Cent	Income Median	1955 Playwrights Per Cent	Income Median	1954 Playwrights Per Cent	Income Median	1953 Playwrights Per Cent	Income Median
0 - 1500	38.9	$ 400	47.9	$ 600	38.1	$ 850	54.3	$ 450	46.7	$ 500
1500 - 2500	14.8	1750	6.3	2000	7.1	1974	5.7	1750	10.0	1700
2500 - 5000	18.5	3075	16.7	3100	19.1	3250	8.6	3500	20.0	4030
5000 - 10000	9.3	8150	8.3	5973	4.8	5000	2.9	7187	-	-
10000 - 15000	-	-	2.1	10000	4.8	13319	2.9	12000	6.7	12500
15000 - 25000	-	-	2.1	16100	4.8	19974	-	-	-	-
25000 - 50000	13.0	35000	4.2	37128	9.5	29000	11.4	37500	10.0	47208
50000 - 100000	5.6	95000	8.3	65133	7.1	50000	8.6	67000	6.7	70740
100000 & over	-	-	4.2	166315	4.8	190334	5.7	122500	-	-
Total N =	100.0 (54)		100.0 (48)		100.0 (42)		100.0 (35)		100.0 (30)	
Median		$2040		$1830		$2758		$1076		$1600
Per cent all Playwrights	43.5		38.7		33.9		28.2		24.2	

164

Foreign Productions

About a fifth of the playwrights earning from original plays also earned from foreign production rights to plays. In addition, about a tenth who had no income from originals during the five years earned from foreign rights to their previous works. Together, then, for these two groups--less than one playwright in five (18.5 per cent of all playwrights)--foreign production rights to plays produced a five-year median personal income of $420. On the average, less than one in ten (8.9 per cent) drew income from this subsidiary source to plays each year.

Unlike the two-fifths of book writers earning from foreign rights to books, however, the small portion of playwrights deriving personal income from foreign rights to plays realized sizeable median incomes each year. (See Table LXIV, page 166.) The yearly medians are typical of those earned by all playwrights from originals and by all playwrights from all playwriting activities in tables already presented.

Of the five years studied, the year 1956 had both the largest median income from foreign productions and the largest participation by playwrights in such income. The 11.3 per cent of all playwrights earning from foreign productions in 1957 produced one-twentieth of the total income earned by all playwrights from plays that year.

Motion Picture Rights

Approximately a fourth of all playwrights (24.2 per cent)--a higher participation than for foreign productions --drew subsidiary income from motion picture rights to plays in this five-year period. On the average, however, less than a tenth realized such income each year. And about a

Table LXIV.

Playwrights' Income From Foreign Productions By Income Classes,
(1953-1957)

Annual Income (dollars)	1953 Playwrights Per Cent	1953 Income Median	1954 Playwrights Per Cent	1954 Income Median	1955 Playwrights Per Cent	1955 Income Median	1956 Playwrights Per Cent	1956 Income Median	1957 Playwrights Per Cent	1957 Income Median
0 - 1500	57.1	$ 405	50.0	$ 453	36.4	$ 593	37.5	$ 501	50.0	$ 254
1500 - 2500	28.6	1907	16.7	1613	18.2	1642	18.8	1737	7.1	2300
2500 - 5000	-	-	-	-	18.2	3556	12.5	3771	14.3	3359
5000 - 10000	-	-	16.7	7000	9.1	8000	25.0	5930	21.4	7000
10000 - 15000	14.3	11000	-	-	-	-	-	-	-	-
15000 - 25000	-	-	16.7	21000	9.1	20000	-	-	7.1	17618
25000 & over	-	-	-	-	9.1	40000	6.2	27000	-	-
Total N =	100.0 (7)		100.0 (6)		100.0 (11)		100.0 (16)		100.0 (14)	
Median		$1214		$1392		$1701		$2010		$1756
Per cent all Playwrights	5.6		4.8		8.9		12.9		11.3	

166

fourth earning personal income from motion picture rights did not have any income from originals during the five years.

While the number earning income from foreign rights to plays was roughly the same portion of playwrights as those earning from motion picture rights, the latter was far more lucrative. Of the years studied, 1956--as for foreign productions--had the largest participation by playwrights in motion picture rights income, but 1957 was by far the best year in median income--$15,000 from this source, Table LXV, page 168.

Motion picture rights, of course, provide a real boost to the playwright's income for those fortunate enough to earn it and accounts for a large portion of the total play income. To illustrate, all the personal income earned from motion picture rights to plays in 1957 by the tenth of playwrights reporting such income that year accounted for a fifth (20.6 per cent) of the total playwriting income derived by all playwrights.

The year 1954, on the other hand, points up the wide fluctuation in size of earnings from this source. With only a fraction less playwrights earning in 1954 than in 1957, the 1954 median ($1,660) is only an eighth that of 1957. And with fewer playwrights deriving personal income from this source in 1953 and 1955 than in 1954, both medians (1953 and 1955) are far greater than that for 1954. But in 1954 movies were experiencing one of their worst slumps, fighting for an audience that was rapidly shifting to the television home screen. Probably this occurrence accounted primarily for the very low median.

The five-year median income earned by the fourth of all playwrights reporting such income in one or more of the

Table LXV.

Playwrights' Income From Motion Picture Rights By Income Classes,
(1953-1957)

Annual Income (dollars)	1957 Playwrights Per Cent	Income Median	1956 Playwrights Per Cent	Income Median	1955 Playwrights Per Cent	Income Median	1954 Playwrights Per Cent	Income Median	1953 Playwrights Per Cent	Income Median
0 - 1500	15.4	$ 735	20.0	$ 500	36.4	$ 281	50.0	$ 106	28.6	$ 301
1500 - 2500	7.7	1750	6.7	1500	-	-	8.3	2120	14.3	2056
2500 - 5000	-	-	6.7	4500	-	-	-	-	-	-
5000 - 10000	23.1	7500	40.0	7750	36.4	8400	8.3	9000	28.6	8750
10000 - 15000	-	-	6.7	11750	-	-	-	-	-	-
15000 - 25000	30.8	15000	-	-	-	-	8.3	16500	-	-
25000 - 50000	15.4	25000	20.0	40500	27.3	27000	16.7	25000	14.3	45000
50000 & over	7.7	74196	-	-	-	-	8.3	60000	14.3	56806
Total N =	100.0 (13)		100.0 (15)		100.0 (11)		100.0 (12)		100.0 (7)	
Median		$15000		$7500		$8201		$1660		$8000
Per cent all Playwrights	10.5		12.1		8.9		9.7		5.6	

five years was $2,400--almost four times that earned by all playwrights from originals and almost twice that earned by book writers for motion picture rights to books. Proportionally, there were three times as many playwrights deriving motion picture rights to plays as book writers deriving such rights to books.

Television Rights

Television rights, in contrast, are not the important source of subsidiary income motion picture rights provided for playwrights. Probably they never have been for several reasons: (1) TV showings are for a one-time exposure only, except in the case of re-runs, and, therefore, much too expensive for most producers and sponsors who would like Broadway's best, (2) the time-lapse of a play is generally two-hours--too long for most television presentations; and (3) television programs must not only be geared to a "general" audience, they must also meet certain standards of morals--a censorship which the legitimate stage is not subject to.[2]

The average (five-year median) of $100 is, thus, not surprising for the 18.5 per cent of all playwrights earning subsidiary income from television rights.

Table LXVI, page 170, reveals that the same portion of playwrights earned from television as earned from motion picture rights in 1957. Yet, the median personal income derived from television rights was less than one-fifteenth of that from motion pictures. Almost a third of the playwrights earning from television were earning from previous works since they had no income from original plays during the five years covered.

Proportionally, three times as many playwrights as

Table LXVI.

Playwrights' Income From Television Rights By Income Classes, (1953-1957)

Annual Income (dollars)	1957 Play-wrights Per Cent	1957 Income Median	1956 Play-wrights Per Cent	1956 Income Median	1955 Play-wrights Per Cent	1955 Income Median	1954 Play-wrights Per Cent	1954 Income Median	1953 Play-wrights Per Cent	1953 Income Median
0 - 1500	53.8	$ 450	55.6	$ 57	66.7	$ 270	55.6	$ 500	50.0	$ 500
1500 - 2500	7.7	2250	11.1	2000	16.7	1800	22.2	2054	50.0	1608
2500 - 5000	23.1	3000	11.1	4037	-	-	11.1	3675	-	-
5000 - 10000	7.7	6000	11.1	7500	16.7	6750	11.1	5000	-	-
10000 - 15000	-	-	11.1	14431	-	-	-	-	-	-
15000 & over	7.7	15836	-	-	-	-	-	-	-	-
Total N =	100.0 (13)		100.0 (9)		100.0 (6)		100.0 (9)		100.0 (4)	
Median		$ 927		$ 500		$ 840		$ 500		$1000
Per cent all Playwrights	10.5		7.3		4.8		7.3		3.2	

book writers drew subsidiary income from television rights.
And the highest paid writers from this source were playwrights in every year except 1955. The book writers' five-
year median, however, was twice that for playwrights--$200.

As a portion of the total playwriting income earned,
television rights provided the smallest amount from any subsidiary source in 1957. The tenth of playwrights earning
from television rights that year contributed only 3.7 per
cent of the total playwriting income earned by all playwrights.

Other Subsidiary Rights

Slightly more lucrative to the playwright than television subsidiary income were other miscellaneous rights--
radio, amateur, and road productions. In all, almost one
playwright in two (46.0 per cent) drew income from this
source between 1953 and 1957. Approximately three-fifths
of these also had income from originals, while about a third
(a seventh of all playwrights) had playwriting income only
from this source.

Not only were median incomes from other subsidiary
rights slightly higher than television rights but the regularity of earnings for the group as a whole was better, Table
LXVII. Yet the five-year median income from other subsidiary rights was only slightly higher than television rights--
$270. The year 1954 for other subsidiary rights' income--
unlike motion picture, television, foreign production rights
and even originals--was the top median income year despite
the fact no playwright earned as much as $10,000, from this
source.

All 1957 income earned from other subsidiary rights
made up 11.7 per cent of the total personal income earned
from playwriting in 1957. It was more than twice that earned

Table LXVII.

Playwrights' Income From Other Subsidiary Rights By Income Classes,
(1953-1957)

Annual Income (dollars)	1957 Playwrights Per Cent	1957 Income Median	1956 Playwrights Per Cent	1956 Income Median	1955 Playwrights Per Cent	1955 Income Median	1954 Playwrights Per Cent	1954 Income Median	1953 Playwrights Per Cent	1953 Income Median
0 - 1500	63.0	$ 450	62.5	$ 230	69.2	$ 392	55.9	$ 158	59.4	$ 200
1500 - 2500	6.5	2300	7.5	1639	7.7	2300	17.7	2050	9.4	1700
2500 - 5000	17.4	3250	10.0	3213	12.8	3000	17.7	2820	21.9	3258
5000 - 10000	8.7	6750	17.5	5200	7.7	8201	8.8	5000	6.3	7100
10000 - 15000	2.2	10434	-	-	2.6	10000	-	-	3.1	14406
15000 - 25000	-	-	-	-	-	-	-	-	-	-
25000 & over	2.2	30583	2.5	25288	-	-	-	-	-	-
Total N =	100.0 (46)		100.0 (40)		100.0 (39)		100.0 (34)		100.0 (32)	
Median		$ 985		$ 942		$ 993		$1100		$ 975
Per cent all Playwrights	37.1		32.3		31.5		27.4		25.8	

172

from foreign productions, and three times as much as that
from television rights.

The Playwriting Specialists

An extremely small portion of the playwrights--10.5
per cent--earning from playwriting between 1953 and 1957
reported their entire personal income only from this source.
Because the number involved here, however, is so small--
it accounts for only three per cent of total writer response--
little value can be attributed to any detailed analysis. Yearly medians, for example, run from less than $2,000 (1953)
to almost $70,000 (1954), with the latest year (1957) income
data showing a median income of $3,000. (See Table
LXVIII.) The latter figure is about three-fourths of that
earned by book writers deriving personal income solely from
books.

Such separate treatment does serve to point out the
irregularity of income for playwrights from playwriting activities and to emphasize the extremely small portion who
earn only from the one endeavor avowed to be their profession. These facts are not surprising, however, when one
considers that of the approximately 300 first-class plays
optioned for Broadway in any one year (true at least of the
50's) only a tenth of this figure actually are produced. Some
of these latter 30-odd plays, unfortunately, are something
less than successful and may be losing ventures, even for
the writer.

Of those reporting personal income earned solely
from playwriting, approximately half are married, but working spouses are not the rule; some had working spouses but
in no case did the spouse show income for more than one
year of the five. The working spouse's contribution to fam-

Table LXVIII.

Income Of Playwrights Reporting Earnings Solely From Playwriting, By Income Classes, (1953-1957)

Annual Income (dollars)	1957 Playwrights Per Cent	1957 Income Median	1956 Playwrights Per Cent	1956 Income Median	1955 Playwrights Per Cent	1955 Income Median	1954 Playwrights Per Cent	1954 Income Median	1953 Playwrights Per Cent	1953 Income Median
0 - 1500	33.3	$ 400	37.5	$ 1000	50.0	$ 800	40.0	$ 217	50.0	$ 426
1500 - 2500	-	-	12.5	1551	-	-	-	-	12.5	1700
2500 - 5000	33.3	3000	-	-	-	-	-	-	-	-
5000 - 10000	11.1	7000	12.5	5200	-	-	-	-	12.5	5700
10000 - 15000	-	-	12.5	10000	-	-	-	-	-	-
15000 - 25000	-	-	-	-	16.7	20300	-	-	-	-
25000 - 50000	-	-	-	-	16.7	47435	-	-	12.5	47208
50000 - 100000	11.1	63875	12.5	61267	-	-	20.0	69100	12.5	75272
100000 & over	11.1	200628	12.5	246521	16.7	212149	40.0	109097	-	-
Total	100.0		100.0		100.0		100.0		100.0	
N =	(9)		(8)		(6)		(5)		(8)	
Median	$3000		$3375		$10749		$69100		$1577	
Per cent all Playwrights	7.3		6.5		4.8		4.0		6.5	

174

ily income was less than $250 yearly.

We must remember, of course, there were others earning--and some quite handsomely--from playwriting activities besides the tenth in Table LXVIII, but they earned income from other sources as well. In 1953, for example, 43.5 per cent of all playwrights earned income from playwriting while only a seventh of these earned personal income solely from this one source that year. Comparable figures for other years are:

Year:	Per cent Earning From Playwriting	Per cent Earning Only From Playwriting
1954	50.0	8.1
1955	56.5	8.6
1956	70.2	9.2
1957	78.2	9.3

Consequently, with such a small group drawing 100 per cent of its personal income solely from playwriting and only a small portion earning enough regularly to meet a minimum of financial obligations, the remaining playwrights looked elsewhere for income.

In summary, the irregularity of earning from playwriting activities indicates the precariousness of the profession. Less than a third of all playwrights (31.5 per cent) derived personal income from playwriting every year between 1953 and 1957. Less than a tenth (8.1 per cent) earned for four of the five years; 16.1 per cent drew income for three years--the same percentage earning for two of the five years; and 28.2 per cent earned income from playwriting in only one year of the five studied. Nor was there any consistent pattern of the combinations playwrights put together for this income. Table LXIX reveals that less than a third --the highest portion--earned playwriting income only from

Table LXIX.

Combination Of Sources Of Playwriting Income And Per Cent of Playwrights Affected (1953-1957)

	Per Cent
Original Plays Only	30.7
Other Subsidiary Rights Only	15.3
Originals and Other Subsidiary Rights	10.5
Originals, Motion Picture and Other Subsidiary Rights	4.8
Originals and Television Rights	4.0
Originals and Motion Picture Rights	4.0
Motion Picture Rights Only	4.0
Originals, Foreign Productions, and Other Subsidiary Rights	3.2
Television Rights Only	3.2
Originals, Foreign Productions, Motion Picture & Television Rights	2.4
Originals, Foreign Productions, Motion Picture & Other Subsidiary Rights	2.4
Originals, Television and Other Subsidiary Rights	1.6
Originals, Foreign Productions, and Motion Picture Rights	1.6
Originals, Foreign Productions, Television and Other Subsidiary Rights	1.6
Originals, and Foreign Production Rights	1.6
Originals, Foreign Productions, Motion Picture, Television, and Other Subsidiary Rights	1.6
Foreign Production and Television Rights Only	1.6
Foreign Production and Other Subsidiary Rights Only	.8
Originals, Motion Picture and Television Rights	.8
Originals, Motion Picture, Television, and Other Subsidiary Rights	.8
Foreign Production, Motion Picture and Other Subsidiary Rights	.8
Motion Picture and Other Subsidiary Rights Only	.8
Television and Other Subsidiary Rights	.8
Total	100.0

(N = 124)

original plays but that there was considerable overlapping in the subsidiary sources. Twenty-three different combinations were needed to account for the playwrights' total playwriting activities.

Other Writing Income

Free Lance

Beside playwriting activities, one playwright in every two (49.2 per cent) had income from other free lance writing as well. On the average, 35.5 per cent of all playwrights earned personal income from some kind of free lance writing other than plays each year. In 1953, with a third of them earning such income, the top free lance median personal income was produced. (See Table LXX.)

By no means did more playwrights earn free lance writing income in 1953 than in any other year, however. The year 1956 with almost 40 per cent participation was the best "employment" year for the group earning from free lance writing other than plays, though the lowest median personal income was also earned that year.

Really, it is difficult to speak of an average yearly income for playwrights from free lance writing other than plays but it is approximately $957 (five-year median). Obviously, if a playwright can successfully produce and sell a play, he will; otherwise, it may be financially wiser to do some other kind of writing in the meantime. And playwrights seem to fare about the same as book writers--no better, no worse--in the other free lance writing areas and amount of income earned.

There was, as already mentioned, some duplication in free lance income for a portion of playwrights and book

Table LXX.

Playwrights' Other[1] Free Lance Writing Income By Income Classes, (1953-1957)

Annual Income (dollars)	1957 Playwrights Per Cent	1957 Income Median	1956 Playwrights Per Cent	1956 Income Median	1955 Playwrights Per Cent	1955 Income Median	1954 Playwrights Per Cent	1954 Income Median	1953 Playwrights Per Cent	1953 Income Median
0 - 1500	41.7	$ 275	51.0	$ 365	41.5	$ 786	43.9	$ 721	40.5	$ 575
1500 - 2500	14.6	1800	12.2	2337	14.6	2047	9.8	2042	9.5	2071
2500 - 5000	20.8	2830	10.2	3295	9.8	3401	12.2	3500	11.9	2800
5000 - 10000	4.2	6359	10.2	7242	14.6	6421	12.2	8550	11.9	6600
10000 - 15000	-	-	6.1	13195	7.3	11000	2.4	10270	14.3	13326
15000 - 25000	8.3	16739	8.2	21937	7.3	23091	14.6	19045	11.9	18992
25000 - 50000	6.3	26400	2.0	45000	4.9	32850	2.4	26530	-	-
50000 & over	4.2	63425	-	-	-	-	2.4	60500	-	-
Total N =	100.0 (48)		100.0 (49)		100.0 (41)		100.0 (41)		100.0 (42)	
Median		$1900		$1481		$2094		$2083		$2450
Per cent all Playwrights	38.7		39.5		33.1		33.1		33.9	

1. Books, magazines, royalties, ASCAP, songwriting, any kind of free lance writing other than playwriting.

writers. For playwrights, more than a third (36.3 per cent) derived personal income from books during the five years studied. About a tenth of them realized approximately the same amount from books and plays; 47 per cent made more money from books, and 43 per cent made more money from playwriting, during the five years. Because Table LXX includes all playwrights earning from books, the yearly median incomes are rather constant for other free lance writing. Almost seven-tenths (69.2 per cent) of those writers earning from plays and books earned steadily year in and year out.

"F.L.-Emp" Writing

More than one playwright in two (55.7 per cent) earned from "F.L.-Emp" writing--motion picture and television writing either salaried or original--for the five years, 1953-1957. Proportionally, this participation was higher than for those earning from other free lance writing than plays. On the average, however, approximately the same earned each year from both sources--35 per cent.

"F.L.-Emp" writing income got a real boost in 1954 over 1953 when more than three-fifths of the playwrights reporting from this source earned from television productions. The median income of $5,500, Table LXXI, page 180, was almost double that of 1953, and the percentage earning increased by 40 per cent. Playwrights deriving personal income from motion pictures--the other source of "F. L.-Emp" writing--decreased by 8.3 per cent during this period.

Whether it was from motion pictures or television-- or both--the 39.5 per cent of all playwrights deriving income from "F.L.-Emp" writing in 1957 drew a median personal income of $8,250 from this source--a median almost three

Table LXXI.

Playwrights' Income From "F.L.-Emp" Writing By Income Classes, (1953-1957)

Annual Income (dollars)	1957 Playwrights Per Cent	Income Median	1956 Playwrights Per Cent	Income Median	1955 Playwrights Per Cent	Income Median	1954 Playwrights Per Cent	Income Median	1953 Playwrights Per Cent	Income Median
0 - 1500	14.3	$1167	21.6	$ 900	23.8	$ 913	22.5	$ 550	32.4	$ 914
1500 - 2500	12.2	1762	13.7	1500	11.9	1750	5.0	1662	14.7	1800
2500 - 5000	12.2	3165	9.8	3600	7.1	4500	20.0	3175	11.8	3745
5000 - 10000	16.3	7750	15.6	7078	19.1	7183	15.0	6400	11.8	7100
10000 - 15000	12.2	13000	13.7	13500	7.1	11700	2.5	12000	8.8	12000
15000 - 25000	12.2	20650	3.9	19050	2.4	17820	12.5	18480	-	-
25000 - 50000	8.2	32500	11.8	31950	19.1	35500	12.5	27000	11.8	39500
50000 - 100000	10.2	65000	5.9	66600	7.1	52400	10.0	60700	8.8	66000
100000 & over	2.0	174000	3.9	105006	2.4	105000	-	-	-	-
Total N =	100.0 (49)		100.0 (51)		100.0 (42)		100.0 (40)		100.0 (34)	
Median		$8250		$5630		$5858		$5500		$5500
Per Cent all Playwrights	39.5		41.1		33.9		32.3		27.4	

times that for 1953. And for 1957, the median for total
personal income of $20,212 (all sources) for this same
group, Table LXXII, was two and one-half times the 1953 median of $8,072. Motion picture and television writing in-
come in 1957 accounted for two-fifths of the total earned by
these playwrights.

Playwrights deriving income from "F.L.-Emp" writing consistently have the highest yearly median incomes
(from all sources) of any group, emphasizing again the importance of motion pictures and television[3] in the mid-fifties
as lucrative outlets for the playwrights' talents.

Playwrights having "F.L.-Emp" writing income
were in the rather unique position of having no writer in
their midst earn less than $2,500 in 1957--a distinction no
other group of writers enjoyed. Of added significance is
that only in 1953 did more than a fourth of this group earn
less than $5,000.

More than three times as many playwrights as book
writers earned from "F.L.-Emp" writing in the five-year
period. The median (five-year) personal income earned by
this 55.7 per cent of all playwrights was $2,700 or almost
twice the median earned by book writers from the same
source. "F.L.-Emp" income was second only to non-writing sources in the playwrights' overall personal income.

Directed Writing

While writing for television and motion pictures gave
additional income to more than half of all playwrights--ac-
counting for almost half of the income earned in 1954 and
1955 by a third of the playwrights--directed writing activities
were not nearly as lucrative and were beneficial at best only
to one playwright in every seven.

Table LXXII.

Total Income Earned (All Sources) By Playwrights Deriving "F.L.-Emp" Writing Income, By Income Classes, (1953-1957)

Annual Income (dollars)	1957 Playwrights Per Cent	Income Median	1956 Playwrights Per Cent	Income Median	1955 Playwrights Per Cent	Income Median	1954 Playwrights Per Cent	Income Median	1953 Playwrights Per Cent	Income Median
0 - 1500	-	$ -	-	$ -	2.4	$ 750	5.0	$ 619	5.9	$1186
1500 - 2500	-	-	3.9	2110	2.4	2315	5.0	2214	5.9	2202
2500 - 5000	6.1	4500	15.7	3400	14.3	3922	12.5	3249	17.7	3752
5000 - 10000	18.4	7405	13.7	7325	26.2	7500	20.0	7105	32.4	7412
10000 - 15000	14.3	12125	13.7	13758	9.5	12147	10.0	10689	11.8	12150
15000 - 25000	28.6	20784	17.6	20278	7.1	20610	20.0	18455	2.9	19450
25000 - 50000	12.2	41281	13.7	31770	16.7	36000	12.5	43450	11.8	35975
50000 - 100000	16.3	69487	11.8	62900	11.9	56500	10.0	61706	8.8	65000
100000 & over	4.1	156500	9.8	122000	9.5	128287	5.0	146600	2.9	111000
Total N =	100.0 (49)		100.0 (51)		100.0 (42)		100.0 (40)		100.0 (34)	
Median		$20212		$16931		$12147		$11342		$8072
Per cent "F.L.-Emp" Income is of Total Income	40.8		33.3		48.2		48.5		35.9	

182

Such activities as ghostwriting, staff work for magazines and newspapers, translations, reviews and criticisms are not as well suited to the playwright as to the book writer, which explains in part why so few playwrights are active in this field. Yet, for the few who were fortunate enough to have directed writing assignments, 1957 was a good year, Table LXXIII. Here, again, however, because of the small response involved, the value of any detailed analysis is perhaps questionable.

Nevertheless, for the something less than one-fifth of all playwrights reporting earnings from directed writing assignments, only in 1957 did payments for such service exceed $15,000. On the average, with about 10 per cent of the playwrights reporting such personal income yearly, a median (five-year) of about $1,300 was earned. This figure is about twice that earned by book writers from the same source, though the proportion of book writers earning each year was higher (14.0 per cent).

As with "F.L.-Emp" writing, the directed writing median personal income for 1957 was more than twice the 1953 median income. Here, however, similarity ceases. The 1954 median for the tenth of all dramatists deriving income from directed writing was second only to 1957, not so with "F.L.-Emp" writing. Nor do playwrights earning from directed writing show any of the consistency or regularity within income classes shown by those earning from motion picture and television writing.

Viewed in retrospect, 59.7 per cent of all playwrights derived all personal income from writing of some kind as compared with 46.3 per cent of all book writers who did. The playwrights' five-year median personal income of $8,620, however, was almost twice that for book writers--

Table LXXIII.

Playwrights' Directed Writing Income By Income Classes, (1953–1957)

Annual Income (dollars)	1953 Playwrights Per Cent	Income Median	1954 Playwrights Per Cent	Income Median	1955 Playwrights Per Cent	Income Median	1956 Playwrights Per Cent	Income Median	1957 Playwrights Per Cent	Income Median
0 - 1500	33.3	$ 410	20.0	$ 400	33.3	$ 253	33.3	$ 432	30.8	$ 285
1500 - 2500	8.3	1726	10.0	1935	8.3	1805	13.3	2149	-	-
2500 - 5000	25.0	3120	20.0	4000	33.3	3000	13.3	3423	7.7	4797
5000 - 10000	25.0	6000	40.0	6825	16.7	6250	13.3	8850	23.1	7400
10000 - 15000	8.3	11579	10.0	11539	8.3	11586	26.7	12073	15.4	11245
15000 & over	-	-	-	-	-	-	-	-	23.1	15000
Total N =	100.0 (12)		100.0 (10)		100.0 (12)		100.0 (15)		100.0 (13)	
Median		$3210		$4500		$2975		$2847		$7400
Per cent all Playwrights	9.7		8.1		9.7		12.1		10.5	

$4, 804.

As concerns marriage-linked dependence, 66.2 per
cent of playwrights earning only personal income from writing of some kind are married; 75 per cent of book writers
are. But, unlike the book writer's dependence on his working spouse's income (1953-1957)--two-thirds had working
spouses contributing 47.2 per cent of the family income or
$4, 947 yearly--55.1 per cent of playwrights had working
spouses who contributed only 15.2 per cent of the total family income or $1, 800 yearly. Book writers earning only
from writing of some kind are, therefore, much more dependent on their working spouses' income than are playwrights. Married male playwrights--77.6 per cent of those
married earning only from writing--are even less dependent
on marriage-linked income; only 47.4 per cent had working
wives who added 7.3 per cent, or $785 yearly to the family
income.

More than a third of all playwrights reporting personal income only from writing of some kind, however, earned less than $5, 000 in 1957, Table LXXIV, page 186. Al-
most a tenth of these (8.1 per cent) reported no personal income at all that year though half reported income from working spouses. (All of the latter were female playwrights, however).

Figures for the non-earning playwrights average 17.6
per cent (of those earning only from writing--10.5 per cent
of all playwrights) for the five years; it should be pointed out
some of these playwrights turned professional during the period and naturally would not have been earning from writing
prior to the time. But, to state it in more meaningful
terms, of all playwrights who did not have "outside" work
(occupations other than writing) about one in every six earned

Table LXXIV.
Playwrights' (Reporting Earnings Only From Writing) Total Income, By Income Classes (1953-1957)

Annual Income (dollars)	1957 Play-wrights Per Cent	1957 Income Median	1956 Play-wrights Per Cent	1956 Income Median	1955 Play-wrights Per Cent	1955 Income Median	1954 Play-wrights Per Cent	1954 Income Median	1953 Play-wrights Per Cent	1953 Income Median
0 - 1500	21.6	$ 275	27.0	$ 10	32.4	$ 0	33.8	$ 0	33.8	$ 0
1500 - 2500	4.1	2084	8.1	1784	2.7	1759	5.4	2047	2.7	2057
2500 - 5000	12.2	3000	8.1	3583	12.2	3511	8.1	3374	12.2	3000
5000 - 10000	13.5	7361	12.2	7640	14.9	7100	16.2	7250	20.3	7000
10000 - 15000	8.1	11750	10.8	12536	6.8	11035	5.4	10387	9.5	13000
15000 - 25000	14.9	22086	9.5	21112	4.1	20300	10.8	21212	8.1	19234
25000 - 50000	9.5	36982	9.5	31770	13.5	35817	6.8	42100	5.4	43604
50000 - 100000	12.2	65000	9.5	61267	8.1	57250	8.1	61644	6.8	67244
100000 & over	4.1	200628	5.4	181198	5.4	172862	5.4	135050	1.4	111000
Total N =	100.0¹ (74)		100.0¹ (74)		100.0¹ (74)		100.0¹ (74)		100.0¹ (74)	
Median		$8822		$7820		$6013		$5837		$5495

1. The "unemployed" playwrights--those having no personal income from any source--totaled:

   8.1 per cent in 1957 (half had income from working spouses)
   13.5 per cent in 1956 (a tenth had income from working spouses)
   20.3 per cent in 1955 (a fifth had income from working spouses)
   24.3 per cent in 1954 (a sixth had income from working spouses)
   23.0 per cent in 1953 (less than a sixth had income from working spouses)

nothing each year between 1953 and 1957.[4]   About two-fifths
of these reported working spouses.   Half the spouses worked only one year out of five; half worked all five years.   It
seems there could have been many join the 40.3 per cent
who used non-writing occupations to supplement writing incomes.

How did they manage to survive?   Some were forced
to live off previous earnings indicated by their comments
written across the questionnaire.   For the rest, one writer
summed it up rather neatly with this comment:

> These categories (income categories on the
> questionnaire), which apparently include only
> directly earned income, leave out some of
> the most important items--what may be
> called the scrounging ones: grants, fellow-
> ships, prizes, a stay at a foundation; but
> chiefly personal loans.

Some playwrights, of course, did include amounts received
as prizes, or awards, but these sums are included with the
non-writing income earners.

Non-Writing Activities and Income

Interestingly enough--though not at all surprising--
the two-fifths of all playwrights who went outside the field
of writing to add to their yearly income kept primarily to
their "own" fields of livelihood, that is, to jobs closely related to or dependent upon the play--acting, directing, producing, and so on.   Almost a fourth, Table LXXV, page
189, turned to acting with about an equal portion having jobs
completely unrelated to the theatrical profession.

What about the degree of regularity in employment
in these non-writing occupations as sources of playwrights'
incomes?   Half of the playwrights listed the job and income
from it for all five years under study; an additional tenth

showed it steadily for four years. We know nothing of the amount of time involved in these non-writing jobs. We do have the presence or absence of income from year to year as a measure of regularity, although it tells us nothing of seasonality. Naturally, some of the non-writing occupations are only temporary--or stop-gap measures--to fill-in or tide the playwright over to his next check from the sale of a play or some other piece of writing.

Seemingly, only about a fifth or less sought an outside job as a one-shot supplement (one-year column, Table LXXVI) to their incomes during this period. On the other hand, fifty per cent of the playwrights reporting income from non-writing sources listed the same source each year; an additional tenth listed the same source for four of the five years; and 18 per cent the same for three. Thus, better than three-fourths of the playwrights who had income from sources other than writing, actually had regular income from these sources and writing was more an avocation.

Another way of looking at the non-writing occupations indicates that almost 60 per cent of the playwrights listing acting and teaching (a third of all jobs) as outside sources of income reported them for the entire five years; those in designing, real estate, those with investments, family business and social work are all regularly engaged in these jobs or sources each year as a supplement to their writing incomes.

For the two playwrights in five who derived personal income from non-writing sources between 1953 and 1957, they drew a yearly median income of $3,149--more than a thousand dollars a year less than the half of all book writers earning from such source.

Of the years studied, 1955 had the highest partici-

Table LXXV.

Type Of Job Held By Playwrights To Supplement Writing Income
(1953-1957)

Occupation	Per Cent
Acting	24.0
Producing-Directing	10.0
Teaching, including playwriting, speech, etc.	10.0
Editing--TV, magazine, press, research	20.0
Scenic, Costume design	2.0
Publicity, Recordings, Advertising	8.0
Public Relations	6.0
Real Estate	4.0
Investments	4.0
Clerk, Typist	4.0
Military Service	4.0
Family Business	2.0
Social Investigator	2.0
Total (N = 50)	100.0

pation of playwrights in non-writing sources of income; over
a third of all playwrights earned--though next to the lowest
yearly median $4,180 was produced that year, from this
source, Table LXXVII, page 191. On the average, 31.5 per
cent of all playwrights earned from non-writing sources each
year--much less than the 44.6 per cent of all book writers
who did.

No playwright earned between fifty and a hundred
thousand dollars from non-writing sources, although two and
one-half per cent on the average earned one hundred thousand or over. Approximately a fourth of the playwrights
having non-writing income earned between $5,000 and
$10,000 from this source each year; and an equal portion
earned $10,000 and over.

For many of these two-fifths of all playwrights, non-
writing income accounted for the major share of their personal earnings each year, Table LXXVIII, page 193, as it

Table LXXVI.

Degree Of Regularity Of Playwright In His Non-Writing Job

Occupation	Per Cent Reporting				
	5 Years	4 Years	3 Years	2 Years	1 Year
Acting	28.0	20.0	11.1	33.3	20.0
Producing-directing	8.0	60.0	-	-	-
Teaching	12.0	-	11.1	-	20.0
Editing	12.0	20.0	22.2	33.3	40.0
Designing	4.0	-	-	-	-
Publicity	8.0	-	22.2	-	-
Public Relations	4.0	-	22.2	-	-
Real Estate	8.0	-	-	-	-
Investments	8.0	-	-	-	-
Clerk	-	-	-	16.7	20.0
Military Service	-	-	11.1	16.7	-
Family Business	4.0	-	-	-	-
Social Investigator	4.0	-	-	-	-
Total	100.0	100.0	100.0	100.0	100.0
N =	(25)	(5)	(9)	(6)	(5)
Per cent of Total	50.0	10.0	18.0	12.0	10.0

190

Table LXXVII.

Playwrights' Income From Non-Writing Sources By Income Classes, (1953-1957)

Annual Income (dollars)	1957 Playwrights Per Cent	1957 Income Median	1956 Playwrights Per Cent	1956 Income Median	1955 Playwrights Per Cent	1955 Income Median	1954 Playwrights Per Cent	1954 Income Median	1953 Playwrights Per Cent	1953 Income Median
0 - 1500	5.1	$ 380	11.1	$ 925	20.9	$ 507	17.5	$ 650	21.6	$ 575
1500 - 2500	7.7	1500	13.9	2000	9.3	2000	12.5	2000	5.4	2000
2500 - 5000	28.2	3330	22.2	3250	27.9	3094	20.0	3300	29.7	3500
5000 - 10000	28.2	6600	30.6	6200	16.3	7050	25.0	6557	24.3	6000
10000 - 15000	12.8	11000	8.3	14500	14.0	10841	12.5	11000	10.8	11500
15000 - 25000	7.7	18480	5.6	16583	4.6	16500	7.5	16300	2.7	17000
25000 - 50000	7.7	28500	5.6	31860	4.6	35900	2.5	25000	2.7	25000
50000 - 100000	-	-	-	-	-	-	-	-	-	-
100000 & over	2.6	100000	2.8	100000	2.3	100000	2.5	100000	2.7	100000
Total N = Median	100.0 (39)	$6000	100.0 (36)	$5000	100.0 (43)	$4180	100.0 (40)	$5025	100.0 (37)	$3955
Per cent all Playwrights	31.5		29.0		34.7		32.3		29.8	

did for book writers deriving income from the same source.
But for the five years, the median income earned from non-
writing sources--$3,149--accounted for only 45 per cent of
the total median personal income earned by these playwrights
from all sources--$7,003. For book writers, the compar-
able figure was 60.3 per cent of their total personal income.

Only in 1955 did the median personal income from
non-writing sources account for less than half of the total
personal income earned by playwrights reporting such income. Since the highest median income was earned in 1955,
however, from original plays, and it was the second-best
year for motion picture rights and other subsidiary rights
to plays, other free lance writing, and "F.L.-Emp" writing
income as well, it would seem logical to expect the total in-
come--including the portion earned from writing activities--
for this group to be high also. This is true. Table LXXVIII
reveals that the median earned in 1955 from all sources by
the 34.7 per cent playwrights with non-writing income that
year was second only to the 1957 median of $10,350.

The same reasoning works in reverse for the 1954
incomes. Almost three-fourths of this group's personal income earned that year came from non-writing sources. The
reasons, pointed out earlier for 1954, were: the worst year
for income earned from plays (except for those deriving income only from playwriting)--originals, motion picture and
television rights, the second lowest medians earned from
foreign production rights to plays, and the second lowest median income earned from "F.L.-Emp" writing.

There naturally is keen competition for writing jobs
available on an occasional basis when one's own field isn't
paying off. Directed writing income in 1954 was second
highest in the five years. And free lance writing other than

Table LXXVIII.

Total Income All Sources For Playwrights Deriving Non-Writing Income, By Income Classes, (1953-1957)

Annual Income (dollars)	1957 Playwrights Per Cent	1957 Income Median	1956 Playwrights Per Cent	1956 Income Median	1955 Playwrights Per Cent	1955 Income Median	1954 Playwrights Per Cent	1954 Income Median	1953 Playwrights Per Cent	1953 Income Median
0 - 1500	-	$ -	5.6	$ 1215	4.6	$ 966	2.5	$ 675	10.8	$ 1025
1500 - 2500	5.1	1550	5.6	2280	7.0	2000	10.0	2071	5.4	1921
2500 - 5000	18.0	3443	22.2	4000	20.9	4180	25.0	3828	24.3	4000
5000 - 10000	23.1	6600	25.0	6405	27.9	6785	22.5	6654	27.0	7206
10000 - 15000	15.4	11511	2.8	10300	11.6	12236	15.0	12153	13.5	13139
15000 - 25000	25.6	19385	22.2	19054	16.3	18213	12.5	17981	10.8	16165
25000 - 50000	2.6	41343	8.3	28000	-	-	5.0	36125	2.7	28939
50000 - 100000	5.1	59252	2.8	75118	7.0	56002	2.5	64454	2.7	87585
100000 & over	5.1	103200	5.6	117750	4.7	111500	5.0	118750	2.7	100000
Total	100.0		100.0		100.0		100.0		100.0	
N =	(39)		(36)		(43)		(40)		(37)	
Median		$10350		$7912		$8400		$6793		$6665
Per cent Non-writing Income is of Total Income	58.0		63.2		49.8		74.0		59.3	

Table LXXIX.

Playwrights' Total Income All Sources By Income Classes, (1953-1957)

Annual Income (dollars)	1957 Playwrights Per Cent	1957 Income Median	1956 Playwrights Per Cent	1956 Income Median	1955 Playwrights Per Cent	1955 Income Median	1954 Playwrights Per Cent	1954 Income Median	1953 Playwrights Per Cent	1953 Income Median
0 - 1500	9.3	$ 526	12.3	$ 990	11.1	$ 752	10.7	$ 675	14.6	$ 879
1500 - 2500	5.1	1860	7.0	1947	5.6	1918	7.8	2047	6.8	2000
2500 - 5000	15.3	3294	14.9	3569	17.6	3511	16.5	3500	18.5	3955
5000 - 10000	18.6	7398	19.3	7412	23.2	7100	22.3	6933	24.3	7000
10000 - 15000	11.0	12023	11.4	13253	10.2	11795	9.7	11208	11.7	13069
15000 - 25000	19.5	20205	13.2	20278	9.3	19256	12.6	18930	9.7	18750
25000 - 50000	6.8	39101	8.8	29885	9.3	35817	7.8	35000	4.9	40000
50000 - 100000	9.3	65000	7.0	64133	8.3	56500	6.8	64454	7.8	66122
100000 & over	5.1	135565	6.1	122000	5.6	128287	5.8	125950	1.9	105500
Total N =	100.0 (118)		100.0 (114)		100.0 (108)		100.0 (103)		100.0 (103)	
Median		$10440		$8550		$8000		$7500		$6800
Per cent all Playwrights	95.2		91.9		87.1		83.1		83.1	

194

plays in 1954 showed a higher percentage of dramatists active in this field as well.

But, whether the playwright earns from plays,
books, magazines, other kinds of writing or from non-writing sources, on the whole, playwrights, like book writers,
have a high degree of "employment" each year. In 1957,
95.2 per cent of all playwrights earned personal income;
throughout the five years, 87.9 per cent earned each year.
Like book writers, however, a third or more each year
(except in 1957) earn less than $5,000, whatever the source
of income, Table LXXIX.

Playwrights deriving personal income each year,
from whatever the source, earn better than book writers.
The 1957 personal median for playwrights (all sources) of
$10,440 was more than $1,600 higher than that for book
writers and $2,000 higher than for all writers. In fact,
yearly median incomes for playwrights earning personal income are higher than those for book writers in all years except 1953.

The five-year median personal income of $7,873
(see Table LXXX, page 196) for all playwrights was almost
$1,000 more than for all book writers and $1,200 higher
than for all writers as a whole.

Table LXXX is a comparative summary of the yearly median personal incomes with that for the five years for
all playwrights earning from the different areas of writing,
non-writing sources, and total income from all sources. Included, as for book writers, are the working spouses' incomes.

Married playwrights--66.9 per cent--are not as
common as book writers or all writers as a whole. Fewer
playwrights also have working spouses. Only 51.8 per cent

Table LXXX.

Playwrights' Yearly Median Personal Incomes From All Sources
And Spouses' Income (1953-1957)

Playwrights' Income From:	5-Year Median Income (1953-1957)	1957	1956	1955	1954	1953
Plays	$ 684	$1548	$1400	$1692	$1337	$1477
Other Free Lance Writing	957	1900	1481	2094	2083	2450
"F.L.-Emp" Writing	2700	8250	5630	5858	5500	2900
Directed Writing	1329	7400	2847	2975	4500	3120
Non-Writing Sources	3149	6000	5000	4180	5025	3955
Total Personal Income	7873	10440	8550	8000	7500	6800
Spouses' Income	1800	4400	5000	5000	4652	4861
Family Income	10795	12074	11500	9678	9375	8431

of the playwrights--compared with 56.5 per cent book writers; 53.8 per cent all writers--had working spouses during
the five years studied, and only slightly more than half of
these spouses (55.8 per cent) earned income for all five
years. (For book writers, 87.3 per cent had working
spouses with five-year incomes.)

The working spouse's five-year median income of
$1,800--half that for all writers--was only 15.2 per cent of
the total playwright family income. While the five-year median for working spouses of playwrights was slightly more
than half that earned by the book writer's working spouse,
the percentage contributed to family income was less than
half of either book writers (34.9 per cent) or all writers
(34.4 per cent).

Male playwrights, however, have many more working wives (76.7 per cent) among their ranks than do male
book writers or all male writers. The amount (8.5 per
cent) contributed to family income, however, is only a few
hundred dollars--$889--yearly.

Very few female playwrights--23.3 per cent--re-
ported working husbands--much, much lower, proportionally,
than for book writers or all writers as a whole. Yet, for
those playwrights with working husbands, 68.2 per cent of
the family income--or $11,040 yearly--is earned by the hus-
band.

As with book writers, the largest portion of yearly income (five-year median) comes from non-writing for the
two-fifths of all playwrights earning such income; "F.L.-
Emp" writing accounts for almost as much, and more than
half of all playwrights earned from this source. On a yearly basis, "F.L.-Emp" writing median incomes are the highest of any source every year except for 1953. Playwriting

income, however, accounted for less than 20 per cent of the
personal income earned by playwrights yearly, and less than
10 per cent for the five-year period.

Summary

Slightly more than one writer in four is a play-
wright--that is, he earned some personal income from playwriting between 1953-1957.

Playwrights--numbering less than half that of book
writers--earn less regularly from plays than do book writers
from books, and the playwright's yearly income (five-year
median) of $684 from playwriting is much less than half that
of the book writer from his books.

For the five years studied, less than 1 playwright
in 5 drew personal income from foreign production rights to
plays; about 1 in 4 realized personal income from motion
picture rights; less than 1 in 5 from television rights; and
almost 1 in 2 earned personal income from other subsidiary
rights to plays. As was true for book writers, motion picture rights to plays were by far the most lucrative; there
were three times as many playwrights as book writers, however, earning such income. The median (five-year) earned
by playwrights was almost twice that earned by book writers
from this source.

Additional income from television rights went to
three times as many playwrights as book writers, but the
book writer's median (five-year) income from this source to
his books was twice that of the playwright to his plays.

A very small portion of playwrights--a tenth--re-
ported earning their sole personal income only from playwriting during the five years. But, working spouses are
not the rule for these writers even though the five-year me-

dian personal income was only $542, and four out of five
are male.

Other free lance writing income provided fewer
playwrights with personal income than book writers. "F.L.-
Emp" writing, on the other hand, gave three times as many
playwrights additional income as book writers. Playwrights
earned almost twice as much as book writers from this latter source--motion picture and television writing either as
salaried or original works.

Playwrights proportionally in number, however,
did not fare as well as book writers from directed writing
assignments, though the five-year median earned was better
than for book writers.

Altogether, 59.7 per cent of all playwrights earned
all personal income from writing of some kind as compared
with the 46.3 per cent of book writers who did. And with a
larger proportion of playwrights earning only from writing,
their five-year median personal income of $8,620 was almost
twice the $4,804 median earned by book writers. The dif-
ference is attributal to a great degree to the "F.L.-Emp"
writing done by playwrights.

Playwrights earning only from writing of some
kind, unlike book writers earning such income, were not dependent on their working spouses' incomes. Two-thirds of
these playwrights are married and more than half did have
working spouses as compared with the two-thirds of the married book writers with working spouses. But, only 15.2 per
cent of the family income--$1,800 yearly--was contributed
by the playwright's working spouse compared with 47.2 per
cent, or $4,947 yearly, by the working spouse of book writ-
ers earning only personal income from writing of some kind.

Playwrights are much less dependent on non-writing sources of income than are book writers. The total median personal income earned (five-year median) by the two-fifths of playwrights and more than half of all book writers from non-writing sources are not greatly different for the five years--$7,003 and $7,464, respectively. For the playwrights, however, only 45 per cent--$3,149--of the total yearly income was earned from non-writing sources compared to the 60 per cent--$4,479--earned from this source by book writers.

Playwrights, deriving personal income from whatever source, earn better than book writers. The five-year personal median income of $7,873 for all playwrights (all sources) compares with the $6,952 personal median income for all book writers from all sources. Book writers, however, have a slightly higher proportion of their group--93 per cent--earning personal income each year than do playwrights with 87.9 per cent earning.

Playwrights, nevertheless, appear to be less able to pursue their chosen career of playwriting than are book writers with books. Seven in ten playwrights earned from originals during the five years compared with 9 in 10 novelists. The playwright's five-year median personal income from playwriting accounted for less than a tenth of his total earnings; for book writers, book income was almost a fourth--23 per cent--of his total earnings from all sources.

* * *

Dividing writers for convenience on the basis of whether they reported income from books or plays (Chapter IV and V) still leaves a small portion of writers unaccounted for except as they are treated generally in Chapter III. That is, 16.4 per cent of all writers reported no income from books or plays in the five years studied. And no provision unfortunately was made on the questionnaire for the writer

to tell us whether he considered himself a novelist, a playwright, a magazine writer, etc.

Again for convenience, therefore, this group of
writers[5] is referred to in Chapter VI as "other" writers
and specific treatment of their incomes from writing and
non-writing sources is presented there.

Notes

1. As with novelists, because of the difficulty in categori-
    zing from the questionnaires who is a playwright and
    who is not, all who reported any income from play-
    writing are included in the analyses here as playwrights.
    Where there is overlap of income, e.g. the same writ-
    er has income from both playwriting and books, such
    overlap is discussed.

2. Perhaps equally significant is the comment of Vance
    Bourjaily, former editor of Discovery and one of the
    best of the young novelists who has tried his hand at
    TV playwriting. (See HARPER'S, October 1959). He
    compares the novelists' and playwrights' positions.
    "Almost all television dramas made from stage plays,"
    he says, "are not really adaptations; they are only
    condensations, and are no more genuine works of
    television art than those quaint, first efforts to achieve
    art in photography by costuming models and grouping
    them to resemble the figures in famous paintings."

    Of novels, he explained, "The approach is so solemn,
    the plays are so portentously over-produced and over-
    cast--at the expense of adequate rehearsal or enough
    time and care spent on writing--that the result can
    only be tedious and artificial ... Short stories have
    provided better source material for television plays
    because the dimensions of a one-hour television play
    are rather like those of a short story ... The short
    story, too, has a singleness of effect and mood which
    would have robbed of variety an extended work like a
    three-act play, a movie, or a novel."

3. Vance Bourjaily (HARPER'S, October 1959) thinks,
    "Important television dramatists work no more in
    a field which offers small scope for their ambitions,

and which, in addition, does not pay very well. An
hour-long script paid $2,500 (1955); to have four
such scripts assigned a year was above average.
The name writers may have got slightly higher fees,
and as many assignments as they wanted, but even
so the payments were far below the forty or fifty
thousand dollars they could earn from writing a
pair of movie scripts in a year. For a moment
television seemed to offer them excitement, reputa-
tion, opportunity to be truly creative--a way might
even have been found of perpetuating their work.
This moment was soon over; when television offer-
ed merely less money for more work, of course
they left."

4. Some of these playwrights earning only from writing
of some kind for the five years reported one-year
earnings only, four years with no income; others
reported four years' earnings, one year with no
income. Some had two years income, three years
without, etc. The ratio of 1 in 6 is simply a mean
for those playwrights who had no income from writing of some kind for one or more of the five years.

5. There were 65.5 per cent of the writers counted as
book writers, 28.3 per cent counted as playwrights;
10.3 per cent were counted as both book writers
and playwrights.

Chapter VI

"Other" Writers

Of the 16.4 per cent of all responding writers who reported no personal income earned from either books or plays, 1953-1957, a very small group of writers (2.3 per cent of all writers) reported <u>no personal income</u> earned from <u>any</u> source for the entire five years.

About nine-tenths of this latter group are married, less than half of whom reported working spouses. And while the five-year median income for their working spouses was over $6,000, these writers as a group are older people with a median age of more than 57 years. Because they did not earn personal income, however, they are not included here in the tabulations for "other" writers.

For the remaining 14.1 per cent of all writers, therefore, the same general analyses are used where feasible as for book writers and playwrights in the preceding chapters. First, a look is taken at sex differences, age, 1957 median personal incomes, and absolute dollar range paid for these writers' services. Next, an attempt is made at some sort of classification of these writers on the basis of their writing and non-writing incomes. Specific analyses are made of incomes, of degree of "employment," and of dependence on the working spouse before examining the total personal income earned and total family income for these writers for the five-year period. Comparisons are presented intermittently with book writers and playwrights throughout the discussion.

203

Almost two in three of other writers (those earning neither from books nor plays) are male, the majority of whom are between ages 40 and 60. A majority of the females, however, are between 30 and 50 years of age, (Table LXXXI, page 205)--the youngest concentration for any group of female writers.

With more than 90 per cent "employment," four-fifths of all other writers were between 30 and 60 years of age, while all other age groups were all "employed" in 1957. The highest median personal income of $9,000, however, was earned that year by the 30-year olds (a fifth of the group) who also had the widest range of dollars paid for services. The second highest median--$8,304--was derived by the 60-year olds, also with the second widest range of actual dollar income. Accounting for more than a third of the group--the largest segment--the 40-year olds earned the third largest median personal income of $7,000.

Writing Income

Free Lance

Almost four-fifths (79.0 per cent) of other writers earned personal income from writing of some kind (other than books or plays) between 1953 and 1957. Of these, almost two in three earned from free lance magazine writing.

As a portion of all other writers, those earning from free lance magazine work in one or more of the five years make up half the group. For this 50 per cent of other writers, free lance magazine writing was not particularly lucrative even though more than three-fourths of them earned something each year; the five-year median personal income from this source was only $440. Yearly medians from free lance magazine writing for this group were considerably

Table LXXXI.

Other Writers' Median Personal Income And Dollar Range By Age And Sex, 1957

Age Group	Male Per Cent	Female Per Cent	Total Per Cent	Median Age	Median Income	Per Cent Earning Income	Range
20 - 29	2.5	-	1.6	29	$4400	100.0	$ 0- 4400
30 - 39	15.0	31.8	21.0	35	9000	92.3	0-42000
40 - 49	40.0	22.9	33.9	45	7000	95.2	0-26000
50 - 59	22.5	31.8	25.8	53	6489	93.5	0-25000
60 - 69	17.5	4.5	12.9	63	8304	100.0	298-27600
70 - 79	2.5	4.5	3.2	74	2207	100.0	200- 4215
80 +	-	4.5	1.6	86	2500	100.0	0- 2500
Total	100.0	100.0	100.0				
N =	(40)	(22)	(62)				
Median				46	$7100		

better, however, as this breakdown indicates:

Year	1957	1956	1955	1954	1953
Median Income	$1616	$975	$700	$1000	$1145
Per cent of Group Earning	71. 0	83.9	87.1	74.2	74.2
Per cent All Other Writers	35.3	41.7	43.3	36.9	36.9
N =	(22)	(26)	(27)	(23)	(23)

For this half of all other writers, who may be
loosely referred to as "free lance magazine writers, " 22. 6
per cent earned personal income only from free lance writing for magazines; 35.5 per cent earned additional personal
income from other kinds of writing; and 41.9 per cent earned personal income from non-writing sources.   Though the
latter two incomes--those from other kinds of writing, and
non-writing sources--are treated specifically in the following
sections, the total personal yearly earnings for these "free
lance magazine writers" are presented in Table LXXXII,
page 207, to show how this half of other writers fared on
total incomes.

These writers have the rather unique position of
being the only group to have a larger five-year median personal income--$6, 035--than any single yearly median.   Pri-
marily, the reason for it is that such a large portion of them
were "employed" each year.   For instance, in 1955 and 1956,
100 per cent of them earned personal income; in no case do
less than 96 per cent earn each year.   But between 40 and
50 per cent of them earn $5, 000 or less each year in per-
sonal income from all sources.

Thus, for these steady earners, personal income
derived from free lance magazine writing accounts for a
fifth or less of their yearly total personal incomes, on the
average--a characteristic true of both book writers and

Table LXXXII.

Other Free Lance Magazine Writers' Total Personal Income,
By Income Classes (1953-1957)

Annual Income (dollars)	1957 Writers Per Cent	1957 Income Median	1956 Writers Per Cent	1956 Income Median	1955 Writers Per Cent	1955 Income Median	1954 Writers Per Cent	1954 Income Median	1953 Writers Per Cent	1953 Income Median
0 - 1500	23.2	$ 660	22.6	$ 600	22.6	$ 915	20.0	$ 902	13.3	$ 728
1500 - 2500	6.7	2395	3.2	2400	6.5	1850	-	-	10.0	1700
2500 - 5000	16.7	4000	25.8	3914	22.6	4350	23.3	4000	26.7	3984
5000 - 10000	30.0	7964	25.8	6614	22.6	6400	30.0	6762	23.3	6550
10000 - 15000	10.0	12000	12.9	11396	9.7	11335	16.7	11383	16.7	11601
15000 - 25000	10.0	20000	6.5	19750	12.9	16425	10.0	19000	6.7	17908
25000 & over	3.3	27600	3.2	30100	3.2	29375	-	-	3.3	28425
Total N =	100.0 (30)		100.0 (31)		100.0 (31)		100.0 (30)		100.0 (30)	
Median		$5889		$4850		$4854		$5735		$4921
Per cent of Group Earning	96.8		100.0		100.0		96.8		96.8	
Per cent of Other Writers	48.4		50.0		50.0		48.4		48.4	

playwrights.

Eighty per cent of these "free lance magazine writers" are married, and 68 per cent reported working spouses. Both figures are higher than for all writers, book writers, or playwrights. The working spouse contributed 66.1 per cent, or $4,920 yearly to family income, and more than half of the working spouses were wives of writer husbands.

By adding the working spouse's income to that of the writer's and arraying in frequency, we have a five-year median family income of $8,139 for this half of all other writers. The median personal income earned from free lance magazine writing thus becomes even less significant.

Other Writing Income

Apart from a few of these other writers--under 5 per cent--who had free lance writing income from royalties or ASCAP, slightly more than two-fifths--41.9 per cent--had personal writing income from other than free lance work for one or more of the five years studied. More than a third of this group--38.5 per cent--had personal income from "F. L.-Emp" writing, 69.2 per cent had income from directed writing assignments, and less than 10 per cent had income from both sources.

The majority of these writers--more than 53 per cent--appear to be staff writers for magazines and newspapers primarily, for it is the major or sole source of personal income to more than a third of them.

For those other writers, then, who earned personal income from writing (other than free lance) an average of 69.2 per cent of them earned each year. (See below.) As a per cent of all other writers, however, this figure is only 29.0 per cent. In other words, of the 41.9 per cent other

writers earning personal income from other kinds of writing,
more than two-thirds of them earned each year from this
source as indicated:

Year	1957	1956	1955	1954	1953
Median Income	$6500	$5350	$5000	$8000	$8775
Per cent of Group Earning	80.8	73.1	61.5	65.4	61.5
Per cent All Other Writers	33.9	30.6	25.8	27.4	25.8
N =	(21)	(19)	(16)	(17)	(16)

Even though more than two-thirds of this group
earned each year and more than a third earned only personal
income from these writing sources, the five-year median income for all earning in one or more of the five years was
only $3,146. The low median ($3,146)--little more than
half of the lowest individual yearly median of $5,000 de-
rived in 1955--is caused primarily by the large portion
(more than two-fifths) having income from these sources of
writing in three years or less; almost a fourth had personal
writing income from other than free lance writing for only
one of the five years.

More than four-fifths--86.2 per cent--of this group
are married, higher than for either book writers or playwrights earning from other kinds of writing. The portion
with working spouses, however, is the lowest of the three
groups--54.6 per cent compared with two-thirds of the book
writers, and 55.1 per cent of the playwrights who had working spouses. Working spouses of this group of other writers
contributed 15.3 per cent of the family income--about the
same portion as for playwrights--but only $1,225 yearly,
also lowest for the three groups.

Non-Writing Activities and Income

Like many of the book writers and playwrights who found it necessary during the five years to add to their personal incomes from non-writing sources, more than three-fifths (62.9 per cent) of other writers also sought income from these sources. More than a third of them--35.9 per cent--had personal income only from non-writing sources.

Again, though we do not know the amount of time involved in these non-writing jobs, almost three-fifths (59.0 per cent) reported five-year personal incomes from the same source. Thus, with steady incomes, we do have a good measure of the regularity of these non-writing sources, Table LXXXIII, page 211. Slightly more than four-fifths (82.1 per cent) reported personal income from the same source three or more of the entire five years.

Writers engaged in government service--17.9 per cent--made up the largest portion of other writers earning personal income from non-writing sources. And together accounting for about a fourth of other writers deriving personal income from non-writing sources were those who taught or did secretarial work between 1953 and 1957.

More than half of all other writers (51.6 per cent) earned personal income each year from non-writing sources, Table LXXXIV, page 212. Though the yearly medians are not particularly high, they are steady both in the amount in the per cent of other writers earning.

The importance of this source of income to other writers is readily apparent in examining the five-year medians. For the five years, the 62.9 per cent of other writers who earned non-writing income for one or more years drew a median personal income of $4,000 from non-writing

Table LXXXIII.
Type Of Job Held (By Other Writers) And Degree Of Regularity To Supplement Writing Income (1953-1957)

Occupation	Per Cent Reporting	5 Years	4 Years	3 Years	2 Years	1 Year
Government Service (Fed, State, Local)	17.9	21.7	33.3	16.7	-	-
Teaching	12.8	8.7	33.3	16.7	25.0	-
Secretarial, Clerk	12.8	4.3	-	33.2	25.0	33.3
Engineer, Builder	7.7	8.7	33.3	-	-	-
The Arts--Radio, TV, Music	7.7	4.3	-	-	25.0	33.3
Public Relations	7.7	8.7	-	16.7	-	-
Consulting	7.7	8.7	-	-	-	33.3
Editor	5.1	8.7	-	-	-	-
Lecturing	5.1	-	-	16.7	25.0	-
Salesman	5.1	8.7	-	-	-	-
Executive	2.6	4.3	-	-	-	-
Dentist	2.6	4.3	-	-	-	-
Family Business	2.6	4.3	-	-	-	-
Investments	2.6	4.3	-	-	-	-
Totals	100.0	100.0	100.0	100.0	100.0	100.0
N =	(39)1	(23)	(3)	(6)	(4)	(3)

1. About a tenth listed multiple jobs or sources of income; about half were property or investment incomes every year; the rest was fill-in work such as done by agents, teachers on a one-shot basis.

211

Table LXXXIV.

Other Writers' Personal Income From Non-Writing Sources By Income Classes, (1953-1957)

Annual Income (dollars)	1957 Writers Per Cent	Income Median	1956 Writers Per Cent	Income Median	1955 Writers Per Cent	Income Median	1954 Writers Per Cent	Income Median	1953 Writers Per Cent	Income Median
0 - 1500	9.1	$ 700	6.1	$ 730	12.5	$ 790	9.7	$1116	12.9	$ 415
1500 - 2500	3.0	2491	3.0	2400	6.2	2306	6.4	2143	3.2	2400
2500 - 5000	39.4	4000	42.4	4000	31.3	4500	29.0	3980	35.5	3969
5000 - 10000	27.3	7000	30.3	7300	34.4	6900	38.7	6750	29.0	6500
10000 - 15000	9.1	13960	9.1	13600	6.2	11700	6.4	11200	9.7	12500
15000 - 25000	12.1	19746	9.1	18234	9.4	17000	9.7	15000	9.7	15000
25000 & over	-	-	-	-	-	-	-	-	-	-
Total N =	100.0 (33)		100.0 (33)		100.0 (32)		100.0 (31)		100.0 (31)	
Median		$4800		$4938		$5126		$5006		$4500
Per cent all Other Writers	53.2		53.2		51.6		50.0		50.0	

sources. This figure approximates closely two-thirds of the total personal income earned by these writers each year from all sources--higher than for book writers, playwrights or all writers. The individual high-year median for non-writing sources for 51.6 per cent of other writers earning that year was 1955 with a personal income of $5,126. Yet, as was the case with other writers earning from free lance magazine writing, on the average between 40 and 50 per cent earned less than $5,000 each year. Not one earned as much as $25,000.

Altogether this group of other writers--free lance magazine writers, staff writers for magazines or newspapers, and those who had no income from books, plays, or magazines but did have income from other kinds of writing or non-writing occupations--experienced the second highest degree of full "employment" for its members of any group during the five years studied (book writers were highest, playwrights lowest). More than nine-tenths of them derived personal income annually.

And while the total personal income five-year median for other writers--$5,938--was lower than for either book writers or playwrights, the individual yearly medians, Table LXXXV, closely approximate those for all writers as a whole.

Other writers incomes tend to be highly concentrated in the middle and upper middle income groups. No individual was paid as much as $45,000 in any of the five years--a figure less than one-fourth of that earned by the top-paid book writer and less than one-sixth that paid the top playwright.

Paralleling closely all writers as a group, the figures for other writers show about three-fourths of them mar-

Table LXXXV.

Other Writers' Total Personal Income All Sources By Income Classes, (1953-1957)

Annual Income (dollars)	1953 Writers Per Cent	1953 Income Median	1954 Writers Per Cent	1954 Income Median	1955 Writers Per Cent	1955 Income Median	1956 Writers Per Cent	1956 Income Median	1957 Writers Per Cent	1957 Income Median
0 - 1500	12.7	$ 530	14.6	$ 1024	19.6	$ 915	13.8	$ 660	15.3	$ 660
1500 - 2500	5.5	1700	1.8	2250	4.4	1900	3.5	2395	3.4	2395
2500 - 5000	23.6	3969	20.0	3872	21.4	4536	25.9	4000	25.4	4000
5000 - 10000	25.5	6500	30.9	6800	23.2	6900	27.6	8689	27.1	8689
10000 - 15000	18.2	11800	16.4	11383	10.7	11668	12.1	12000	8.5	12000
15000 - 25000	10.9	15322	12.7	20000	12.5	16000	12.1	19746	13.6	19746
25000 & over	3.6	34212	3.6	31750	7.1	31562	5.2	26800	6.8	26800
Total N =	100.0 (55)		100.0 (55)		100.0 (56)		100.0 (58)		100.0 (59)	
Median		$6000		$6762		$5702		$7100		$7100
Per cent all Other Writers	88.7		88.7		90.3		93.6		95.2	

ried (74.2 per cent) and 54.3 per cent of these with working spouses. Other writers, however, have a larger percentage of the family income--43.5 per cent--contributed by the working spouse than do spouses of all writers as a whole, book writers, or playwrights.

The amount added to family income by other writers' spouses each year--$2,900--is lower than for all writers and book writers but higher than for playwrights. These figures for other writers' working spouses are clearly explained by the fact that 58 per cent of the working spouses are wives (second only to playwrights in proportion) of other male writers, and the wife contributes 7.4 per cent of the family income, or $787 yearly, while the 42 per cent who are working husbands add 64.5 per cent to the family income or $5,640 yearly.

The five-year median family income of $8,038 for other writers is the lowest family income for all groups, including all writers. But for more than a third of other writers--the 37.1 per cent earning personal income only from writing of some kind--the family income is a bit higher at $8,900.

Summary

Apart from those writers who earned personal income from books and plays was 16.4 per cent of all writers who earned from neither source. Included in the latter figure are the 2.3 per cent of all writers who earned no personal income from any source between 1953 and 1957.

For the 14.1 per cent of "other" writers who did earn personal income--but not from books or plays--two in three are male.

Free lance magazine writing accounted for half of

all "other" writers earning personal writing income while seventy-nine per cent of all "other" writers earned personal income from writing of some kind for one or more of the five years studied.

Though magazines were not a lucrative source of personal income, more than a fifth of those earning derived personal income only from this source. The working spouse thus contributed heavily to these free lance magazine writers' family incomes (66.1 per cent, $4,920 yearly).

More than a third of "other" writers who derived personal income from writing of some kind, drew personal income solely from this source. Their five-year median writing income was the highest--$7,151--of any group of "other" writers earning from whatever source. And, less dependence on the working spouse's income was evident for these writers as well since the total family income median moved up only to $8,900.

Like book writers and playwrights, many "other" writers (62.9 per cent) sought personal income from non-writing sources; almost three-fifths had five-year personal incomes from the same non-writing source.

Non-writing sources, however, are not particularly lucrative to these three-fifths of "other" writers even though such income accounts for two-thirds of their total personal income earned each year. The $4,000 five-year median is more than that earned by playwrights and less than that earned by book writers from this source.

As a group "other" writers averaged 91.3 per cent who derived personal income annually--second most fully "employed" group. Two reasons seem apparent for this high incidence of earning. First, only half had any free lance writing income; the rest, thus, would have to seek other means of livelihood. And, secondly, supporting this point of view is the fact that two-thirds of the group are male, 85 per cent of whom are married and living with spouse, therefore their responsibility as breadwinners for their families.

One might speculate further that since these "other" writers are a bit younger than all writers as a group (a median age of 46), perhaps they are not yet well enough established to make a go of it simply from free lance writing. But in all fairness to this point of view, we must point out that some of these writers have obviously found their niche in that they have become established (staff) writers in magazines, newspapers, or some other media such as TV, motion pictures, or music (ASCAP). About 15 per cent of the group seems to fit this classification easily.

"Other" writers average income (five-year median), nevertheless, of $5,938 is lowest for any group of writers. And even though working spouses of "other" writers contribute proportionally more of the family income than do those of other groups, the median of $8,038 for family income is lower than that for book writers, playwrights, or all writers as a whole.   *   *   *

With the incomes of different types of writers having been analyzed specifically in the preceding discussions (Part II), Chapter VII of Part III now examines the writers' tax problems and presents the arguments for a revision of present taxing practices applicable to free lance writers, before summarizing the findings of this study, Chapter VIII. Chapter IX discusses the implications for the writer's future on the basis of what we now know of the free lance author and his income.

Part III

Problems For Writers

Chapter VII

Tax Problems

> ... How many loopholes there seem to be
> in the tax laws for everybody else but the
> writers.
> --Farrar[1]

Unquestionably the progressive income tax is unfair
to writers whose incomes show wide, yearly fluctuations. We
have only to examine the book writer's low- and high-year
incomes from books and the playwright's low- and high-year
incomes from plays over the five years, 1953-1957, to illustrate this vividly and emphatically. The approach can best
be made by expressing the low year as a per cent of the
high-year income.

Methodology

Of necessity, all those writers who earned income
from books or plays only one year out of five have been e-
liminated for this analysis. The rest were first arrayed on
the basis of the five-year median personal incomes from
books and plays, and the group median (dollar) determined
for both book writers and playwrights.

Next, with both groups divided in half by the dollar
median, the median per cent ratios were calculated separately for each half. Essentially this was done to see if there
was any similarity between the two halves, and if so, how
closely those in the half below the median income (based on
the five-year average) parallel those in the half above on the
basis of the median per cent of the low income to high income

years. But more importantly, they were divided in order
to eliminate any undue influence in the overall analysis
which the large amounts of money acquired from book clubs
and motion picture rights might have--skewing the ratios.

For each individual, then, the amount he earned
from books or plays in the low income year was divided by
the amount he reported in the high income year to find his
per cent of low to high years, and at the same time reveal
the fluctuation for at least two years of his income. These
percentages were arrayed and a median established for each
group.

Income Fluctuation

Book Writers

For all book writers the median percentage is 29.0
per cent, (Table LXXXVI, page 221). In other words, the
average book writer earned in his low income year from
books only 29 per cent of the amount he drew in his highest
income year during the five years. Yet, he was fully taxed
on the highest amount which would only seem just if this sum
was typical of his regular yearly earnings.

Take as an example, the average book writer whose
highest figure earned from books was $6,850; this means he
earned only $1,985 in his low income year (to meet the me-
dian 29 per cent characteristic of the average book writer).
He was taxed on $6,850 without consideration that in other
years he made much, much less than this amount from his
profession of writing books. A book writer thus reporting
these two amounts of income could fall in the lower half
(column 2) on Table LXXXVI, assuming he earned income
from books in only two out of the five years, for his five-year
median income from books would then be $1,767.

Table LXXXVI.

Relation Of Low To High Years Of Personal Income From Books Of Book
Writers Who Reported Income In More Than One Year,
(1953-1957)[1]

Per Cent Scale	For Half Below 5-Year Median Dollar Income[2]		For Half Above 5-Year Median Dollar Income[2]		All Book Writers	
	Book Writers Per Cent	Median Per Cent	Book Writers Per Cent	Median Per Cent	Book Writers Per Cent	Median Per Cent
(1)	(2)		(3)		(4)	
.05- 9.0	22.5	4.0	16.9	5.5	19.7	4.0
10.0 - 19.0	19.4	16.0	14.6	14.0	17.0	14.5
20.0 - 29.0	13.2	25.0	13.8	25.0	13.5	25.0
30.0 - 39.0	13.9	33.0	10.0	34.0	12.0	33.0
40.0 - 49.0	9.3	44.5	14.6	44.0	12.0	44.0
50.0 - 59.0	9.3	52.5	11.5	53.0	10.4	53.0
60.0 - 69.0	4.6	64.0	8.5	64.0	6.5	64.0
70.0 - 79.0	3.9	75.0	6.2	74.0	5.0	75.0
80.0 - 89.0	2.3	83.0	2.3	82.0	2.3	82.5

221

Table LXXXVI. (continued)

Relation Of Low To High Years Of Personal Income From Books Of Book Writers Who Reported Income In More Than One Year, (1953-1957)[1]

Per Cent Scale	For Half Below 5-Year Median Dollar Income[2]		For Half Above 5-Year Median Dollar Income[2]		All Book Writers	
	Book Writers Per Cent	Median Per Cent	Book Writers Per Cent	Median Per Cent	Book Writers Per Cent	Median Per Cent
(1)	(2)		(3)		(4)	
90.0 - 99.0	.8	99.0	.8	90.0	.8	94.5
100.0	.8	100.0	.8	100.0	.8	100.0
Total N =	100.0 (129)		100.0 (130)		100.0 (259)	
Median	26.0		32.5		29.0	

1. 90.2 per cent of all book writers earned some income from books for two or more years, 1953-1957.

2. The median used here is $1,767, which is the five-year dollar average median income from books for this group of authors.

222

For the half of book writers below the five-year median dollar income in column 2, the median percentage of the low to high years was 26.0 per cent--lower than for the group as a whole but only slightly; for the half above the five-year average dollar median (column 3), it was 32.5 per cent. Even this latter figure, however, means that for book writers earning $1,800 or more yearly from books, their low income year was only 32.5 per cent of their highest income year from this source.

To cite another example, the book writer in the upper half who drew $12,482 dollars from books as his highest earning for the five years in turn drew only $4,060 his lowest year.

What is more astonishing is the proportion of book writers who in their lowest income year drew less than half the amount they earned from books in their highest income year. For the half below the five-year median dollar income, more than three-fourths--78 per cent--earned less than 50 per cent of their highest income from books in their lowest year.

For the half above the five-year median, the proportion was 70 per cent. And for all book writers earning personal income from books for two years or more of the five (which included 90.2 per cent of them), 74 per cent had incomes in their lowest year that were less than half the amounts they earned in their highest year. Almost a fifth of all book writers (19.7 per cent)--the largest single portion--earned less than 10 per cent of their high year's income in their lowest income year; almost as many--17.0 per cent--earned less than a fifth but at least a tenth of their high year's income. These two groups account for more than a third of all book writers.

Few there are who have real steadiness in year to
year incomes from books it would seem. Less than four
per cent of all book writers earning income from books show
as little as 20 per cent variation in year to year incomes--
that is, the amount they earned in their lowest year was at
least 80 per cent of their highest year's income.

Playwrights

The playwright's income fluctuates even more than
the book writer's. The median percent of low to high years
for playwrights as a whole is 23.0 per cent (Table LXXXVII,
page 225) compared to the 29.0 per cent for all book writers.

That the playwright's earnings from plays is also
less regular than the book writer's from books, however, is
emphasized by the fact fewer playwrights could report more
than one year's income from plays. Only 71.8 per cent of
all playwrights--against the nine-tenths of all book writers--
had two or more years' earnings from plays in the five-year
period.

The playwright who earned $5,400 in his high year
and a low of $1,250--a median per cent of 23.0 which is
average for all playwrights--could at the same time have also
been in the half below the five-year median (column 2) as
well. These two figures--again assuming only two years'
income--when added together and divided by five produce a
five-year median of only $1,330. And the median per cent
for the lower half is also 23.0. More than three-fourths--
75.6 per cent--of the playwrights in the half below the five-
year median dollar income, like book writers, earned less
than 50 per cent of their highest income in their lowest
year's earnings.

Because playwrights as a rule draw larger incomes

Table LXXXVII.

Relation Of Low To High Years Of Personal Income From Plays Of Playwrights Who Reported Income In More Than One Year, (1953-1957)[1]

Per Cent Scale (1)	For Half Below 5-Year Median Dollar Income[2] (2)		For Half Above 5-Year Median Dollar Income[2] (3)		All Playwrights (4)	
	Playwrights Per Cent	Median Per Cent	Playwrights Per Cent	Median Per Cent	Playwrights Per Cent	Median Per Cent
.05 - 9.0	15.5	3.0	27.3	3.0	21.3	3.0
10.0 - 19.0	17.8	14.5	20.5	13.0	19.1	13.0
20.0 - 29.0	24.4	22.0	13.6	23.5	19.1	23.0
30.0 - 39.0	11.1	33.0	15.9	35.0	13.5	34.0
40.0 - 49.0	6.7	45.0	4.5	47.5	5.6	46.0
50.0 - 59.0	2.2	58.0	4.5	50.0	3.4	50.0
60.0 - 69.0	6.7	60.0	9.1	67.5	7.9	61.0
70.0 - 79.0	2.2	78.0	-	-	1.1	78.0

Table LXXXVII. (continued)

Relation Of Low To High Years Of Personal Income From Plays Of Playwrights Who Reported Income In More Than One Year, (1953-1957)[1]

Per Cent Scale (1)	For Half Below 5-Year Median Dollar Income[2] (2)		For Half Above 5-Year Median Dollar Income[2] (3)		All Playwrights (4)	
	Playwrights Per Cent	Median Per Cent	Playwrights Per Cent	Median Per Cent	Playwrights Per Cent	Median Per Cent
80.0 - 89.0	6.7	85.0	4.5	84.0	5.6	85.0
90.0 - 99.0	-	-	-	-	-	-
100.0	6.7	100.0	-	-	3.4	100.0
Total	100.0		100.0		100.0	
N =	(45)		(44)		(89)	
Median	23.0		21.0		23.0	

1. 71.8 per cent of all playwrights earned some income from plays for two or more years, 1953-1957.

2. The median used here is $1,330, which is the five-year dollar average median income from plays for this group of playwrights.

for their successes than do book writers, it might be expected that the portion of playwrights (in the half above the
five-year median dollar income) who earn less than 50 per
cent of their highest income in their lowest year would be
larger also than the corresponding portion of book writers.
This is true. More than three-fifths--81.8 per cent--of the
playwrights in this category realized less than half of their
high year's income in their lowest year's earnings. As an
example, the playwright who earned $29,000 in his high
year, drew less than $7,000 in his low year for a median
per cent of 21.0. And again, it was necessary for this individual to figure his tax on the $29,000 without any consid-
eration that he made much, much less than this amount
from his profession of playwriting in other years. The
$29,000 also probably put him in the prohibitively high tax
rates one encounters after reaching the $25,000 net mark
in any one year.

For all playwrights who earned income from plays
in two or more years of the five in this study, 78.7 per
cent of them made less than half of their high incomes in
their low year. More than a fifth--also the largest single
portion of playwrights as it was for book writers--earned
less than 10 per cent of their high income in the low year.
But in contrast to book writers, 9 per cent of the play-
wrights--more than twice the proportion of book writers--
experienced 20 per cent or less variation in year to year
incomes. This would seem to imply a larger portion of
playwrights are able to maintain steadier incomes than is
the case for book writers, though playwrights as a whole as
pointed out in an earlier chapter experience more irregularity in year to year earnings than do book writers.

In summary, then, (1) more book writers in the

half below the five-year median dollar income earned less
than 50 per cent of their highest income in their lowest year
than was the case for playwrights in the same category.
But (2) for those in the half above the five-year median dollar income, more playwrights earned less than 50 per cent
of their highest income in their lowest year than did book
writers. As a group, (3) slightly more playwrights than
book writers earned less than half their high year's income
in their lowest year's earnings.

These figures seem staggeringly high, and only
serve to emphasize the tax problems writers face because
of the wide fluctuation in year to year incomes. We can
appreciate the situation more fully, perhaps, if we speculate
what the problem would be like for the lawyer, or the teacher, or the engineer, if he earned this year only 23.0, or
29.0 per cent of his last year's income (as in the case of
the average playwright or book writer) while performing
relatively the same kind of job.

Such a situation would explain rather quickly also
why a large portion of us would thus seek additional income
to meet minimum economic obligations either from sources
closely related to one's chosen field of work or else in a
field completely apart from the individual's profession, e.g.
the case already presented as typical of the American free
lance writer.

Tax Problems

The United States is one of the few Western na-
tions that penalizes writers with punitive taxation. The doc-
tor whose income averages $20,000 a year over a five-year
period is far better off than a writer who makes $5,000 a
year for four years, and in the fifth year hits a movie jack-

pot that raises his income in that year to $80,000. Yet, among good writing professionals, this irregular pattern is quite often the rule rather than the exception. In five years, assuming that both men are single, the doctor will pay $32,000 in taxes, the writer will give up $52,196. There is, thus, this real advantage in steady income.

But, a writer's income is not steady. Most writers' incomes are not. Even if his income is in the lower brackets, the writer's yearly tax return will frequently prove to be more complicated than that of many small-sized corporations. He may have worked part of the time for a salary, like a clerk, part of the time for fees, like a consulting engineer, but he may also have lived part of the time like a capitalist on his rents and royalties. His work will have involved business expenses that are hard to estimate: How much should he charge off for that month of research at the Huntington Library in Pasadena? And that party to which he invited two editors and some people they wanted to meet: Would he be justified in deducting the cost of it-- what cost?--as business entertainment?

One of the most vexatious matters professional writers face, especially in pursuit of work that requires research expenses, is the quarrelling they must go through each year with the Federal Tax people to have these expenses honored.

Several years ago, a noted book writer[2] took his family on a long cruise in a boat he had bought for the purpose of taking the sea voyage to gather material for a book. He was gone for many months, with his wife and two small children. Upon his return, he entered the total cost of the trip--less the amount for food his wife and children actually had consumed--as a deductible business expense.

This deduction--which ran into some $8,000--was challenged by the Internal Revenue Service. He appealed to the U. S. Tax Court, which every taxpayer has the privilege of doing through payment of a $10 fee, and, through his attorney, argued in favor of his deduction. It was firmly established by the U. S. Tax Court that if a writer goes anywhere to collect information for a story, article, book, movie, or whatever he can deduct the total cost of the trip. It was also established that merely because he takes his wife and children along is no sign that the trip is not a business one. (If it had been classified as a vacation, the writer, of course, would not have been able to deduct his own expenses.) The writer naturally cannot deduct the actual cost incurred by his wife and children during the trip.

Yet, Max Wylie[3] in his preparation of the book, Assignment: Churchill, ran up bills of over $1,500. None of it was accepted by the Federal Tax people. In his long labor of the novel, Trouble In The Flesh (based on the life of Eugene O'Neill), he had bills in excess of $3,000. Two trips to the coast, several to New England, to South Jersey to visit the former Mrs. O'Neill, and one to Phoenix, Arizona. All of these were certified through cancelled checks, hotel receipts, train tickets, desk calendar. Only half the total was permitted as a legitimate deduction.

Or, consider Pat Frank's trip to South America in 1949.[4] He secured an assignment from a Collier's editor to do three short articles. When he returned from Caracas, notes and pictures for two of the three articles in his bag, his editor was gone, and no one could recall his assignment to do three articles in South America. Perhaps he could use the material as a basis for fiction pieces they suggested. This he did, selling one story to Collier's and one elsewhere.

He asked a tax expert whether he could deduct expenses for researching the two short stories. The taxman's opinion was no. Later, Frank discovered this opinion was incorrect.

The reason our tax courts are months and even years behind in their dockets is that the tax law is not only complex, but bewilders even the experts. Frank discovered the expert's wrongness too late to do anything about it.

The complexities in income reporting which the author may have are infinite. For instance, one prominent writer[5] established a plan to pool his income from books (except foreign and movie income) and set up a "kitty" with his publishers, from which they would pay the writer $20,000 a year. In 1953, an advance of $8,000 was paid against the next novel, and in 1954 $2,000 more (included in the $20,000 each year, of course).

This advance of $10,000 was part of a contract deal offered to total $50,000 on two novels, payable $1,000 a month for 48 months beginning in January 1953, with the extra $2,000 payable on that first month. The novelist could not write; he was "blocked off"; he tore up his contract. But, the publisher had already paid out $8,000. The writer then signed with a second publisher who bought up the $8,000 from the first and agreed to resume the $1,000 a month (to a total of $26,000 advance) when the writer began to write again, thus the acceptance in 1954 of the $2,000. The deal was then terminated once more for the same reasons. A long, difficult novel sometimes involves this and more--the publishers do not always press, nor do they suggest a return of the advance. Yet, how does a writer explain all this on his form 1040 to Uncle Sam? To the Federal Tax people this is income, all earned in one year, and taxable as such.

When another writer[6] told a tax examiner that it took him only nine months to write a book, the examiner asked, "Then why did you say in your '56 return that Forbidden Area took longer than two years?"[7] The author explained that the book actually began in 1942 when he was in Australia during World War II. His war experiences there were combined in 1950 with the new military and political situation and he wrote an article on how the United States could be attacked. That article contained the skeleton of the book's plot. In 1954, he used the material to write a serial--what might be called the rough draft of his book. He wrote the novel in 1955; it was published in 1956. He could document all of this.

Nor or these cases the exceptions. Rather they are more often the rule. Typically, a writer may receive--

> from various magazines, fees for writing articles or stories, and much smaller fees for writing book reviews.

> from publishers, pay for reporting on the literary quality of several manuscripts, usually at $25 a report, and they might also have called him into consultation about the revision of other manuscripts.

> from another publisher, a check for editing and writing an introduction to a book that was on its way to becoming a classic. (The introduction might also have been published as a magazine article and might have been used as the basis of a lecture, since the writer tries to make each separate project yield a double or triple income.)

> from one of the minor book clubs, a small monthly retainer for serving as a member of its editorial board.

> from several universities, fees for lecturing, usually $100 a night and traveling expenses.
>
> from staffing a writers' conference, $250 a week and expenses, (and with more free time he might have taught at other conferences, on a sort of Chautauqua circuit).
>
> from his own publisher, a report about the sale of books he has written in the past. (There perhaps would not be many dollars in his actual royalty account, but sums might be owed for subsidiary rights--for a soft-cover reprint or for a translation into Spanish or Swedish.)

By a combination of all these means, the author reflects, he has managed to survive. He has not lost much time through illness, fortunately. Someday, someday he would get a windfall, a sudden check from a book club or an award from a foundation, and it would enable him to write the book he has been planning for as long as he can remember ... without ever having time--or money enough--to get to work on it.

There are various stratagems writers have used to assure themselves of continued income, and at the same time not have to pay taxes at the prohibitively high rates after a man passes the $25,000 net income mark. For example:

> 1. A writer is offered $200,000 for the rights to his book for a motion picture. Instead of taking it in one lump-sum payment (which would make him liable for taxes up to $140,000), he can specify, instead, that he be paid $25,000 a year for eight years.

His total taxes on it (depending, of course, on what other income he may earn in each of the eight years) most likely will be only $50,000 or so altogether. But it is extremely

important--according to tax court rulings--that the agreement specify flatly and irrevocably that the writer cannot demand payment of the residue owed him whenever he wants
it. In other words, if the writer has the privilege in the
agreement of asking for the remainder due him and getting
it at any time, then the Tax Court has held that, in fact,
the whole amount of the agreement is taxable income in the
year in which the agreement was made. In short, the agreement must be irrevocable that he be paid only $25,000 a
year and that he has no rights to the other due him until it
actually is due to be paid, at which time, of course, it
immediately becomes subject to the income tax.

> 2. A writer might exchange his services,
> as a writer, to someone who needs the
> services of a writer, in exchange for
> some service which the other person
> may render to him.

There is some question on the validity of this method, particularly as it regards business expenses. If the exchanged
service is in keeping with the person's livelihood--a writer
produces a speech in exchange for having his house painted
(by either a professional housepainter or a friend)--the writer must pick up the value of the produced speech (his normal charge) and declare it as income. If the person offer-
ing the exchange service is engaged in some other profession than that of house painting, he is not required to report
the value of his received service as income. There are so
many facets that color the situations, however, where there
is a mutual exchange of personal services, that again, even
the experts cannot agree on the interpretation. Writers and
others using the device have reasoned that since no money
passes hands, in either case, there is no tax situation and
that both parties are exempt from having to report the trans-

action since no "income" was represented. They reason it
as the old barter system pure and simple. But even in barter where there is an exchange of goods involved the value
of such goods is subject to taxing as income. If there is a
mutual exchange of personal services between two parties--
neither party performing a service that is his usual source
of livelihood--the value of such services is not taxable income generally.

> 3. A writer consults tax lawyers and/or
>   certified public accountants or studies
>   tax rulings so he can proceed with sure-
>   ness both in claiming the deductions he
>   does take or in claiming losses that other
>   people might overlook.

For example, writers should remember that they
are just as eligible to use the provisions (e.g. loopholes)
of the tax law, to their own advantage, as are the rich or
those in the business of studying taxes for their profession.

As an illustration, consider the case of the writer
who took a first trust note when he sold a piece of property:

> The trust note was for $20,000, payable in small
> monthly installments. But the time came when the
> writer wanted cash for his other activities. He
> sold the note, which had a face value of close to
> $20,000, for $15,000. This gave him a carry-
> forward tax loss of $1,000 a year for five years.
> This carry-forward (of losses) was one of the
> vital points he kept in mind in making his de-
> cision to sell the note, rather than to borrow
> money against it and hold it until the entire
> $20,000 had been paid to him over a period of
> years. He knew he could use the $15,000 to
> finance undertakings that would make him far
> more than $20,000, and at the same time he
> would have a $1,000 automatic deduction each
> year for five years. Also, when he sold the
> property, he received in cash (over and above
> the $20,000 note) approximately what he had
> paid for the property originally. [8]

Estimates are that tens of thousands of persons, who have the right to claim carry-forward tax losses, do not do so because they are not aware of their rights. A writer, like his fellow citizens, these days must--and often does--give a great deal of time, thought, and effort to his tax records, and to the tax rules and regulations in effect in his community, his state, and his country.

Much has been written--some of it rather humorously, some quite seriously--about the plight of the writer and his taxes:

> For instance, there have been bills introduced in Congress to make it possible for writers to depreciate their bodies, as manufacturers depreciate machinery. And arguments have been advanced on the theory that the writer is not unlike
>
> (1) the oil well (allowed an annual depletion of 27.5 per cent)--a writer can just as suddenly run dry and start belching unsalable gas;
>
> (2) the farmer (whose surplus is bought by the government or else the government pays him money not to produce)--the writer's unsalable stories keep better than Idaho potatoes; or
>
> (3) he has capital losses on stories he cannot sell.
>
> In the latter, he is like the small manufacturer who builds cabin cruisers of a special type, for a limited market, isn't he? The manufacturer builds ten boats that sell, and two that for some reason he cannot sell at all. That is a capital loss. "Ah," the tax examiner replies with a raised finger. "But the writer has invested nothing tangible in a short story. The manufacturer invests materials. He has to pay salaries."

For some years, the Authors League has spon-

sored legislation in Congress which would make it possible
for writers (and other professional, self-employed persons)
to set aside a certain sum of money each year, for retirement purposes, and to deduct this as a business expense,
similar to corporate executives deducting retirement payments from their income before computing what they owe in
taxes. Congressional leaders, however, have found it difficult to believe that writers, and kindred self-employed
persons, deserve any "special" treatment.

One faint ray of hope has been the Jenkins-Keogh
bills, H. R. 9 and H. R. 10. The bill allows a self-employed person to deduct from gross income each year a limited
amount of self-employment income contributed by him to a
restricted retirement fund or paid in as premiums to pur-
chase an insurance policy with retirement features. He can
deduct annually up to $5, 000 or 10 per cent of self-employ-
ment income, whichever is less, but not more than a total
of $100, 000 during his life time. There is a five-year
carryover of unused deductions, subject to certain limitations.

An individual who has reached age 50 before the
effective date is allowed to deduct an additional amount, to
help him build up an adequate interest in the fund or obtain
more than a token annuity. In his case, the normal deduction limit is increased by one-tenth for each year of age
over 50 and not over 70.

The contribution, plus accumulations, becomes
taxable when distributed, and may be withdrawn at any time.
However, where withdrawals take place before age 65, the
tax is 10 per cent greater than otherwise payable, but the
payment is treated as having been received pro rata during
the taxable year and the four preceding years. Lump-sum
payments after age 65 are given special treatment, under the

bill's provisions.

Briefly, the tax problems authors face, then, are three--partly because of the wide fluctuations in his income as indicated but partly because of statute rulings:

(1) The author's inability, under present income tax law, to accumulate the means for professional survival or to provide a reserve for retirement.

(2) Denial of social security benefits to authors, otherwise eligible, because of receipt of royalties from books written long prior to retirement and the fact that an author may be engaged, although unprofitably, in the writing of another work.

(3) Arbitrary classification of income from inherited property as "income in respect of a decedent," and the consequent denial to an author' heirs of the right to take depreciation on literary property they have inherited at the market value on which estate taxes have been assessed.

These three problems are shared by all persons who, by their independent effort, create works protected by the Copyright Act--novelists, playwrights, poets, historians, biographers, composers, scientists, painters, and sculptors. The case for remedying these problems was presented before the Ways and Means Committee in the House of Representatives (Eighty-fifth Congress, Second Session) concerning general revenue revision as it relates to the writer and other self-employed persons. These arguments presented before the Committee and in defense of the Jenkins-Keogh bills, state the writers' income position well. They appear here in excerpt form: [9]

(1) The Problem of Professional Survival

(a) The creation of a literary work is a protracted

process which does not produce income until it is
completed.

One overwhelming handicap faced by most authors
who write independently is the inability to accumulate the means for professional survival, the funds
to support themselves and their families while they
are writing. This is not a problem because authors are profligate or inept or do not receive substantial return on their work. It is a problem
faced by authors who are frugal, successful, and
who make money.

The problem is due to an inexorable condition of
the author's calling. From the beginning to the
end of his career, the author's life is a series of
prolonged periods devoted to the creation of literary property; during these periods the work he
is creating does not produce any income for him.
(We are speaking of authors who write independ-
ently--who do not render services to others in exchange for salary or fees.)

Income is only realized intermittently when the
property created, the book or play, is put to use
by publication, performance or other means.

These periods of unremunerative creation vary in
length from months to years, depending upon the
writing habits of the individual author, the degree
of initial preparation required, the nature of the
work, and a variety of other circumstances.

One such period will often be followed consecutive-
ly by another, since creative work does not always
culminate in a literary property which the author
can exploit. Often a work in progress is aban-
doned uncompleted. Sometimes a play (or novel)
will not be presented to the public for many years
because of problems encountered by the producer
or publisher, and, frequently, the product of these
months or years of unremunerated writing is published (or performed) and fails.

The financial failure of a book or novel is a risk
inherent, indeed inevitable, in a writing career.
It is an experience which is suffered by great writ-

ers as well as novices. A 'flop' is as common-
place in the theater (or book publishing) as dry
holes are in the oil industry or operating losses in
any manufacturing enterprise.

Ironically, an author may fail with a work which has
great merit and receives its recognition years later, too
late to benefit him although it may benefit others who can exploit it profitably after it has passed into the public domain.

To survive professionally--to devote his time and
talent exclusively to writing--an author must have
a reserve to draw on to support himself and his
family during these recurring, prolonged and unremunerated periods of writing. The professional
author is limited to one source, the proceeds of
work he has already created. From these he must
be able to accumulate his reserves for continued
professional survival.

But today it is difficult to do this. Profits from a
successful novel or a play, particularly when substantial,
are decimated by high income taxes since payments are of
necessity received within a brief period of time.

(b) Concentration of income

The profitable life of most novels, which may have
taken as much as four or five years to write, is
usually no more than 10 to 14 months; a successful play will run for an equal or slightly longer
period ... It is rare for a hit to survive for more
than two years on Broadway. Copies are sold,
and tickets are purchased, because the work is a
success, and when it is a success. Unlike a pa-
tented device or process, there is no long term
substantial demand for a book or play; or, more
accurately, no continuous demand on a basis which
is profitable to the owner of the property, the author. After its initial success, a novel or bio-
graphy will continue to be read for years by many
thousands of people, but the return to the author
is negligible. For example, readers avail themselves of free copies on public or school library
shelves.

Consequently, the author, as owner of the property (the literary or artistic composition and the rights in it secured by copyright), derives the greater part of his royalty or rental income within a span of a few months. As owner, he will have leased one or more of the separable property rights in the work; a novelist will lease (or license) the limited right of publication; a playwright will lease the limited right of performance in this country and Canada. If the work is successful, additional rights will be leased; the novelist may license publication of book club and paperback editions; the playwright will lease the right of amateur performance of his property. All of these additional licenses are usually made at the time of the initial success when the demand is great. Occasionally an author will be able to lease or sell one of the most valuable property rights he possesses, the right to make a motion-picture version, in this same period because the interest in that right is stimulated by the current success of the property.

Although there are several means by which an author may put his literary property to work--the incomes for such subsidiary rights have already been treated in the preceding chapters--the conditions of the market compel him to exploit most of them within one or two successive tax years. Except in unusual cases the author cannot defer the leasing or sale of rights until later tax periods.

(c) <u>Present income tax procedures are a serious obstacle to literary and artistic careers.</u>

Because profits are received in one or two successive tax years, present income tax rates make it impossible to support an author over the long pull of his career, or to provide a reserve for retirement. An unfortunate consequence is that many writers of talent are prevented from devoting their time and ability to creative writing. They can only afford to write as salaried employees; or turn to unrelated work to support themselves. Because creative writing requires sustained, con-

centrated effort, these people cannot afford to make
valuable contributions to our culture. And, para-
doxically, as salaried writers they will over a lifetime earn more income and pay less income tax
than they would have done as independent authors
under our present tax structure.

(d) Need for statutory revision

These problems merit the most serious consideration. It is a matter of public interest that creative talent be encouraged and not deterred from
pursuing careers in literature and the arts. This
is not to say that unless there is a tax reform all
writing will cease, but we do say that unless the
author is given equitable treatment many persons
capable of creating valuable work will not do so
because they cannot afford to.

Secondly, these problems deserve consideration
because they involve inequitable treatment of a
group of taxpayers caused by the peculiar conditions under which their property is created and
exploited, difficulties and inequities of a kind
which Congress has seen fit, in the past, to rem-
edy in other areas. Income from other rapidly
depleting assets is given special consideration;
taxpayers are permitted to cushion the effect of operating losses, in other enterprises, by carryback
or carryover provisions.

The code does not contain any provisions which
solve the author's problems. It deals specifically
with taxation of income from literary property in
two instances: Section 1302, which was intended
to assist authors, and sections 1221 and 1231,
which discriminate against them.

(e) Section 1302

Section 1302 was designed to permit--in limited
circumstances--allocation of profit from a literary
work over the period of its creation. It was not
intended to solve the problem of permitting the author to accumulate the resources for professional
survival, to live under the unique conditions which
characterize his career. Even in terms of its

narrow purpose, the section has not afforded adequate relief for these reasons:

> (i) The author is only permitted to allocate
> profits received in a single tax year if his
> receipts are no less than 80 per cent of
> all profit derived from the work (a) during
> that year; (b) in all preceding years; and
> (c) in the year following.

This requirement is impossible to satisfy in most
instances. Although the profits from a successful book or
play are generally concentrated over a period of a few
months, that period frequently overlaps two taxable years.
Plays are ordinarily produced in the fall, and if successful
would run into the succeeding year. Similar patterns are
prevalent in book publishing. The sale of movie rights frequently fall in the succeeding tax year.

> Consequently, although 50, 60 or 75 per cent of
> all income from a literary property may be re-
> ceived in the first year of its publication or per-
> formance--a concentration which under prevalent
> tax rates is disastrous--relief is denied because
> of the 80 per cent requirement and the taking into
> account of income received in the subsequent 12
> months.

> (ii) If an author meets the 80 per cent re-
> quirement he is only permitted to allocate
> the profits from the book over a maximum
> of 36 months, although the actual writing
> may have entailed many months more.

The inequity of this limitation is emphasized by
the more favorable treatment given to other taxpayers in similar circumstances. An inventor is
entitled to allocate his profits up to a maximum
of 60 months; and lawyers and others qualifying
under section 1301 may allocate their income over
the entire period in which the services were rendered, without limitation of time.

(f) Sections 1221 and 1231

> When owned by its author, a novel (and the copy-
> right on it and the rights secured thereby) cannot
> be treated as a 'capital asset' (Sec. 1221) or 'prop-
> erty used in trade or business' (Sec. 1231). The
> same property can be transformed into one of these
> classifications of 'capital assets' the moment it is
> acquired by a purchaser, although he makes the
> same use of the property as the author did. He
> can depreciate the property, and the proceeds of
> its sale (if held for 6 months) may be treated as
> a capital gain.

This anomalous condition is recognized in the language of the two sections. Copyrights and literary property
are not disqualified as such from capital gains treatment;
they are only disqualified so long as they are held by the author. There is no justification in logic or policy for this
discrimination. The owner of buildings held for rental purposes, it is argued, is not denied capital gains treatment
because he was the individual who constructed them. A corporation similarly is not denied capital gains treatment upon
the sale of machinery used in its business because it constructed that machinery itself rather than purchased it from
someone else.

> Obviously, the only basis of distinction should be
> the manner in which the property is used by its
> owner. The same property may be an item held
> for sale in the ordinary course of business by one
> owner; it may be a capital asset or property used
> in the course of a business in the hands of another
> owner. The profits on the sales of buildings are
> taxable at ordinary rates if the owner's business
> is building and selling; they are taxable at capital
> gains rates if the owner was in the business of
> renting.
>
> Authors are entitled to like treatment. If one au-
> thor derives his profit by a continual process of
> selling his copyrights or rights therein, then his
> gains should be taxed as ordinary income. But
> where a novelist, for example, follows the usual

practice of his profession and retains ownership of copyright on all of the works he has ever written and derives his income by leasing (licensing) rights therein for limited periods of time, he should be entitled, as is the owner of any other type of rental property to treat the gain from an isolated sale of one of his copyrights, or of a right or rights secured thereby, as a capital gain.

The same considerations of public policy which prompted Congress to extend the privilege of capital gains treatment to inventors exist here. Moreover, the risks of failure faced by an author, and the sacrifices he makes in the creation and development of a literary property, are as formidable as those faced by the purchaser of common stock or any other risk-taking investor; authors require at least as much incentive, and have, as we have indicated, as great a need for an opportunity to increase their capital. If extending the privilege of capital gains treatment to authors is considered a reward, we sincerely suggest that rewarding creative talent in this manner is not bad public policy.

(g) Recommendations for statutory revisions

In the light of the foregoing discussion, we respectfully suggest for consideration (i) two revisions in the method of taxing ordinary income derived from the exploitation of literary property; (ii) a revision of section 1302; (iii) revision in the capital gains section; and (iv) the adoption of individual retirement provisions in the manner proposed by Representative Keogh in H. R. 10, 84th Congress, 1st session.

> (i) An author (or one whose 'basis is determined by reference to the authors') should be permitted as a deduction from annual gross income derived from lease or license of literary property, a reasonable allowance for depletion of that property amounting to 25 per cent of such gross income.

Such a provision would take into account the fact that literary properties are usually rapidly depleting assets, created by arduous effort over long, unremunerative periods of time, and at a considerable risk.

The second method of meeting the problems, and recognizing these factors, would be to permit the author to compute his tax upon income derived from the lease, license, sale, or other use of literary property as follows:

All income derived from the taxpayer's literary properties in the taxable year shall be aggregated with similar income (if any) received in any one or more of the 4 preceding taxable years. Such aggregated income shall be divided into 5 equal installments which shall be allocated, respectively, to the current taxable year, and to each of the 4 preceding years. The tax attributable to such income in the current and preceding 4 years shall be computed as if received in each of these years on the allocated basis. The tax payable by the author in the current taxable year shall be the tax attributable to such allocated income in that year, and the difference in each of the 4 preceding years between the tax attributal to such income on an allocated basis and the tax attributed to such income prior to allocation.

The privilege of reallocation in this manner would be available from year to year.

We respectfully submit that such a method of computation would not cause any significant loss of tax revenue, nor would it impose any administrative difficulties. The practice of averaging and reallocating income is well established; it is applied not only under section 1320 but under other sections (e.g. secs. 172, 1301) in areas where the amounts of income and of income tax greatly exceed those which would be involved here.

> (ii) As an alternative, and one which in all candor we believe would not meet the problems as adequately, we recommend that section 1302 be amended to (a) permit allocation of gross income from literary property in any taxable year in which gross

income is not less than 40 per cent of the
gross income derived from such property
in the current year and in previous taxable years; (b) permit the taxpayer to allocate such income over the period in
which the work was created (or, at the
very least, subject to the same maximum
time limitation applicable to patents--60
months).

(iii) We recommend that the provisions of sections 1221 and 1231 of the Internal Revenue Code, absolutely excluding copyrights
or literary property from capital gains
treatment, be eliminated, and that the
taxpayer whose personal efforts created
a copyright on literary or musical or
artistic composition or similar property,
be permitted to treat the sale of the copyright, or any separable right therein as
the sale of a capital asset (or an asset
used in trade or business) so long as such
transaction is not the usual and ordinary
means by which the taxpayer exploits his
copyrights, literary property, or the rights
therein.

(iv) At present, it is impossible for authors
as well as other self-employed persons in
many fields of endeavor to make adequate
provision for retirement in the absence of
benefits and safeguards which are extended to salaried employees under the Internal
Revenue Code.

It seems clear, therefore, that the only opportunity
which authors and other self-employed individuals will have
to establish reserves for retirement is by the enactment of
an individual retirement act to permit them to establish vol-
untary pension plans. The league believes that an enactment
of the type proposed by Representative Keogh in H. R. 10
would adequately meet this problem.

(2) Denial of Social Security Benefits to Retired Authors on
    the Mistaken Theory That Royalties from Past
    Works Must Be Treated As Income From Current
    Employment

The Social Security Administration has ruled that if
an author continues to write between ages 65 and 72 (or 60
and 72 if a woman), he or she will lose social security benefits even though what is written produces no income, should
the author at the same time receive royalties (exceeding
$1,200 annually) on literary property created and licensed
for use before retirement. Benefits would also be suspend-
ed if the total royalties from earlier and current works exceed $1,200.

> The Social Security Administration ruling ... is
> another example of arbitrary and important equa-
> ting of rental income produced by literary prop-
> erty with wages of compensation received for ser-
> vices rendered.
>
> This is due to a misinterpretation by the Social
> Security Administration of section 203 of the Social
> Security Act (42 U.S.C. 403), which requires
> that social security benefits be reduced or denied
> entirely to eligible authors if they continue to work
> or engage in self-employment and thereby earn
> more than $1,200 annually.
>
> Congress did not intend that benefits would be
> suspended if a person received income from his
> property (whether it be stocks, bonds, or copy-
> rights), or even from services performed in the
> past, so long as he did not earn $1,200 annually
> from current work or employment. For this sec-
> tion provides that an eligible individual is entitled
> to benefits whenever he is not working; receipt of
> dividends, interest or royalties on literary prop-
> erty, no matter how substantial, would not deprive
> an author of social security benefits if he did not
> write. And benefits are not denied to a person
> who works, so long as he does not earn more than
> $1,200 annually.

The Social Security Administration has taken two
unrelated factors (i) the receipt of royalties for
the use of literary property written before age 65,
and (ii) the current writing of a new book or play
and combined them to achieve disqualification. As
a result, an author could continue to write so
long as such writing produced less than $1,200
annually, even though he received substantial a-
mounts of income from various types of property--
real estate, securities, mortgages. But if he received royalties from literary property, produced
in the past, he would have to stop his current
writing or lose his social security benefits.

Much valuable writing is done by authors who have
reached 65.

(3) Discriminatory Tax Treatment of Income Re-
ceived By Authors' Heirs From Inherited
Literary Property

Discrimination in the tax treatment of an author's
literary property haunts him not only during his career but
even after his death.

At death, the literary property the author created
passes to his heirs and estate, and many subse-
quently produce profit in the form of royalties on
copies of a book sold (or performances of a play
presented) after his demise. The Internal Revenue Service has taken the position that such payments for posthumous uses are 'income in respect
of a decedent' under section 691 of the code.

As a result, an author's heirs are denied the
right, which legatees of similar rental property
have (under sec. 1014 of the code), of taking the
fair market value of the inherited property at the
time of death and recovering its value by deducting an allowance for depreciation from the income
it produces, before computation of taxes. But the
fair market value of the inherited literary property is included in the estate for the purpose of as-
sessing estate tax.

The purpose of section 691 is to insure that income (wages, fees, commissions) earned by a

person during his lifetime does not escape income
taxation because he died before it was paid--to pre-
vent such accrued income from being considered
as part of the estate.

But royalties paid to an author's heirs on copies
of a book sold after his death are not income which
the author had earned or was entitled to receive
before his death--though paid under a publishing
contract in effect at his death.   In a publishing
contract (or other license agreement), the author,
as the owner of literary property, grants to the
publisher the right to make a limited use of the
property--the right of publication--in a limited
area, e.g., the United States.   The license fixes
the rentaly (or royalty) to be paid for such use as
the publisher may make during its term.   The license agreement is not a contract of employment;
royalties are not payment for services rendered,
and the author does not sell anything to the publisher; he retains title to the copyright.

The contract simply fixes the rate of royalties to
be paid if and as the publisher used the right of
publication; it does not impose any obligation on
the publisher to pay specified amounts or at any
specified time, nor does it vest in the author any
right to receive specified amounts of royalties.
Nothing accrues to him at the time the contract is
signed.   Only as and when copies of a book are
sold (or performances of a play are staged) do
royalties become payable as to those particular
copies or performances.   If copies of a book are
not sold, the author has no claim for royalties nor
any rights against the publisher, except to termi-
nate the lease.

Consequently, at the time of an author's death, the
only income which could have accrued to him under a publishing contract would be unpaid royalties due on copies sold
before his death.   As for copies sold after death, royalties
are paid to the heir, as owner of the property right used by
the publisher (the right of publication) for its use.

These are fundamental principles of contract law,

applicable to contracts and licenses of literary property; the
Internal Revenue Service has taken a diametrically opposed
position and is equating rental paid for the use of literary
property with wages or compensation earned by an individual
before his death.

> An author's heirs are thus denied rights given to
> persons inheriting other income producing property
> even when subject to leases. The owner of an
> apartment building may, during his lifetime, have
> rented all of the apartments on leases effective
> for a long time beyond the date of his death. None-
> theless, when his heirs inherit the building and
> receive rent, they are not required to treat it as
> income earned by the deceased owner, although the
> rent for the entire term (before and after the
> owner's demise) was established as an obligation
> by the lease at the moment it was signed during
> the owner's lifetime. Posthumous rent is consid-
> ered as income produced by the inherited building.
> And even though the owner may have fully depre-
> ciated the building before his death, his heirs are
> entitled to establish a new cost basis for it, at
> fair market value, and to deduct from subsequent
> rents an allowance for depreciation, thus obtaining
> a significant tax saving.

> In effect, heirs are entitled to establish a cost
> basis for inherited property, much as a purchaser
> is permitted to do for purchased property, except
> that it is established at fair market value rather
> than at purchase price. This underlines the incon-
> gruous treatment given to literary property, for
> when it is sold to a stranger he is entitled to take
> his purchase price as the cost basis of the prop-
> erty (copyrights and the works they protect)--even
> though the income which the literary property pro-
> duces for him thereafter may be payable under
> long-term license agreements which the author had
> previously executed.

> Again, the failure to make a distinction between
> income produced from the leasing or licensing of
> literary property, and compensation for services
> or wages, operates to the detriment of authors,

in a manner which is both illogical and unfair.

We believe that the inequities and hardships which
we have described are sufficient, as such to merit
the committee's consideration. There is ample
precedent for relieving unintended hardships which
result from the impact of broadly drawn statutes
upon the unique economic conditions of a particular
group of taxpayers. The case for relief is even
stronger here because authors are actually discriminated against--they are denied privileges
which are extended to other taxpayers holding similar property for the same purposes.

Moreover, the consequences of the provisions and
interpretations, which we have discussed, trans-
cended the welfare of author-taxpayers, and have
a considerable effect on important national values
and purposes. Obviously tax statutes can stimu-
late and encourage--or deter and inhibit--activi-
ties which are of public concern. Frequently,
statutory changes are enacted for precisely that
purpose.

We believe that in the case of authors, these statutory provisions (and administrative decisions) are
definite obstacles for persons who would otherwise
write professionally; and conversely that there has
been a deplorable lack of effort to encourage writing.

We have no doubt that with or without tax reforms
many authors will continue to write. But we also
have no doubt that the obstacles inherent in these
statutory provisions will deter many people of
talent from continuing to write independently, and
will continue to penalize those who do. This is
particularly unfortunate, since most creative writing is done by individuals whose income is derived
from their copyrights, who do not work for hire.
Many authors could write independently, since royalty income can be adequate for self-support, were
it not for these existing tax provisions.

Dan Lacy, Managing Director, American Book Publishers Council, also spoke in behalf of the author concern-

ing copyrights at this hearing. What he had to say is e-
qually significant in the case.[10]

> The council welcomes this opportunity to present
> its views on the policy questions relating to the
> taxation of income from copyrighted material. In
> a very real sense our statement is supporting and
> supplementary to the testimony being presented to
> the committee by the Authors League. It is the
> author who is directly affected by the methods of
> Federal taxation applied to income from copy-
> righted works. We believe, however, that the pub-
> lic also has a great interest in this question be-
> cause of the effect of taxation upon the professional
> authorship and upon the quality and quantity of pub-
> lished material which can be made available for
> study, research, public information, recreation
> and cultural improvement.
>
> Copyrights and patents are two of the very few
> forms of property specifically provided for in the
> Constitution of the United States. Article I, sec-
> tion 8, of the Constitution gives the Congress the
> power 'To promote the progress of science and
> useful arts, by securing for limited times to au-
> thors and inventors the exclusive right to their
> respective writings and discoveries;'. The purpose
> of this constitutional provision was obviously to
> promote the public welfare by encouraging inven-
> tors and writers to carry on their work. The
> patent and copyright laws of the United States spell
> out the details of the property rights conferred
> upon inventors and authors and in general give the
> author, playwright, and composer a sound and
> salable title to his creative work for a limited pe-
> riod of years.
>
> As members of this committee well know, however,
> with the great growth of income and estate taxa-
> tion it is not gross income which counts in these
> times, but the income that remains after taxes.
> In this respect, we believe present Federal tax
> law has gradually evolved so as to discriminate
> against income from copyrights as compared with
> income from other forms of property. Thus the
> constitutional encouragement of authorship by grant
> of the copyright privilege is to a considerably ex-

tent being nullified by the tax laws.

It is necessary here to give some attention to the
special characteristics of the income derived from
copyrights and to the way in which professional authors earn their living in order to see clearly the
special impact upon them of the present tax laws.
We are concerned here not with the writer who is
in a salaried position or who is paid on a regular
monthly basis, and whose tax problems are sub-
stantially those of any salaried employee. We are
rather concerned with the author who is an independent businessman devoting himself to the creation of a special class of property--copyrighted
literary works--and whose income is derived from
the exploitation of this property. Several points
need to be borne in mind. First, this is an extremely speculative enterprise. A particular novel,
if it happens to be a 'best seller' and to be the
choice of one of the major book clubs, and the subject of a motion picture, can be very remunerative,
but for every novel that reaches this level of success there are many dozens--indeed hundreds--of
relative failures which return only a slight income
to the author in compensation for the several years
of work that may have gone into their productions.

In the second place, for most American writers
several years' work and preparation necessarily go
into the creation of a single major piece of writing. The income from one successful book is
hence his compensation for several years of otherwise unpaid effort. The income from his successful book must also repay him for the years that
have been devoted to the preparation of books that
in the outcome were unsuccessful, just as the returns from a single successful oil well may have
to cover the expenses of many unsuccessful test
drillings.

In the third place the income from a successful
book is concentrated in a very short period of
time. Few novels, even the most successful, sell
actively for more than 1 to 2 years. The sale of
movie rights generally comes simultaneously with
the peak sale of the novel itself and so does any
book club income that may be received. The in-

come from certain types of copyrighted matter,
for example, textbooks and standard musical com-
positions, are spread more evenly over a longer period of time, but in general a characteristic of almost all copyrighted income is its concentration in
very short periods separated by long periods with
little or no income.

Finally, since the author is an independent businessman with no company-provided disability or
sickness insurance, with no guaranteed annual income, and with no company-financed pension or
retirement plan, the income he receives from his
widely spaced successes must not only reimburse
him for the years that went into their preparation,
but must also provide the capital to finance him
while he is working on his next book and with the
means to set aside savings to protect him against
the contingencies of illness or disability, to provide for the education of his children, and to provide for his own retirement and old age.

What the author of copyrighted material needs to enable him to meet this situation without the necessity of aban-
doning professional authorship to seek other means of support,
and without the risk of becoming a burden upon the state,
Mr. Lacy feels, is in essence three things:

1. A means of spreading peaks of income over
    the periods in which they were actually earned
    and for which they must actually provide sup-
    port for the author.

2. The termination of certain discriminations a-
    gainst copyrights as a class of property, so
    that when an author realizes a bona fide capi-
    tal gain from disposing of a copyright he will
    be able to treat it for tax purposes as any oth-
    er kind of property owner is able to treat a
    similar income from the sale of his property.

3. A means of deferring tax liability on sums set
    aside to provide pensions or annuities compar-
    able to that enjoyed by employees who partici-
    pate in company-sponsored pension plans.

In all three of these cases authors and other creators of copyrights are presently discriminated a-
gainst--obviously without deliberate congressional
intention--by various aspects of the tax laws.

Spreading of Income

The Congress has recognized the special need of
the author to have some means of spreading his
income for tax purposes, and has provided that
both inventors and writers may spread or average
their income over a period of time if the inven-
tion or the copyrighted work took two years or
more to complete and if 80 per cent of the income derived therefrom was received in a single
calendar year. There is, however, a discrimination against authors as compared with inventors
in that the income received from a patent may be
spread over a period of 5 years and that received
from a copyrighted work may be spread only over
3 years, even though it is probable on the whole
that a longer period of time goes into the creation
of a typical copyrighted work than into the creation
of a particular patentable idea of an individual inventor.

In addition to this discrimination the congressional
intent with respect to authors is in large degree
frustrated by the 80 per cent requirement. The
income from a successful book is concentrated
within a relatively short period, usually not more
than 24 months. However, it is rare that so much
as 80 per cent falls within a single calendar year.
This is particularly true since the typical publishing season and principal theater season runs from
fall to spring, thus normally dividing the peak income between the latter half of one calendar year
and the first half of the succeeding year. Relatively minor changes in the language of the spreading provision could greatly increase its effective-
ness in achieving the purpose intended by the Congress.

Capital Gains Treatment

The Congress has undertaken by means of certain
provisions of section 1235 of the code to provide

a special incentive to inventors in that patents may
be sold by an inventor and profits from the sale
taxed as long-time capital gain. This is true
whether the inventor is a 'professional' inventor
or not, and whether the sale is for a lump sum or
is for a payment over a period of time based on
the actual use of the product--in other words, on
a royalty basis. In contrast to this preferential
position afforded the creators of patents, the creator of copyrights suffers disadvantages with respect
to capital gains experienced by the owner or creator of no other class of property. The author
under no circumstances can realize a capital gain
from the sale of a copyright, whether it be in the
normal course of his business or as an isolated
transaction, whether it be in its entirety or for a
divisible part of the copyright, and whether it be
for a lump sum or for a royalty payment. The
Constitution assigns the same purpose to patents
and to copyrights and gives them both the same
preferential position within the Constitution.   There
would appear to be no sound reason for not extending to the creators of copyrights the benefits now
extended to the creators of patents.   There would
certainly appear to be every reason not to impose
a special disability upon the creators of copyrights
that not only does not afford them the special benefits given inventors, but denies them rights available to the owners of property of every other kind.

Funding of Retirement Provisions

In common with all other self-employed professional workers, the author is discriminated against in
providing for his own retirement as contrasted
with the employee of a corporation. If the corporation sets aside funds to provide for the retirement of its employees on the basis of an approved
plan, those funds are not taxed until they are actually disbursed to the employee as retirement income. This wise provision of the Congress has
been the basis of now very widespread arrange-
ments by American Corporations that provide for
the comfortable retirement of their employees,
supplementing the governmental provision made
through the social security system. Probably few
tax measures have been as well conceived or as

beneficient in their consequences.

The individual author struggling to sustain himself
as a private creator of goods in our society has
no such opportunity to provide for his retirement.
In this situation he is, of course, joined by the
attorney, the physician, and the practitioners of
many other professions. The disadvantages of not
being able to make a tax-exempt provision for future retirement income is particularly onerous in
its impact upon the author because the occasional
years in which he might otherwise be able to set
aside a substantial sum for his retirement are
also years in which, as we have previously pointed
out, his tax rate is extraordinarily high.

The effect upon the internal revenue from changes
of this character would be negligible. The total
annual income of authors from copyrights is probably no more than $100 million on which there is
now probably a tax liability of no more than $15
million annually. The changes here proposed would
remove none of that $100 million from taxation.
Their only effect would be to defer or spread out
certain tax payments with a corresponding leveling
out of tax rates. Even this effect would apply only
to those authors whose successful work over the
years is paid for in very brief periods of peak income. Probably loss of tax revenue would doubt-
less be in the neighborhood of one or at very most
two million dollars a year initially, which would
be reduced as deferred tax income is received.

Small as the effect on tax revenue would be, the
social impact of the proposed changes would nevertheless be substantial. Only a handful of men and
women in the United States who are without independent means now feel free to devote themselves
wholly to authorship. Gladly they would accept
the hazards of an occupation whose rewards are
rarely large and always highly speculative, if the
returns from the occasional and hoped-for success
could be used to bridge the unpaid years of effort
in between. But the present impact of taxation on
peak income, coupled with the ineffectiveness of
the present well-intended spreading provisions,
make it all but impossible for an author to sustain

himself and his family and provide for his old age
even when the works he creates are distinguished
and successful. In consequence, almost all American authors are compelled to turn to other, more
dependable and regular, but less creative means
of livelihood and do such writing as they can in the
weary margins of their time. There is no way we
can measure the loss to American culture and
scholarship from this deadening influence upon
creative work, but surely it is grave. This is, of
course, an unintended policy; no one has deliber-
ately sought a tax policy that would discourage authorship. But nevertheless we have fallen into a
situation in which our tax policies, far from carrying out the constitutional injunction to encourage
authorship, act positively to discourage creative
writing and intellectual effort as a profession.

No special privileges are sought, but we do make
the following recommendations, intended to place
authors on the same footing as inventors and as
other creators and owners of property:

1. The adoption of improved spreading provisions
    along the lines recommended at these hearings
    by the spokesman for the Authors League.

2. Placing copyrights on the same basis as pat-
    ents so far as capital gains treatment is con-
    cerned.

3. The adoption of the legislation proposed by
    Representative Keogh (H. R. 10), similar leg-
    islation to extend to the self-employed the op-
    portunity, within reasonable limits, to make
    provision for voluntary pension plans.

This inequity of tax provisions is not just the concern of the professional writer and his sponsoring organizations. Besides the testimony of Mr. Lacy speaking as a representative of the American Book Publishers Council in support of the statement presented by Howard Linsay for the
Authors League, others who voiced their agreement and support of these proposals included--

a) the American Federation of Television and Radio Artists

b) the American Veterinary Medical Association

c) the National Association of Retail Druggists

d) the American Osteopathic Association

e) the Southern California State Dental Association

f) the Chamber of Commerce of the United States

g) the Illinois State Bar Association

h) the New York Stock Exchange

i) the Medical Society of the County of New York

j) the National Association of Insurance Brokers, Inc.

k) the Conference of Actuaries in Public Practice

l) the American Medical Association, and

m) members of both the House of Representatives and the Senate of the United States Congress.

Henry S. Reuss, Representative from Wisconsin, is author of H. R. 2490, one of the several bills--before the Ways and Means Committee on general revenue revision--identical with the Jenkins-Keogh bills. Thus far none has been voted out of committee to the floor for a vote, however.

One brief study in 1956 of writers' income in support of the Curtis Bill, H. R. 7873, made by the Western Writers of America Tax Spread Committee, determined that 400 per cent was not an unusual fluctuation over a period of 15 years in the 17 cases presented as evidence.[11]

The extreme fluctuations, of course, cannot be controlled by the writer. But under present laws, he pays on everything as current income in most instances; one year he may be in the 50 per cent bracket--the next he may show a loss.

Not only writers suffer from tax inequalities, how-

ever. Some of these people have been alluded to in the preceding statements. Others, a great pitcher or boxer, for
instance, cannot hope to remain in the high income brackets
for more than fifteen years, and a star outfielder or tennis
champion, twenty. The athlete does have this advantage.
He can cash in on his fame so long as he lives, operating
a tavern, selling golf clubs or swimming pools, or, if he
played football, bonds.

When an author's mind rebels against further creation and it is said that he has dried up, or worse, when his
brain refuses to function because of physical disability, as
happened to Mencken, then he is through altogether.

There is another difference. At the end of his career, the athlete (or general, or Eisenhower) can write his
memoirs, and whatever money he receives from publication
will not be regarded as income, but capital gains. But when
a writer is finished ... he is finished.

Notes

1. Larston D. Farrar, Successful Writers and How They
    Work, Chapter XX. (Some of the ideas for background
    material to this chapter were gleaned from his treat-
    ment of taxes.)

2. Ibid., p. 262.

3. Personal interview with and note from the author, June
    1959; copy in this writer's files.

4. Pat Frank, "The Taxman Cometh," Writer's Digest, Vol.
    39, No. 4, April 1959, pp. 29-35, 63 ff.

5. Because this information was given in confidence, iden-
    tity has been concealed and circumstances modified
    slightly to maintain anonymity; the facts are true as
    reported.

6. Frank, op. cit., p. 30.

7. The author knew instantly what the examiner was driving
   at: Under a recent ruling an author or inventor can
   spread over a three-year period income received from
   a single work in a single year, providing he required
   more than two years to plan and complete that work.
   The author had received the bulk of income from his
   novel in 1956, and spread it back through 1954 and 1955.
   It modified and increased his taxes for the two earlier
   years, but altogether it saved him a few hundred dollars
   by lowering his taxable income in 1956.

8. Farrar, op. cit., p. 234.

9. "General Revenue Revision," Hearings before the Ways
   and Means Committee, House of Representatives, 85th
   Congress, Second Session, Parts 1, 2, and 3, Government Printing Office, Washington, 25, D. C., January
   7-31, and February 3-7, 1958.

10. Ibid.

11. Letter to the author from Noel Loomis, Chairman, Tax
    Spread Committee, Western Writers of America; copy
    on file.

Chapter VIII

Summary

The average independent professional American writer does not earn the bulk of his living from his free lance writing.

To recap, Table LXXXVIII lists the average (five-year median) incomes for the various sources writers used to earn their livelihood, 1953-1957; it also gives the per cent of all writers reporting each source for one or more of the five years.

Table LXXXVIII.

Five-Year Median Incomes For Individuals Reporting Specified Sources

Source	Per Cent of All Writers Reporting for one or more years	Median Income
Free Lance Writing Only	42.9	$3438
Books	65.5	1600
Magazines	46.6	444
Plays	28.3	684
"F. L.-Emp" Combined	25.0	1849
Motion Pictures	12.4	2700
Television	18.5	585
Directed Writing Combined	20.8	1893
Staff Writing for Magazines or Newspapers	12.5	1200
Other	8.7	700
Non-Writing Income	51.1	4078
Personal Income All Sources	(100.0)	6667
Spouses Income	53.8	3600
Family Income	100.0	9097

Currently, the typical American free lance writer, earning a total personal income of $6,667 from all sources, will have been born in a metropolitan area, has a Middle Atlantic or Midwestern background and now resides in the metropolitan New York area or on the West Coast.

He is 49 years of age, married, and has one or two dependent children, if in fact he has any at all. The writer is far better formally schooled than is his counterpart in the population at large, and he comes from a home in which his father is or was a professional man or white collar worker, though the chance of his father having also been an author is very slight.

Writers as a Group

Two writers in three are male. The one in three who is a female is, on the average, slightly older, but all writers--unlike most other professionals--continue at their work far beyond the usual years of retirement.

The proportion of male writers who are married is much higher than for the population at large, though female writers are more likely to be divorced and single or widowed than married. Three-fourths of all writers are married-- higher than for the population at large--and have fewer dependent children.

Both the struggle for woman suffrage and the great depression of the early thirties seem to have influenced the number who turned to writing as a career, for more present women writers, proportionally, turned to writing as a career in the decade of the '20's and more men in the decade of the '30's.

Those writers earning from books earn more regularly than those earning from plays. And, of all writers,

two in three are writers of books--1 in 4 is a playwright--
in that they earn personal income from books and plays in
a five-year period.

Younger writers are becoming professional earlier
than older writers did. Perhaps this is attributable partly to
the lack of a defined apprenticeship at present which was
more characteristic of the profession in years past.

Casualness of the Writer Labor Market

(1) Writing provides less substantial support for
writers than other income sources.

Even though more than three-fifths of all writers
earned income from writing of some kind in all five years,
1953-1957, more than half of all writers received more income from non-writing sources (including the working
spouse's income) than from writing. The average (five-year
median) income earned from writing of any kind was $2,828;
the average received from non-writing sources was $3,103.

(2) Few writers are single specialists; few earn
even the major portion of their income each
year from free lance writing.

One writer in 10 derives his sole income from
books; less than 1 in 30 derives his sole income from playwriting; and less than 1 in 50 derives his sole personal income from free lance magazine writing. In 1957, about a
fourth of all writers drew more than half of their personal
income from books; 8.2 per cent drew more than half from
plays; and 4.1 per cent drew more than half of their personal income from books and plays combined. Slightly more
than a fifth of all writers earn their sole personal income
from free lance writing.

Altogether, 46.6 per cent of all writers earn all
personal income from writing of some kind. Six in 10 of

these, however, have personal writing income from other
than books, plays, free lance magazine writing, and royalties. And while two writers in five (of all writers) earn
personal income from other kinds of writing than free lance,
a fourth to two-fifths of the latter earn such income only
one year out of five.

> (3) There is great dependence on non-writing occu-
> pations as a supplement to the writer's person-
> al income earned from writing, but occasional
> non-writing employment is rare.

More than half of all writers derive personal income from non-writing sources in five years' time, and
non-writing occupations are steady sources of personal income for a large portion--almost a third of all writers--
who earn such income each year.

Writers who earn personal income from non-writing
sources, however, earn less from writing than do those who
earn personal income solely from writing whether the latter
have working spouses or not. This fact seems to imply
that if a writer can earn enough from writing--whatever kind
of writing it may be--he will work only at writing and nothing else.

> (4) The writer is greatly dependent on marriage-
> linked income.

More than half--53.8 per cent--of all married writers have working spouses who contribute heavily, adding
more than a third (34.4 per cent) or $3,600, to the family
income annually. Age has little to do with whether the
spouse works or not; the working spouse is steadily employed.
But writers without working spouses are better earners both
at writing and non-writing occupations than writers whose
spouses must work--or by choice do work.

The married writer without working spouse earns
on the average (five-year median) $5,478 yearly from writ-
ing of all kinds, $10,637 from all sources. The married
writer with working spouse earns $3,200 yearly from writ-
ing, $6,210 from all sources of personal income. These
facts thus seem to indicate that among writers there is dependence on the working spouse's income by a large portion
of writers devoting themselves entirely to writing while the
husbands or wives work either (a) as writers, too, or (b)
as non-writers.

> (5) Casualness in this labor market is also indicat-
> ed by the different writing sources and various
> combinations used by the writer to earn per-
> sonal income.

The majority of writers derive personal income
from six clusters of sources, the largest being a combination of book-magazine and non-writing occupations (but less
than a fourth of all writers had this combination). The second cluster is a combination of book and non-writing occupations (for 10 per cent of all writers), and the third cluster
is book writing only (9.8 per cent). The fourth and fifth
clusters--book-magazine writing, and playwriting-other occu-
pations--account for an equal number of writers (7.1 per
cent each). Completing this group are those writers combining playwriting-"F.L.-Emp" writing activities (5.7 per
cent).

> (6) Writers' family incomes are larger than family
> incomes for the population at large.

Income

> (1) The free lancer who derives his sole personal
> income from free lance writing earns about
> $3,400 a year.

For the few more than a fifth of all writers earning
their sole personal income from free lance writing, there is
great dependence upon the working spouse's income, however.
On the average, 49.8 per cent is contributed to family income by the working spouse, or $4,400 yearly. One writer
in 10 earns no free lance income in a five-year period.

> (2) Motion picture writing is by far the most lucra-
> tive type of writing done, but only a small por-
> tion of all writers do such writing.

Of all writers, about 1 in 13 will realize such income over a five-year period, and much less than this ratio
--1 in 20--in any one year's time. These writers are a
group of young men primarily, whose median age is 45 years.

> (3) Writers for television are younger than any other
> group of writers; most are men; but the income
> earned is much less lucrative than from motion
> pictures.

About a fifth of all writers will earn income from
television in five years' time, but less than 1 in 10 will realize such income each year.

> (4) About 4.5 per cent of all writers account for al-
> most half of the income earned from television
> and motion picture writing each year.

A small, exclusive group, earning both from motion
pictures and television, are the really successful income
earners apart from the few high earning free lance writers
of books and plays. This group of motion picture and television writers account for almost half of the income earned
by all writers from these two sources. Such a fact is readily understood when one considers that the five-year median
income from these two sources together for all earning is
$1,849, thus not a source of regular income for many. In
any one year's time, however, those earning from either of

these sources combined will average about $5,000.

      (5) Aside from the five per cent of all writers em-
ployed regularly (earning each year) as staff
writers for magazines and newspapers, directed
writing assignments provide additional outlets for
fewer writers' talents than does motion picture
and television writing.

The magazine and newspaper staffers who earn regularly each year draw a steady income of about $6,000.
These are older writers--51 median--more than two-thirds
of whom are men. Other directed writing activities--ghost-
ing, advertising copy, translations, etc. --provide relatively
few--about 1 in 12--with income. This is the kind of "fill-
in" income used by writers when other sources are not paying off; less than half of those who earn from this source
(including the staffers in the group) earn from this source
each year and the five-year median is extremely low--about
$700.

      (6) Not only are non-writing occupations more regu-
lar than writing for writers, but, typically they
pay better.

Over the five years studied, non-writing income is
the highest average income earned by any group of writers
from any source and accounts for a larger portion of the
average income than any other source. Primarily this is
so because of the regularity in income--not from the overly
large payments characteristic of motion picture or book club
awards earned perhaps in one year out of five, or if more
regularly, by far fewer writers. Over 80 per cent of those
having non-writing income earn such income each year.
Three-fourths of these writers are male--49 year median
age--earning an average of $4,078 yearly from this source.

      (7) Other writing and non-writing occupations apart
from free lance writing do not offer the kind of

writing career which the professional writer
seeks. And though the <u>mean</u> of the yearly medians for those writers earning <u>all</u> their personal
income from writing of any kind in any particular year is $5,750, most of this comes <u>not</u> from
free lance writing, but from other kinds of writing.

(8)   For the profession as a whole, books provide the
largest portion (25.2 per cent) of the total writing personal income earned by all writers.

Non-writing accounts for a larger portion of the total
yearly personal income earned by all, however, 28.0 per
cent. Altogether, approximately $38 million dollars was
earned in 1957 by writers and their working spouses. The
writers' non-writing income and the spouse's income accounted for 40.9 per cent of it. Personal writing income, however, accounted for 72 per cent of total personal income.
Approximately the same amount was earned by working
spouses and by writers from non-writing income sources
(15.5 million) as from all free lance writing ($15.0 million).
The proportion of total contributed by those earning from
plays, motion pictures, and television lead to the conclusion
that these are the most lucrative of all sources but for fewer
people and on a more irregular basis.

(9)   The average writer earns from all sources--ex-
cluding spouse's income--about $6,667 a year,
about the same as the average for all college
teachers, but only three-fourths of that of the
average lawyer, and less than half that of the
average physician.

Book Writers and Playwrights

(1)   Book writers on the average are older than playwrights and, proportionally, there are twice as
many women who are book writers as women who
are playwrights.

The median age for book writers is 50 years; for playwrights, it is 46. The ratios of men to women among book writers is two to one; among playwrights, four to one.

    (2) A larger portion of book writers are married and have working spouses than is the case for playwrights.

More than three-fourths of all book writers are married; 56.5 per cent have working spouses. Sixty-six and nine-tenths per cent of playwrights are married; 51.8 per cent have working spouses.

    (3) Income from books is more regular for book writers and accounts for a larger portion of total personal income than does income from plays for playwrights.

Income is not only less regular for playwrights, the average (five-year median) earned from plays is less than half that earned by book writers from books--$684 as against $1,600.

About four-fifths of all book writers report book income in any one year; though only 58.9 per cent had five-year incomes. About three-fifths of all playwrights report income in any one year, though less than a third--31.5 per cent--had five-year incomes.

About a third as many book writers earn income from books for only one year out of five as do playwrights from plays.

Book income accounts for less than a fourth of the book writers personal income each year (five-year median); play income accounts for less than a tenth on the average of the playwright's personal income. A small group of writers earns from both books and plays. They are steady earners. About half earn more from books; the other half earn more from plays.

The fact that the 70-year olds are highest in median personal play income and second highest in book income suggests either (1) that writing ability and income producing capacity rises with age to death, or (2) that the crop of writers now in their seventies were intrinsically superior to those writers produced in other decades.

The crop of present 70-year olds reached their prime years--their 40's (which age group curiously enough has the highest median earners of personal income from books and second highest from plays)--in the post World War I decade. This period--the 1920's--has frequently been called the second renaissance of American literature.

Perhaps, the lack of a defined apprenticeship characteristic of the older writer accounts for it in part also; and we, thus, have lost something of the creative effort these writers in their 70's have.

Importance of Subsidiary Sources

> (4) Motion picture rights is the most important subsidiary source of income for both the book writer and the playwright.

One book writer in 10 earns from motion picture rights to books in five years' time, but less than 1 in 20 each year. One playwright in 4 earns from motion picture rights to plays; but less than 1 in 10 each year.

Book clubs are second in importance, and paperbacks third, as sources of subsidiary income for book writers from their original books.

Foreign production rights are second in importance, other subsidiary rights third, as sources of subsidiary income for playwrights from their original plays.

> (5) Television rights is the least important subsi-

diary source of income to playwrights, and second least important to book writers.

Proportionally, three times as many playwrights as book writers earn income from TV rights in five years' time, but the book writer's five-year median earning from this source is twice that of the playwright's.

The Book and Playwriting Specialists

The book writing specialists (deriving personal income only from books) are primarily female, and account for less than a tenth of all writers. For the one in four who is male, his income is considerably higher than the female, but for all book writing specialists, the average (five-year median) personal income is only $3,646.

As a consequence, this group of writers has the highest proportion of working spouses of any group--64.3 per cent. The working spouse also contributes heavily to the family income--59.7 per cent, or $4,543 yearly; yet, it remains the lowest group of all in total family income--$5,474.

Adult fiction is still the most important type of book according to its measure of income in 1957 (by 30 per cent of all novelists). General non-fiction is second (28.0 per cent listing it), and juvenile fiction third at 21.0 per cent. No other type of book was reported by as much as a tenth of the book writers.

The playwriting specialists are even rarer than book writing specialists accounting for less than 3 per cent of all writers. There is much less dependence on the working spouse also, even though income from plays is most irregular for this group as a whole. Less than a tenth of all playwrights earn only from playwriting each year.

Other Writing Income

    (6) About the same proportion--1 in 2--of book writ-
ers and playwrights earn additional free lance income apart from books and plays in five years.

More book writers earn regularly, however, (about
44.2 per cent yearly) than do playwrights (about 35.5 per
cent yearly).

    (7) The most lucrative of any source of personal in-
come to both book writers and playwrights alike
was "F.L.-Emp" writing.

For those writers (book writers or playwrights) earning from motion picture or television writing either on a
salary or original basis, they are among the highest personal income earners each year. But less than 1 book writer
in 5 earns in five years' time from this source; less than 1
in 10 earns each year. For playwrights, about 1 in 2 earns
from this source in a five-year period, 1 in 3 yearly.

    (8) About the same portion of book writers and play-
wrights earn from directed writing assignments.

In a period of five years, about 1 in 5 will earn.
Book writers earn more regularly--1 in 7 yearly--but earn
less on the average ($630) than do playwrights--1 in 10 year-
ly--and $1,300 income.

    (9) More playwrights than book writers, proportion-
ally, earn all personal income from writing of
some kind (59.7 per cent against 46.3 per cent);
book writers, moreover, draw less of their total
income (family) from writing than do playwrights.

The book writers earning sole personal income from
writing draw an average (five-year median) of $4,804 yearly,
while the playwright makes almost twice this amount--$8,620
--from the same sources.

There is greater dependence on the working spouse

by the book writer than by the playwright. Two-thirds of
the married book writers earning sole personal income from
writing of some kind have working spouses contributing 47.2
per cent of family income, or $4,947 yearly. Of the play-
wrights married and earning only personal income from
writing of some kind, 55.1 per cent have working spouses
contributing 15.2 per cent of family income, or $1,800
yearly.

>(10) More book writers are dependent upon non-writ-
>ing sources for personal income than are play-
>wrights.

About 1 book writer in 2 earns in five years' time
from non-writing sources; three-fifths earn regularly each
year. For playwrights, about 2 in 5 will earn in a five-
year period, less than one-third regularly each year, and
the latter stick more closely to jobs connected with the theater.

The book writer earning from non-writing sources,
draws on the average, 60 per cent of his personal income--
$4,479--from such sources. Playwrights draw about 45 per
cent, or $3,149, of their personal income from non-writing
sources if they earn from these sources. The largest average income (five-year median) earned by playwrights is
from non-writing sources on the average, though that earned
from "F.L.-Emp" writing is very nearly the same and more
playwrights earn from this latter source than from non-writing sources.

Total personal incomes earned by book writers and
playwrights deriving non-writing income are very nearly the
same--$7,003 to $7,464--as compared with all book writers,
$6,952 and all playwrights, $7,873.

>(11) Playwrights earn better than book writers as a

rule but are less able to pursue their profession
of playwriting than are book writers with books.

The median personal income from plays on the average (five-year median) is lower than for any other source
including other free lance work, directed writing, and the
working spouse's income.

(12) Playwrights, book writers, and "Other" writers
all experience high "employment" yearly.

For playwrights, an average of 87.9 per cent earn
each year; for book writers, an average of 95.2 per cent;
and for "other" writers, an average 91.3 per cent.   A
larger portion of other writers seek non-writing personal
income than either book writers or playwrights, however
(62.9 per cent).

Among these three groups, other writers also have
the greatest dependence on the working spouse's income--
43.5 per cent, or $2,900 is contributed yearly by the
spouse.   But other writers earn least of all in total personal income--$5,938--and also in family income--$8,038--on
the average.

Playwrights' working spouses contribute only 15.2 per
cent--$1,800 yearly; playwrights have the highest personal
income from all sources ($7,873); they also have the highest
family income--$10,795.

Book writers' working spouses contribute more in
dollars--$3,478--but less on a per cent basis than "other"
writers--34.9 per cent.   The book writer's total personal
income averages $6,952 yearly, and his total family income,
$9,935.

Writers' incomes from books and plays show wide
fluctuations in year to year income.   Whatever the varied
causes for such fluctuations, the distribution is very even in

each half of the portion of writers falling within any particular percentage class of low to high income years. That is, even dividing book writers and playwrights on the basis of a five-year median dollar income shows no undue influence of book club, paperback, or motion picture rights monies in one half over the other.

Book writers' median per cent of low to high years shows a bit wider median spread for the half above the five-year median dollar income over the lower half, than is the case for playwrights. But with similar median percentages in each half and for both book writers and playwrights, what in effect the percentages reveal is that the low income earners need tax relief just as badly as the high income earners do. That is, it is just as difficult to maintain a steady though lower income from books and plays as it is to maintain steady but higher incomes year to year from these same sources.

Almost three-fourths of all book writers and playwrights earning personal income from books and plays in two or more years in five realize less than half of their highest year's income in their lowest year's earnings. Both also have at least a third of their group who receive less than 20 per cent of their high year's income in their lowest income year out of five.

Because of the fluctuation in income and the corresponding unjust progressive income tax on high-income years, and because of statute rulings--

(1) denying social security benefits to writers otherwise eligible (only 35.3 per cent of writers-- compared to 52.5 per cent of the population at large--eligible by age were receiving such benefits in 1957), and

(2) denying to writers' heirs the right to take depreciation on inherited literary property,

writers find it difficult indeed to accumulate the means for
professional survival.

The average independent professional writer thus earning insufficient income to live on from his chosen profession
of writing seems to have an excellent case for tax relief
measures.

Chapter IX

Conclusions

To make the findings of this study more meaningful than the summarized results in Chapter VIII, a complete
treatment of the structure of the writing market and a complete economic treatment of all writers would be most help-
ful. Since they are not available, however, and acknowledg-
ing these reservations, this chapter discusses some of the
implications for the free lance author's future on the basis
of what is now known about this type of writer and his income.

Problems which the free lance author faces are of
several types: those which occur personally in his pursuit
of income, those associated with and caused primarily by
the publisher, and those which are perhaps more or less inherent in his calling.

If the author is one of the minority who is a spe-
cialist (earning his sole personal income from books and
plays), he has to depend greatly on his working spouse's income to meet family obligations, for his average income of
$3,400 a year will fall short. Most free lance authors,
therefore, will have to write in several different areas or
capacities, though most of this kind of writing is not what
they would really prefer to do. Or else, they will be forced
to take non-writing jobs which will limit the time and effort
they can afford to devote to their writing.

Because writing provides less substantial support
for authors generally than their other income sources, this

economic barrier to authorship alone limits the time and effort authors can devote to writing. Hence the volume and
quality of writing--both scholarly and creative--authors could
produce are significantly affected. As a consequence, probably affected also is the usefulness to society of the annual
output of books.

Yet books retain a unique and basically important
role in society in spite of the rapid development of the other
communications media. They are the principal means of
serious literary expression. They, along with the scholarly
journals and monographs, are the only feasible vehicles for
scholarly work. Books--and more infrequently magazines--
offer the only practical mechanisms for extending and care-
fully examining questions. Books, with limited circulation
magazines, are the only media that do offer a measure of
national availability to minority views, to new writers, and
to material of limited appeal. And finally, books are the
only medium that gives the user an uncontrolled access to
the whole range of information and culture.

In recent decades, however, the successful exploitation of subsidiary rights has become a very real necessity in publishing economics. Often such subsidiary income represents the difference between an unsuccessful and
a successful book. It is now almost universally believed by
the trade that publishers lose money in the physical production and sale of books as a whole. Thus publishers tend to
seek, and authors to write, books designed to fit the mass
market requirements of book club selections, pocketbooks,
and motion pictures--to the extent that authors' creative capacities run in directions ill-suited to the mass market. The
output of the literature industry thus appears to be not what
somebody wanted to write, but what somebody else wanted to

get written. Writer R's remarks is a case in point. He, at 47, is recent author of a best seller, non-fiction work for which motion picture rights have brought a handsome return:

> Communications is suffering because writers like myself simply cannot afford to leave anything for the young free lancer ... Communications has become sterile ... there's a terrible shocking sameness in this business ... writers are forced to bring out junk just to stay alive.

And Mr. S, age 61, wrote:

> My income at present comes from eleven books still selling, though no one book could support me. I have to bring out a new popular fiction book about every two years to keep the pot boiling.

Among the Authors League membership also are those writers who have adapted to the salable formula for pulp magazines as exemplified in Mrs. T's comments:

> I never have been anything but a professional writer. In 1939, at 23 I started earning enough to live on. I write pulp true confessions, averaging about $3,000 a year.

Once the author has "proved" himself to the publisher, that is, when he produces salable pieces, the publisher frequently offers a retainer or regular advance to that writer. Such a practice makes the free lancer resemble the salaried writer more and more, for the salaried writer is guaranteed space for his writings and is expected to produce a certain number of articles each year. Similarly, the author who has been given the retainer or advance is expected to produce for the publisher, who maintains a list of writers and who has planned a specified number of new books for the year. This practice of a retainer or advance thus guarantees the publisher a "stable of writers" from which he can draw to meet his quota of new books. At the same time, such a practice also curtails the market possibilities for the true free lance.

Another of the reasons for the publisher's tending to seek books geared to the mass market which will guarantee at least a profitable sale is the fact he constantly faces rising manufacturing and distribution costs which narrow his margin on limited-interest works more and more. This is also true in the theater, where drama is arbitrated by "show business." The producer, rather than speculate on something risky, tends to stick to a tried-and-true formula based on the success of the past. As a result, we will continue to have much the same old products, cut to standard lengths.

Some writers, nevertheless, seem intuitively "tuned" to the mass market, and they are not forced to prostitute a higher ambition:

> Mr. U, age 41: Writing to me is 'letting off steam'--it's an avocation, though I've been highly successful with it. In 9 years I've had 13 paperbacks and reprints. But you see, I have three other businesses and I'm completely apart from the writing profession. I don't mix with writers socially; I never cared to. But I love my writing and I write as I want. I follow a schedule--writing from 10 at night until 2 in the morning. I admit I'm a hack. If I knew how the book would turn out when I sat down and started it, I'd never write it in the first place, but that's the way my detective stories and sexies are. When one of my books is a success, it throws me into a ridiculous tax bracket--writing becomes a real luxury for me.

Mrs. V, age 38, writing only for the fun of it but also quite successful in selling her work, is also somewhat typical:

> I get some income from amateur rights from three plays produced on Broadway before 1953. And I sell television rights to short stories written be-

fore 1953 every so often. I am an actress by profession and only write for fun between jobs. My
income combined with my husband's is usually between 30-40 thousand a year but most of it is earned by him as a stage director and by me as an
actress. About a fifth comes from writing (author's italics) and some from inherited income.

One of the biggest problems among the professional
free lance authors of books and plays, however, is that of
writing salable pieces. There is a striking similarity between writers and prospectors of the old West in search of
gold: the one success--or just the thought of it--that keeps
them both going! For the gold prospector the dream is making the big strike--the mother lode; for the writer it is a
dream of writing the book or play that will hit the jackpot.
Such hope is illustrated in these comments:

Mr. W, age 50: My last income from writing was
for a book published in 1948--$300. But I'm still
writing!

Mrs. X, age 60: I brought up a large family and
did various types of work to help out through the
years. I always wanted to write and as soon as
the children were on their way and finances better,
I went at it. I sold my first Junior novel and two
subsequent ones, have another almost ready. I
have also done small town newspaper work for very
little pay.

Mr. Y, age 63: I have actually received very
little income directly from writing, but most of
my life I have held jobs for which I did an enormous amount of writing. During the period covered by this questionnaire, I have written three plays
and a movie, none of which has produced income
to date; I translated another play, and wrote an
enormous amount of publicity copy. It is probable
that this year will show a substantial income from
writing. (author's italics)

Mr. Z, age 37: Short stories published are all I

count. As a staff writer for a business magazine
I consider my work journalism. Two unpublished
novels count for nothing; I have another one in
progress, however.

Mr. AA, age 45: I have sold about 20 magazine
articles, but my main concern is two novels I've
been working on for the past four years.

Mr. BB, age 51: After six years of spare-time
work, I got my first book accepted (1956) but I've
been writing since 1931.

Salability and creativeness, such as that driving the inventor,
are obviously operative in the writing field as indicated by
these and similar comments from respondents. Age and sex
have nothing to do with it. But though man may be driven
to try--whether it be as the inventor of some new machine
or process, as the prospector for gold, or as the writer of
a book or play, it is not the economic accomplishment alone
which sustains him but the prospect of what there might be
that keeps him going.

     For the marginal writer this is a race between
optimism for a future strike and the drain of authorship.
One of the purely economic factors working against this
drive, or the prospect for the future strike, is the out-of-
pocket costs--the cost of research, stenographic service,
postage, paper, art work, etc.--which together may be considered the writer's ventured capital. To wit:

Mr. CC, age 56: It is extremely difficult to market manuscripts with the high postage and express
rates plus agents wanting manuscripts tailored to
their whims, and publishers timid or riding fads.
So you spend your efforts writing for "free" with
the publishers sending no checks. It does flatter
your vanity though.

Mr. DD, age 46: Of four published books, I never
have retained anything. Typing, research, and

expenses amounted to more than the advances plus royalties.

Mrs. EE, age 57: While there was a dribble of royalties in 1953 and 1954, these were more than offset by (1) cost of promotion copies and (2) charge for 1/2 the art work on the 'picture-book. Total art work on the book alone cost $2,112.24. I do not have a breakdown of this situation--just the tax record showing no net income from royalties.

Mrs. FF, age 55: May I add that it's a nuisance to be considered a celebrity when your income doesn't allow you to live up to what the public expects of an author.

To keep going, writers must have some return on the ventured capital and effort. Otherwise they reach the point where they must abandon writing altogether, either because they no longer can afford it or because the recognition does not come and the creative urge dies.

Others of course do write simply because of the urge or the drive to be creative. Those who have a burning desire to write will do so and will find an outlet for their work even though they have to write as an avocation--a situation akin to sex for love rather than sex for money. These writers will continue as long as possible. For example:

Mr. GG, age 55: I think the idea of this study is fine; for four long years I have worked on a long and difficult novel [here the author named what has since become a best seller, non-fiction work], and it will be another year before it is finished--if it ever is. It's been touch and go with me all the way--generous publishers have made advances; I hope the book will recover these.

Mr. HH, age 63: This is the return of a poet. I got my first job with a newspaper in 1917. From about 1919 I have been publishing poetry off and on in national periodicals. Some prose ... a book of prose in 1937.

> Mrs. II, age 70: I have never tried to earn a liv-
> ing by writing--I couldn't--if you thus designate
> the term professional, though I've published novels,
> novelettes, some criticisms, etc.

In any case, whether it be that the author no longer can afford to write, recognition fails to come, or the creative
urge is stifled, the writer turns instead to non-writing jobs,
writing only incidentally. Part of the reason for turning to
other sources of livelihood (characterized by the high degree
of casualness in receipt of income) is due partly to the irregularity in earning from the writer's efforts. The market
becomes oppresive for him:

> Mrs. JJ, age 56: You might be interested in know-
> ing that in 1944, I made $50,000 from a book--
> quite a difference in my present income of $1,800,
> isn't it?

> Mr. KK, age 56: You know, this is the damnedest
> business to be in you ever saw. My income has
> bounced like a rubber ball--from $1,500 ten years
> ago up to $25,000 and back to only a few hundred
> a year.

> Miss LL, age 57: The last few years I have been
> working on a novel, and have sold nothing, alas!

> Mrs. MM, age 47: I couldn't possibly make my liv-
> ing from writing unless I got a job staff writing or
> connected with better paying markets than my pre-
> sent ones.

> Mr. NN, age 33: I've not published since 1951; at
> that time I published a mystery novel and most of
> the income was earned in 1951 and 1952. There
> was some small income from 1952 to the present
> from paperbound sales and foreign rights. I'm
> revising a new novel at the suggestion of my pub-
> lisher.

Similarly, Mrs. OO's point of view adds to the oppressiveness which authors feel:

> Can you call this a profession? I have written 10
> books (3 are book-club selections and best sellers).
> I have 20 more unpublished; I'm still writing and
> hoping. It costs more to write than I can take off
> my tax; at this point writing is an expensive hob-
> by for me.

But perhaps the last remark is more typical of the successful manufacturer with a second, though floundering, business
which he continues to operate either (1) because his relatives
run it, or (2) because of the challenge which it affords. Wis-
dom--in either instance--would decree that both be given up.
However, Mr. Y's comments are much more illustrative of
the oppressiveness:

> To show how little juvenile books may earn, even
> pretty good ones, one of mine was a Junior Liter-
> ary Guild selection (historical novel) and was given
> the top position in the New York Times Children's
> Literary section; the second, lighter in character,
> for two years was on the New York Public Librar-
> y's 'permanent exhibit.'
>
> The income stated--about $500 a year--is derived
> entirely from these two books which it took some
> years to write. A third book, just out, has not
> yet yielded income except for a three hundred dol-
> lar deposit against royalties--to be repaid if the
> book does not earn this sum.

Mr. Y's comments also indicate another of the problems the
author must reckon with--one which again hits the marginal
writer particularly hard. It is the situation occurring when
the published book produces no income. Two or three years'
time invested in a work which does not sell offers no rec-
ompense to the author. He cannot take a loss on his tax for
time, effort, and energy expended; he has no income to
spread even if he could qualify for this tax provision.

Thus authors have been affected seriously (1) by the book industry's emphasis on works with mass sales potential, (2) by the practice toward standardizing the selection of new works according to past successes, and (3) by the decreasing demand for new and experimental works and consequently for new and unproved authors and books of merit but which have a limited audience. With publishers sticking as closely as possible to the "proved" within various genres, and the economic factors of cost working against the young writer, the trade continues to contribute to the difficulty of the young, serious writer and in the process must lose good books because authors simply cannot afford to write them.

Since the writer's book has to be printed before it can be read, the future of literature of necessity depends upon the health of the publishing industry. The conclusion appears warranted that the new mass market for books is working toward conformity rather than diversity in American fiction.

Wide fluctuation in the author's income and his corresponding inability to establish a retirement plan such as that granted (tax-free contributions) to business people make his future even more insecure. Not only does the author lack a pension plan, but in many cases he finds himself completely ineligible even for social security benefits when he does reach retirement age. For low earners and marginal writers, the future is not attractive in authorship.

Looking into the future of books in our country might lead one to think that the shape of things to come will approximate the paperbound rather than the leather or clothbound volume. It seems probable that an increasing number of manuscripts will be excluded from the likelihood of being

preserved between hardcovers. Light fiction, Westerns,
light romances, mysteries, detective stories and science
fiction are written to be hastily and superficially indulged in
and seldom to be remembered or reread. They neither require nor deserve more permanence than the same type of
material which flashes rapidly across the movie or TV
screen or attracts temporarily the listener's attention when
carried over the radio. As mass media seem to supplement
rather than supplant each other, the demand for impermanent
reading matter seems to grow and may reach the point where
most, if not all, fiction will appear in this temporary format.
Only, perhaps, when such writing is recognized to be of en-
during value will it be granted the coat of distinction, in a
reversal of the current practice, and appear as a reprint in
cloth binding.

Bibliography

A. Books

Abbott, Lawrence, Economics and the Modern World, Harcourt, Brace and Company, New York, 1960.

Cheney, O. H., Economic Survey of the Book Industry 1930-1931 (With 1947-1948 Statistical Report), R. R. Bowker Company, New York, 1949.

Cohen, Sydney W., editor, Celebrity Register, Celebrity Register, Inc., New York, 1959.

Contributions to Education, (Dissertation Abstracts) (Published Under the Direction of George Peabody College for Teachers), Cullom and Ghertner Company, No. 206, Nashville, Tennessee, 1938.

Cowley, Malcolm, The Literary Situation, The Viking Press, New York, 1954.

Cowley, Malcolm, Writers at Work, The Paris Review Interviews, The Viking Press, New York, 1958.

Davis, Elmer, Some Aspects of the Economics of Authorship, Fifth of the R. R. Bowker Memorial Lectures, The New York Public Library, New York, 1940.

Deming, William Edwards, Some Theory of Sampling, John Wiley and Sons, Inc., New York, 1950.

Duffus, R. L., Books, Their Place in a Democracy, Houghton Mifflin Company, New York, 1949.

Farrar, Larston D., Successful Writers and How They Work, Hawthorne Books, Inc., Publishers, New York, 1959.

Ferber, Robert, Statistical Techniques in Market Research, 1st ed., McGraw-Hill Book Company, New York, 1949.

Freedley, George and Reeves, John A., A History of the Theater, Crown Publishers, New York, 1941.

Gee, Wilson, Social Science Research Methods, Appleton-
    Century-Crofts, Inc., New York, 1950.

Gill, Robert S., The Author, Publisher, Printer Complex,
    The Williams and Wilkins Company, Baltimore, 1940.

Grannis, Chandler, B., editor, What Happens in Book Pub-
    lishing, Columbia University Press, New York, 1957.

Guinzburgh, Harold K., Frase, Robert W., and Waller,
    Theodore, Books and the Mass Market, University of
    Illinois Press, Urbana, 1953.

Henry, Nelson, Adult Reading, University of Chicago Press,
    Chicago, 1956.

Kunitz, Stanley J., and Haycroft, Howard, Twentieth Century
    Authors, The H. W. Wilson Company, New York, 1942.

Kunitz, Stanley J., and Colby, Vaneta, Twentieth Century
    Authors, First Supplement, The H.W. Wilson Company,
    New York, 1955.

Lacy, Daniel M., Books and the Future: A Speculation,
    New York Public Library, New York, 1956.

Lawrence, Alberta, editor, Who's Who Among North Amer-
    ican Authors, Golden Syndicate Publishing Company,
    Los Angeles, 1939.

Literary Market Place 1959-1960 (The Business Directory of
    American Book Publishing), R. R. Bowker Company,
    New York, 1959.

Mathieu, Aron M. and Coffman, Gratton E., editors, Writ-
    er's Market, 17th ed., Writer's Digest, Cincinnati,
    Ohio, 1959.

Miller, William, The Book Industry, Columbia University
    Press, New York, 1949.

Niehuis, Charlie, Writer's Market, "It's Money in the Bank,"
    Writer's Digest, Cincinnati, Ohio, 1959.

Parker, John, Who's Who in the Theater, 12th ed., Sir
    Isaac Pitman and Sons, Ltd., London, 1957.

Parten, Mildred, Surveys, Polls and Samples, Harper and
    Bros., New York, 1950.

Peterson, Theodore, Magazines in the 20th Century, Univer-
    sity of Illinois Press, Urbana, 1958.

Pine, L. G., editor, The Authors and Writers Who's Who
    and Reference Guide, 4th ed., Burke's Peerage, Ltd.,
    London, 1960.

Schick, Frank L., The Paperbound Book in America, R. R.
    Bowker Company, New York, 1958.

Schulberg, Budd, A Face in the Crowd, Bantam Books, New
    York, 1957. (With an introduction by Elia Kazan.)

Stephan, Frederick F. and McCarthy, Philip J., Sampling
    Opinions: An Analysis of Survey Procedure, John
    Wiley and Sons, Inc., New York, 1958.

Stockton, John R., An Introduction to Business Statistics,
    2nd ed., D. C. Heath and Company, Boston, 1947.

U. S. Bureau of the Census, Statistical Abstract of the
    United States 1960, Eighty-first edition, Government
    Printing Office, Washington, D. C., 1960.

Wain, John, editor, International Literary Annual, Criterion
    Books, New York, 1959.

Warner, J. Loyd and Abegglen, James C., Occupational
    Mobility in American Business and Industry, Univer-
    sity of Minnesota Press, Minneapolis, 1955.

Watt, Ian, The Rise of the Novel, Chatton and Windus, Pub-
    lishers, London, 1957.

Webster's Biographical Dictionary, 1st edition, G. and C.
    Merriam Company, Publishers, Massachusetts, 1958.

Who's Who in America, Volumes 28, 29 and 30, The A. N.
    Marquis Company, Chicago, 1954-55, 1956-57, 1958-
    59.

Woon, Basil, The Current Publishing Scene, Exposition
    Press, New York, 1952.

B. Periodical Articles

Benson, L. E., "Mail Surveys Can Be Valuable," Public
    Opinion Quarterly, Vol. 10, 1946, pp. 234-37.

Blum, Eleanor, "Paperback Book Publishing: A Survey of
    Content," Journalism Quarterly, Vol. 36, No. 4, Fall
    1959, pp. 447-454.

"Book Publication Statistics for 1957," Publishers Weekly,
    Vol. 173, No. 3, January 20, 1958, pp. 33-41.

"Book Publication Statistics for 1958," Publishers Weekly,
    Vol. 175, No. 3, January 1959, pp. 38-74.

Brustein, Robert, "Why American Plays Are Not Literature,"
    Harper's Magazine, Vo. 219, No. 1313, October 1959,
    pp. 167-172.

Clausen, J. A. and Ford, R. N., "Controlling Bias in Mail
    Questionnaires," Journal of the American Statistical
    Association, Vol. 42, No. 240, 1947, pp. 491-511.

DeVoto, Bernard, "Writing for Money," The Saturday Re-
    view, Vol. 16, No. 24, October 9, 1937, pp. 3-4.

"Economics of Publishing," Publishers Weekly, Vol. 178,
    No. 26, December 26, 1960, pp. 20-26.

Fadiman, Clifton, "Party of One: Ah! The Literary Life!"
    Holiday, Vol. 23, No. 3, March 1958, pp. 11-15.

Ferber, Robert, "The Problem of Bias in Mail Returns: A
    Solution," Public Opinion Quarterly, Vol. 12, No. 4,
    1948-49, pp. 669-676.

Ford, Robert N. and Zeisel, Hans, "Bias in Mail Surveys
    Cannot Be Controlled by One Mailing," Public Opinion
    Quarterly, Vol. 13, No. 3, Fall 1949, pp. 495-501.

Frank, Pat, "The Taxman Cometh," Writer's Digest, Vol.
    39, No. 4, April 1959, pp. 29-35ff.

Franzen, R. and Lazarsfeld, P. F., "Mail Questionnaire as
    a Research Problem," Journal of Psychology, Vol. 20,
    1945, p. 294.

Hansen, Harry, "Plain Talk for Aspiring Writers," The Saturday Review, Vol. 37, November 13, 1954, p. 21.

Harris, Seymour E., "Who Gets Paid What," Atlantic Monthly, Vol. 201, No. 5, May 1958, pp. 35-38.

Heilbroner, Robert L., "Mr. Nobody's Byline," The Saturday Review, January 14, 1956, pp. 9-10.

Howells, William Dean, "The Man of Letters as a Man of Business," Scribner's Magazine, Vol. 14, No. 43, October 1893, pp. 429-445.

Kerr, Walter, "Adventures of the Mind, 20: What Ails the Theater?" The Saturday Evening Post, Vol. 231, No. 32, February 7, 1959, pp. 99-100.

Kerr, Walter, "Killing Off the Theater," Harper's Magazine, Vol. 210, No. 1258, March 1955, pp. 55-62.

Lasser, J. K., "The Book Business--With and Without a Profit," Saturday Review of Literature, Vol. 32, No. 44, October 29, 1949, p. 9.

MacLeish, Archibald, "The Isolation of the American Artist," Atlantic Monthly, Vol. 201, No. 1, January 1958, pp. 55-59.

"News, Trends, Statistics in the Book Industry," Publishers Weekly, Vol. 175, No. 3, January 1959, pp. 58-61.

Schick, Frank L., Issue Editor, "Trends in American Book Publishing," Library Trends, Vol. 7, No. 1, University of Illinois Library Quarterly, July 1958, pp. 3-30.

Seaver, Edwin, "The Age of the Jackpot," The Saturday Review Vol. 30, No. 7, February 15, 1947, pp. 9-10.

Shuttleworth, F. K., "Sampling Errors Involved in Incomplete Returns to Mail Questionnaires," Journal of Applied Psychology, Vol. 25, 1941, pp. 588-591.

"Should Publishers Have 50% of Club and Paperback Income," Publishers Weekly, Vol. 178, No. 26, December 26, 1960, p. 22.

Snow, C. P., "Which Side of the Atlantic?" Harper's

Magazine, Vol. 219, No. 1313, October 1959, pp. 163-166.

Stanton, Frank, "Notes on the Validity of Mail Questionnaire Returns," Journal of Applied Psychology, Vol. 23, 1939, pp. 95-104.

"State of the Theater," Theater Arts, Vol. 31, June 1947, p. 23.

Strout, Donald E., "Book Club Publishing," Library Trends, Vol. 7, No. 1, July 1958, pp. 71-77.

Time, Vol. 64, July 19, 1954, p. 83.

Vidal, Gore, "The Perils and Rewards of Going Into Trade," The Reporter, Vol. 17, No. 1, July 11, 1957, pp. 33-36.

Wernick, Robert, "The Queens of Fiction," Life, Vol. 46, No. 14, April 6, 1959, p. 139ff.

"Writing in America," (A Special Supplement), Harper's Magazine, Vol. 219, No. 1313, October 1959, pp. 125-190.

"The Writing World and Writers," Newsweek, Vol. 44, October 25, 1954, p. 106.

C. Publications of Organizations

1956 Annual Survey of the General Book Publishing Industry, American Book Publishers Council, Inc., New York, May 1957.

"Book Sales in 1958, Annual Statistical Release," Bulletin, American Book Publishers Council, Inc., New York, June 15, 1959.

"Campus Emporia," The Biddle Survey, Vol. 28, No. 6, October 6, 1959, p. 2.

Dramatists Guild Bulletin, March 1958.

General Revenue Revision, Hearings Before the Ways and Means Committee, House of Representatives, Eighty-fifth Congress, Second Session, Parts 1, 2, and 3,

Government Printing Office, Washington 25, D. C.,
January 7-31, and February 3-7, 1958.

Health, Education, and Welfare Trends, 1960 Edition, Bulletin, U. S. Department of Health, Education, and Welfare, Washington, D. C.

Illinois Business Review, Bureau of Economic and Business
Research, University of Illinois, Urbana, Vol. 16, No.
6, June 1959, p. 3.

Illinois Business Review, "Business Briefs," Bureau of Economic and Business Research, University of Illinois,
Urbana, Vol. 17, No. 11, December 1960, p. 7.

Illinois Business Review, "Business Briefs," Bureau of
Economic and Business Research, University of Illinois,
Urbana, Vol. 18, No. 2, February 1961, p. 9.

"News Summary," Federal Trade Commission, No. 41,
Washington, D. C., July 23, 1959.

Occupational Outlook Handbook, 1959 Edition, Bulletin No.
1255, Department of Labor, U. S. Government Printing Office, Washington, D. C.

Policies of American Society of Composers, Authors, and
Publishers, (A Report of Subcommittee No. 5 to the
Select Committee on Small Business), Eighty-fifth Con-
gress, Second Session, House Report No. 1710, U. S.
Government Printing Office, Washington, D. C., May
12, 1958.

U. S. Bureau of the Census, 1950 Census of Population:
Classified Index of Occupations and Industries, Washington, D. C., December 1950.

U. S. Department of Commerce, "Current Population Reports, Labor Force," Bulletin, Series P-50, No. 79,
Washington, D. C., December 1957.

U. S. Department of Commerce, Bureau of Census, 1954
Census of Manufactures, Bulletin MC-27A, "Newspapers,
Periodicals, Books, and Miscellaneous Publishing,"
Washington, D. C., 1957.

D. Unpublished Materials

Baker, Kenneth Marne, "Editorial Requirements for Higher-
  Paying Magazines," Unpublished Master's thesis, University of Illinois, Urbana, 1951.

E. Newspapers

"Authors, Too, Are Depleted," Editorial, Champaign-Urbana
  Courier, January 7, 1958.

"Bellamy Sees Pay TV as Theater Aid," Champaign-Urbana
  Courier, "Green Page," September 19, 1960, p. 13.

Boyle, Hal, "You Keep What You Spend," AP Release,
  Champaign-Urbana Courier, October 9, 1959, p. 25.

Cannel, Ward, "Fame at Checkout Counter?" Champaign-
  Urbana Courier, August 5, 1959, p. 20.

Crosby, John, "Artists and Box Offices: Success Once Was
  Cheap and Vulgar," New York Herald Tribune, January
  24, 1961.

Nichols, Lewis, "In and Out of Books," The New York Times
  Book Review, February 1, 1959, p. 8.

Nichols, Lewis, "In and Out of Books," The New York Times
  Book Review, July 3, 1960, p. 8.

"Physician's Income," Champaign-Urbana Courier, January
  27, 1954.

"Serling No Longer Angry," Champaign-Urbana Courier,
  September 27, 1959, p. 23.

Vita

William Jackson Lord, Jr., was born May 10, 1926, in Sabine County, Texas. After graduating from C. E. Byrd High School, Shreveport, Louisiana, in 1944, he entered the United States Army and served for more than two years.

He earned the Bachelor of Business Administration degree in Foreign Trade (1950) and the Master of Business Administration degree in Business Writing (1953), from The University of Texas, Austin.

From 1951-1954 he served as Instructor in Business at West Texas State College, Canyon. Since 1954, he has been Instructor in Business English at the University of Illinois. He is married and has three children.

Among his publications are "Business Letters," (Chapter XXIV for the Management Manual of the National Association of Plumbing and Heating Contractors), "Good Report Writing--An Aid to Effective Communication," Willing Water, Vol. 2, (September 1958) pp 10-11, and "A Knowledge of Letters," (a series in three parts for The Secretary (July, August, and September 1959).

An active member and Committee Chairman of the American Business Writing Association, Delta Sigma Pi, and other organizations, he also presently serves as Communications Consultant to the Franklin Life Insurance Company, Springfield.

Index

Index   311